KEY TO HARDINESS ZONES

...hows eleven ...l zones based on ...annual minimum ...es recorded for the ...to 1986. The zone ...ccompanying the ...his book indicate their lower limits of winter cold hardiness. Extreme summer heat and humidity also play a part in a plant's adaptability; many plants hardy in colder zones grow poorly in warmer, wetter ones.

1	BELOW −50°F BELOW −46°C
2	−50° TO −40°F −46° TO −40°C
3	−40° TO −30°F −40° TO −34°C
4	−30° TO −20°F −34° TO −29°C
5	−20° TO −10°F −29° TO −23°C
6	−10° TO 0°F −23° TO −18°C
7	0° TO 10°F −18° TO −12°C
8	10° TO 20°F −12° TO −7°C
9	20° TO 30°F −7° TO −1°C
10	30° TO 40°F −1° TO 4°C
11	ABOVE 40°F ABOVE 4°C

EYEWITNESS
GARDEN HANDBOOKS

BULBS

EYEWITNESS
GARDEN HANDBOOKS
BULBS

A DK PUBLISHING BOOK

Produced for DK Publishing by PAGE*One*
Cairn House, Elgiva Lane, Chesham,
Buckinghamshire HP5 2JD

PROJECT DIRECTORS Bob Gordon and Helen Parker
EDITOR Charlotte Stock
DESIGNER Matthew Cook

MANAGING EDITOR Francis Ritter
MANAGING ART EDITOR Derek Coombes
PRODUCTION Martin Croshaw
PICTURE RESEARCH Joanne Beardwell

First American Edition, 1997
2 4 6 8 10 9 7 5 3 1

Published in the United States by
DK Publishing, Inc., 95 Madison Avenue,
New York, New York 10016
Visit us on the World Wide Web at http://www.dk.com

Library of Congress Cataloging-in-Publication Data

Bulbs. — 1st American ed.
    p. cm. — (Eyewitness garden handbooks)
    Includes index.
    ISBN 0-7894-1454-6
    1. Bulbs. I. DK Publishing. Inc. II. Series.
SB425.B872 1997
635.9'4—dc21   96-47960
                                                            CIP

Color reproduction by Colourscan, Singapore
Printed and bound by Star Standard Industries, Singapore

CONTENTS

SMALL

CONTRIBUTORS

ROD LEEDS
Consultant

RONALD HEDGE
Dahlias

LINDEN HAWTHORNE
Writer

HOW TO USE THIS BOOK

THIS BOOK PROVIDES the ideal quick reference guide to selecting and identifying bulbs for the garden.

The BULBS IN THE GARDEN section is a helpful introduction to bulbs and advises on choosing a suitable plant for growing in a particular site or purpose, such as for a border, container, or simply as a specimen.

To choose or identify a bulb, turn to the CATALOG OF BULBS, where photographs are accompanied by concise plant descriptions and useful tips on cultivation and propagation. The entries are grouped by size, season of interest, as well as by color (see the color wheel below) to make selection easier.

For additional information on bulb cultivation, routine care, and propagation, turn to the GUIDE TO BULB CARE, where general advice on all aspects of caring for your bulbs can be found.

At the end of the book, a useful two-page glossary explains key terms, and a comprehensive index of every bulb, its synonyms, and common names, together with a brief genus description, allows quick and easy access to the book by plant name.

The color wheel
All the bulbs in the book are grouped according to the color of their main feature of interest. They are always arranged in the same order, indicated by the color wheel below, from white through reds and blues, to yellows and oranges.

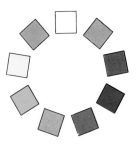

Bulb size categories
The bulbs featured in the CATALOG OF BULBS are divided according to the average height they attain. However, heights may vary from the ones given, according to site, growing conditions, climate, and age.

The categories are as follows:

LARGE
Over 2ft (60cm)
MEDIUM
9in–2ft (23cm–60cm)
SMALL
Up to 9in (23cm)

THE SYMBOLS

The symbols below are used throughout the CATALOG OF BULBS to indicate a plant's preferred growing conditions and hardiness. However, the climate and soil conditions of your particular site should also be taken into account, since they may affect a plant's growth.

HARDINESS
The range of winter temperatures that each plant is able to withstand is shown by the USDA plant hardiness zone numbers that are given in each entry. The temperature ranges for each zone are shown on the endpaper map in this book.

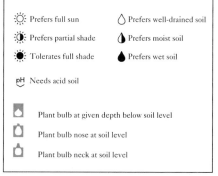

☼ Prefers full sun   ○ Prefers well-drained soil

☀ Prefers partial shade   ◗ Prefers moist soil

☀ Tolerates full shade   ● Prefers wet soil

pH Needs acid soil

▣ Plant bulb at given depth below soil level

◲ Plant bulb nose at soil level

◱ Plant bulb neck at soil level

HOW TO USE THE CATALOG OF BULBS

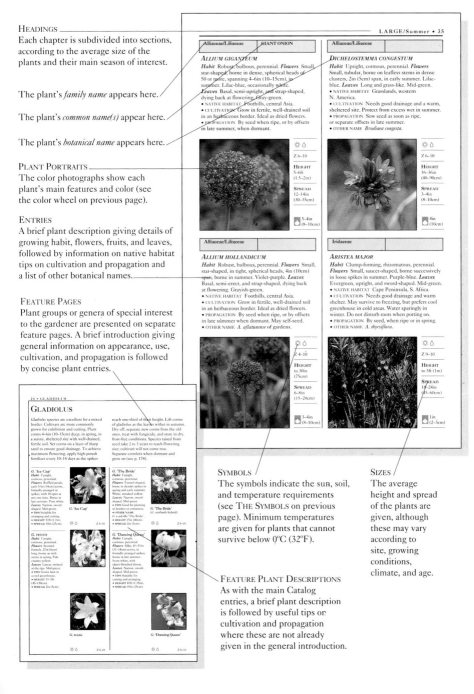

HEADINGS
Each chapter is subdivided into sections, according to the average size of the plants and their main season of interest.

The plant's *family name* appears here.

The plant's *common name(s)* appear here.

The plant's *botanical name* appears here.

PLANT PORTRAITS
The color photographs show each plant's main features and color (see the color wheel on previous page).

ENTRIES
A brief plant description giving details of growing habit, flowers, fruits, and leaves, followed by information on native habitat tips on cultivation and propagation and a list of other botanical names.

FEATURE PAGES
Plant groups or genera of special interest to the gardener are presented on separate feature pages. A brief introduction giving general information on appearance, use, cultivation, and propagation is followed by concise plant entries.

LARGE/Summer • 35

Alliaceae/Liliaceae   GIANT ONION

ALLIUM GIGANTEUM
Habit Robust, bulbous, perennial. *Flowers* Small, star-shaped, borne in dense, spherical heads of 50 or more, spanning 4–6in (10–15cm), in summer. Lilac-blue, occasionally white. *Leaves* Basal, semi-upright, and strap-shaped, dying back at flowering. Gray-green.
• NATIVE HABITAT Foothills, central Asia.
• CULTIVATION Grow in fertile, well-drained soil in an herbaceous border. Ideal as dried flowers.
• PROPAGATION By seed when ripe, or by offsets in late summer, when dormant.

Z 6–10
HEIGHT 5–6ft (1.5–2m)
SPREAD 12–14in (30–35cm)
3–4in (8–10cm)

Alliaceae/Liliaceae

DICHELOSTEMMA CONGESTUM
Habit Upright, cormous, perennial. *Flowers* Small, tubular, borne on leafless stems in dense clusters, 2in (5cm) span, in early summer. Lilac-blue. *Leaves* Long and grass-like. Mid-green.
• NATIVE HABITAT Grasslands, western N. America.
• CULTIVATION Needs good drainage and a warm, sheltered site. Protect from excess wet in summer.
• PROPAGATION Sow seed as soon as ripe.
• OTHER NAME *Brodiaea congesta.*

Z 6–10
HEIGHT 16–36in (40–90cm)
SPREAD 3–4in (8–10cm)
4in (10cm)

Alliaceae/Liliaceae

ALLIUM HOLLANDICUM
Habit Robust, bulbous, perennial. *Flowers* Small, star-shaped, in tight, spherical heads, 4in (10cm) span, borne in summer. Violet-purple. *Leaves* Basal, semi-erect, and strap-shaped, dying back at flowering. Grayish-green.
• NATIVE HABITAT Foothills, central Asia.
• CULTIVATION Grow in fertile, well-drained soil in an herbaceous border. Ideal as dried flowers.
• PROPAGATION By seed when ripe, or by offsets in late summer when dormant. May self-seed.
• OTHER NAME *A. aflatunense* of gardens.

Z 4–10
HEIGHT to 30in (75cm)
SPREAD 6–8in (15–20cm)
3–4in (8–10cm)

Iridaceae

ARISTEA MAJOR
Habit Clump-forming, rhizomatous, perennial. *Flowers* Small, saucer-shaped, borne successively in loose sprays in summer. Purple-blue. *Leaves* Evergreen, upright, and sword-shaped. Mid-green.
• NATIVE HABITAT Cape Peninsula, S. Africa.
• CULTIVATION Needs good drainage and warm shelter. May survive to freezing, but prefers cool greenhouse in cold areas. Water sparingly in winter. Do not disturb roots when potting on.
• PROPAGATION By seed, when ripe or in spring.
• OTHER NAME *A. thyrsiflora.*

Z 9–10
HEIGHT to 3ft (1m)
SPREAD 18–24in (45–60cm)
1in (2–3cm)

---

24 • GLADIOLUS

GLADIOLUS

Gladiolus species are excellent for a mixed border. Cultivars are more commonly grown for exhibition and cutting. Plant corms 4–6in (10–15cm) deep, in spring, in a sunny, sheltered site with well-drained, fertile soil. Set corms on a layer of sharp sand to ensure good drainage. To achieve maximum flowering, apply high-potash fertilizer every 10–14 days as the spikes reach one-third of their height. Lift corms of gladiolus as the leaves wither in autumn. Dry off, separate new corms from the old ones, treat with fungicide, and store in dry, frost-free conditions. Species raised from seed take 2 to 3 years to reach flowering size; cultivars will not come true. Separate cormlets when dormant and grow on (see p. 174).

G. 'Ice Cap'
Habit Upright, cormous, perennial. Ruffled petals, each 5⅓in (14cm) across, formally arranged in spikes, with 10 open at any one time. Borne in late summer. Pure white. *Leaves* Narrow, sword-shaped. Mid-green.
• TIPS Suitable for arranging and cutting.
• OTHER NAME *G. 'Ice Cap'*
• HEIGHT 5½ft (1.7m)
• SPREAD 10in (25cm)
Z 8–10

G. 'The Bride'
Habit Upright, cormous, perennial. Funnel-shaped, borne in slender spikes in spring and early summer. White, streaked yellow. *Leaves* Narrow, sword-shaped. Mid-green.
• TIPS Good for planting in borders or containers.
• OTHER NAME *G. 'The Bride'* (*G. carditaalis* hybrid)
• HEIGHT 15in (40cm)
• SPREAD 2in (5cm)
Z 8–10

G. TRISTIS
Habit Upright, cormous, perennial. Funnel-shaped funnels, 2¼in (6cm) long, borne on wiry stems in spring. Pale creamy-yellow. *Leaves* Linear, twisted at the tips. Mid-green.
• TIPS Grows best in a cool greenhouse.
• HEIGHT 15–38 (45–130cm).
• SPREAD 2in (5cm).

G. tristis
Z 8–10

G. 'Dancing Queen'
Habit Upright, cormous, perennial. Silky, 4½–5⅓in (11–14cm) across, in formally arranged spikes, borne in late summer. Ivory-white, with claret-blotched throat. *Leaves* Narrow, sword-shaped. Mid-green.
• TIPS Suitable for cutting and arranging.
• HEIGHT 4½ft (1.35m).
• SPREAD 10in (15cm).

G. 'Dancing Queen'
Z 8–10

SYMBOLS
The symbols indicate the sun, soil, and temperature requirements (see THE SYMBOLS on previous page). Minimum temperatures are given for plants that cannot survive below 0°C (32°F).

FEATURE PLANT DESCRIPTIONS
As with the main Catalog entries, a brief plant description is followed by useful tips or cultivation and propagation where these are not already given in the general introduction.

SIZES
The average height and spread of the plants are given, although these may vary according to site, growing conditions, climate, and age.

BULBS IN THE GARDEN

BULBS, CORMS, AND TUBERS provide enormous potential for adding color, form, and often fragrance to the garden. One of their primary characteristics is that they bloom for one season only, thereafter lying dormant and unseen. With careful planning, this feature can be exploited to extend or enhance interest in a range of planting designs. Most bulbs bloom in spring or early summer, providing a succession of color before the summer-flowering shrubs and perennials reach their peak. Summer-flowering bulbs, like some alliums or *Galtonia candicans*, for example, are suitable for mixed and herbaceous borders, offering potential for bright highlights or subtle contrasts of color and form in the border.

Autumn- and winter-flowering bulbs lend color and variety in the quieter periods of the year, when much of the garden is fading or dormant. Many bulbs also thrive in pots, which may be used to decorate the home, greenhouse, or patio.

Ideal conditions
With the exception of species native to damp meadows and woodlands, nearly all bulbs grow and flower best in well-drained soil in sun. Warmth and good drainage are particularly important for sun-lovers such as *Nerine bowdenii*, the architectural *Crinum* x *powellii*, and *Amaryllis belladonna*. In areas at their limits of hardiness, these are best grown at the base of a warm wall, preferably within the shelter of house eaves to protect them from excessive rain. Given ideal conditions, these bulbs make the display last well into autumn, when the golden-yellow *Sternbergia lutea* and colorful autumn-flowering crocus and colchicums come into their own.

Bulbs in a mixed border
The deep pink-purple heads of Allium sphaerocephalum *provide strong contrast of form and act as a link to tie in the color theme of a border in shades of pink.*

Mixed and herbaceous borders

The use of bulbs to complement the often short-lived flowering season of perennial and shrubby plants is a tried-and-tested planting technique. It is especially valuable in small gardens, where an unoccupied space can be particularly noticeable. With careful planning, bulbs can provide lively variations of color, tie together color themes, and lengthen the period of interest over many months of the year. Mixed borders that feature a combination of perennials, annuals, shrubs, and biennials provide the greatest opportunity for creating year-round interest with imaginative plant associations. By interplanting with bulbs, an attractive succession of color can be achieved, enlivening the duller months from autumn to spring.

Even before shrubs and perennials come into leaf in spring, the ground can be clothed with a tapestry of snowdrops (*Galanthus*), winter aconites (*Eranthis*), or *Anemone blanda*, in white, pinks, and blues. The early-flowering dwarf hybrid *Narcissus*, small irises such as *I. reticulata*, along with the clear blues of *Chionodoxa* and *Scilla* provide complementary swathes of color beneath the yellow flowers of early-flowering shrubs, such as *Forsythia*, *Corylopsis*, and *Hamamelis*.

As spring progresses, the emerging foliage of perennials can be enlivened and enhanced with a display of spring and early summer bulbs. A sequence that includes tulips, from single earlies such as *Tulipa* 'Apricot Beauty' to single late-flowering tulips such as *T*. 'Greuze', *Hyacinthoides hispanica*, and fritillaries, will provide a succession of subtle or sumptuous color until early summer.

Formal plantings

The strongly upright, sculptural shapes of bulbs such as hyacinths and tulips are ideal in classic spring-bedding designs. They can provide vivid blocks of color, either alone in massed plantings, or in association with

A pageant of color
The strong forms and brilliant hues of tulips make them ideal for massed plantings that are arranged in well-ordered ranks, and give an elegantly formal effect.

lower-growing plants, such as pansies (*Viola*), forget-me-nots (*Myosotis*), or the strongly fragrant wallflowers (*Erysimum*). In general, the flamboyant flowers of hybrid bulbs are the best-suited to formal plantings, although several species, such as *Muscari latifolium* and *M. aucheri*, with neat form and strong color, also lend themselves to edging in less-structured plantings.

The refined appearance of certain summer- or late summer-flowering bulbs, corms, or tubers, for example, dahlias and most gladiolus, makes them ideally suited to formal use. Equally, some bulbs are sufficiently versatile to be used in structured gardens or in more free-form plantings. Many lilies (*Lilium*), for example, provide elegant formality in patio tubs, but combine equally well in relaxed associations with perennials and shrub roses.

Bulbs for bright borders
Here, loose drifts of slender tulips provide colorful highlights in a mixed border and, incidentally, reveal their adaptability to informal and formal planting plans.

The more delicate-looking flowers and form of species bulbs are well suited to planting in informal borders and cottage-style gardens. When grown between low, ground-covering plants, or blooming above clumps of emergent, fresh green, herbaceous foliage, bulbous plants can be used to draw the eye to bright colors and striking contrasts of form.

In high summer, use bulbs such as *Allium caeruleum* and *A. hollandicum*, with their striking, metallic-purple globes, or some of the incomparably elegant, sun-loving lilies, to grow through and complement perennials in full bloom. Use the upright spikes of *Galtonia candicans* or, in warmer gardens, *Eucomis* species, to provide strong vertical accents, and enhance "warm" combinations with the hot colors of *Crocosmia* cultivars such as

'Bressingham Blaze' or 'Lucifer'. In mixed plantings, set the bulbs between other plants in bold but informal drifts, so that the empty space left by flowers and foliage that have died back will be filled by the mature growth of shrubs and perennials.

Naturalizing bulbs
When left undisturbed in conditions that suit them, many bulbs and corms will increase readily by seed or offsets, to create natural drifts of color. This method of growing allows bulbs to be used in areas of the garden that are often unsuitable or impractical for larger flowering plants. To create a natural effect, plant in large, irregular, and informal drifts and use species rather than cultivars. With the possible exception of crocuses and the smaller *Narcissus* cultivars, most species

possess a greater delicacy of form and hue. In addition, their scale and style often makes them more appropriate to natural plantings.

Naturalizing beneath trees

Many bulbs thrive beneath deciduous trees or shrubs, where it would be difficult or impossible to establish larger flowering plants. Early spring- and autumn-flowering bulbs, especially those that need a dry dormancy in summer, often adapt well to these conditions. During summer, dormant bulbs benefit from the protection of a leafy canopy that shields them from excess summer rainfall, and in spring, during active growth, they receive adequate sunlight and moisture beneath the leafless trees. Some woodland bulbs, for example snowdrops (*Galanthus*) and English bluebells (*Hyacinthoides non-scriptus*), prefer a cool, shaded site with slightly moist conditions when dormant. Given a moisture-retentive soil that, ideally, has been enriched with leaf mold, these plants are perfect for creating colonies in a woodland setting.

A natural planting
Clumps of autumn-flowering Colchicum byzantinum *thrive and spread naturally in the light, dappled shade cast by a birch tree.*

Woodland charm
Growing beneath bare branches, Cyclamen coum *and crocuses provide color during late winter and early spring, when most plants in the garden are dormant.*

Spring spectacle
Naturalized crocuses provide the most spectacular effects when planted in bold, sweeping, and irregularly shaped drifts of a single color. The vivid hues are offset by the white blooms of snowdrops.

Naturalizing in turf

Whether on a bank, in a lawn, or in a meadow, bulbs can transform turf into a tapestry studded with jewel-bright color, in spring or autumn. The art of establishing thriving colonies that spread more thickly year by year depends on the observation of a couple of important ground rules. First, the size and vigor of the bulb should match the strength of the grass, and second, mowing must be scheduled to permit the bulb to grow, flower, set seed, and fade naturally before cutting. It is essential to allow full development of the foliage, since the leaves provide the bulb's food storage which, in turn, produces the following year's flower. For early-flowering bulbs, the first cut will be made from mid- to late spring onward; for summer-flowering plants, perhaps grown among taller meadow grasses, the first cut will be in mid- or late summer. Autumn-flowering bulbs are likely to commence growth before the usual mowing season ends, so discontinue lawn-cutting from late summer onward. Do not begin again until the leaves have faded, which may not be until spring.

Where grass is composed of vigorous, hard-wearing species, select larger bulbs, such as the robust species and energetic hybrids of *Narcissus*, or the more resilient Dutch crocus hybrids (*C. vernus*). In finer grade turf, or in thin grass beneath trees, some of the smaller bulbs, such as *Crocus tommasinianus*, the stronger variants of *C. sieberi* and *C. chrysanthus*, and the vigorous, autumn-flowering colchicums, will thrive. Such conditions also suit *Narcissus cyclamineus* and *N. minor*, which would not survive competition from the roots of more vigorous grasses.

Bulbs in containers

There are several reasons for choosing to grow bulbs in containers. For purely decorative purposes, growing them in ornamental pots, window boxes, or other containers provides an added dimension to a garden design. Containers can be placed to make a focal point within a design, or massed together on a terrace or patio, with graduations of height and variation in form, to create exuberant displays of color. Groupings of fragrant bulbs, such as lilies or *Crinum* x *powellii*, in containers around a doorway or window permits their scent to be enjoyed frequently and at close quarters. With careful selection, pot-grown bulbs can provide color from late winter through to autumn. When their display is over, they can be lifted and stored, or planted out in the garden, to be replaced with other plants. It is important to match the size and vigor of the bulb to the scale of the pot. Use the smaller bulbs in window boxes and, for best results, plant them in layers beneath other plants to make the most effective use of space. Most of the tall lilies, and the architectural crinums, need fairly large, deep containers if their tall flowering stems are not to become top-heavy, either physically or aesthetically.

Bulbs under cover

Growing in pots under cover, in an alpine house, greenhouse, or bulb frame, permits each to be grown in controlled conditions to suit individual needs, especially with regard to the type of soil mix, light, warmth, and watering regime. This is particularly useful for cultivating small stocks of uncommon species and, in areas with wet summers, is the most practical way of growing those that need dry conditions during dormancy. In cold and cool temperate regions, many tender or borderline hardy bulbs that would not survive in the open garden, are grown in this way. Some, such as *Watsonia* or *Crinum*, may be moved outdoors during

their flowering period, and later moved back under cover to protect them from moisture and cold during dormancy. Others, such as *Veltheimia* or *Nerine* cultivars, may be transferred indoors where the flowers can be enjoyed.

The alpine house and bulb frame are ideal for small bulbs that are marginally or even fully hardy, but which need carefully controlled watering during growth and protection from rain when dormant, either in summer or winter. A bulb frame is a plunge bed with a removable cover to give overhead protection from rainfall in dormancy, while maximizing light and ventilation.

Bulbs in pots

The white trumpets of Lilium regale *provide the focal point of this tiered arrangement, in which the white is echoed by geraniums and contrasted with the warm tones of terracotta.*

PLANTERS' GUIDE TO BULBS

FOR EXPOSED OR WINDY SITES
Amaryllis belladonna
Anemone
Canna 'Assaut'
Chionodoxa
Colchicum
Crocus
Cyclamen some
Fritillaria dwarf species
Galanthus
Iris reticulata cvs.
Muscari some
Narcissus dwarf species/cvs.
Ornithogalum some
Scilla some
Triteleia
Tulipa dwarf species

FOR SHELTERED SITES
Bulbs that prefer the
protection of a wall
Amaryllis belladonna
Eucomis
Fritillaria persica
Ixia
Nerine bowdenii
Rhodophiala advenum
Scilla peruviana
Sparaxis
Sternbergia lutea
Watsonia
Zephyranthes candida

FOR MOIST SHADE
Bulbs that prefer
moist shade
Anemone blanda
Arisaema most species
Arum italicum
Cardiocrinum giganteum
Eranthis
Erythronium
Fritillaria camschatcensis
Fritillaria cirrhosa
Galanthus
Leucojum aestivum
Leucojum vernum

Narcissus cyclamineus
Narcissus triandrus
Nomocharis
Notholirion
Tulipa sylvestris

FOR DRY SHADE
Bulbs that tolerate
dry shade
Arum italicum subsp.
  italicum 'Marmoratum'
Cyclamen coum subsp. *coum*
Cyclamen hederifolium
Galanthus nivalis forms
Hyacinthoides non-scripta

FLOWERS FOR CUTTING
Allium some species
Amaryllis belladonna
Camassia
Crocosmia
Freesia
Galtonia
Gladiolus some
Ixia
Lilium
Narcissus
Ornithogalum
Ranunculus asiaticus
Sparaxis
Tulipa

ARCHITECTURAL PLANTS
Allium cristophii
Allium giganteum
Canna
Cardiocrinum giganteum
Crinum × *powellii*
Fritillaria imperialis
Lilium most species/cvs.

FOR ROCK GARDENS
Albuca humilis
Allium dwarf species
Bellevalia hyacinthoides
Bulbocodium vernum
Colchicum small species
Crocus

Cyclamen hardy species
Fritillaria many species
Galanthus
Ipheion
Iris dwarf species
Merendera
Muscari
Narcissus dwarf species
Puschkinia
Rhodohypoxis
Scilla some
Sternbergia lutea
Tulipa dwarf species
Zigadenus

FOR ALPINE HOUSES
Albuca humilis
Babiana
Bellevalia
Biarum
Bulbocodium vernum
Calochortus
Colchicum small species
Crocus
Cyclamen some
Fritillaria most species
Iris dwarf species
Leucocoryne
Leucojum
Merendera
Narcissus dwarf species
Rhodohypoxis
Scilla
Sternbergia
Tecophilaea

CATALOG OF
BULBS

Amaryllidaceae/ Liliaceae	

LEUCOJUM AESTIVUM 'Gravetye Giant'

Habit Robust, free-flowering, bulbous, perennial. **Flowers** Clusters of 2–7 drooping bells, borne on long, leafless stems in late spring to early summer. White, with green petal tips. **Leaves** Basal, long, strap-shaped, and semi-erect. Rich green.
• NATIVE HABITAT Garden origin.
• CULTIVATION Thrives in moist, heavy, fertile, even waterlogged soils. Tolerates sun where soil remains moist. May be naturalized in damp grass.
• PROPAGATION By division in autumn or spring.

☼ ◐ ◊

Z 4–9

HEIGHT
30–36in
(75cm–1m)

SPREAD
4–5in
(10–12cm)

1–2in
(3–5cm)

Amaryllidaceae/ Liliaceae	

CRINUM × *POWELLII* 'Album'

Habit Sturdy, bulbous, perennial. **Flowers** Large, fragrant funnels, borne in clusters on leafless stems in late summer or autumn. White. **Leaves** Long, strap-shaped, and semi-upright. Fresh green.
• NATIVE HABITAT Garden origin.
• CULTIVATION In cold areas, plant in a sheltered site by a warm, sunny wall. Needs fertile, moist but well-drained soil that is rich in organic matter. Protect bulb with a deep, dry mulch in winter.
• PROPAGATION Separate small offsets in spring or early summer.

☼ ◊

Z 7–10

HEIGHT
to 3ft (1m)

SPREAD
2ft (60cm)

Nose
level

Hyacinthaceae/ Liliaceae	SUMMER HYACINTH

GALTONIA CANDICANS

Habit Robust, erect, bulbous. **Flowers** Scented, bowing, short-tubed bells, borne in slender spikes in late summer. White. **Leaves** Fleshy, long, semi-erect, and narrowly lance-shaped. Grayish-green.
• NATIVE HABITAT Damp grassland, often in hills and mountains, southern Africa.
• CULTIVATION Excellent for a sheltered, herbaceous border in sun. Needs fertile, moist but well-drained soil.
• PROPAGATION By seed in spring, or by offsets in autumn or spring.

☼ ◊

Z 7–10

HEIGHT
3–4ft
(1–1.2m)

SPREAD
7–9in
(18–23cm)

5in
(12cm)

Araceae	

ZANTEDESCHIA AETHIOPICA 'Crowborough'

Habit Tuberous, perennial. **Flowers** Cowl-like spathe around a golden spike, borne successively from early to mid-summer. White. **Leaves** Glossy, evergreen, and arrow-shaped. Dark green.
• NATIVE HABITAT Garden origin.
• CULTIVATION A hardy cultivar that is deciduous in cold climates. May be used as a waterside plant in up to 12in (30cm) of water. Needs fertile, moist but well-drained soil that is rich in organic matter.
• PROPAGATION By suckers or division in spring.

☼ ◐

Z 8–10

HEIGHT
18–36in
(45cm–1m)

SPREAD
14–18in
(35–45cm)

4in
(10cm)

Hyacinthaceae/ Liliaceae	

CAMASSIA LEICHTLINII

Habit Tuft-forming, bulbous, perennial.
Flowers Star-shaped, 2–3in (5–7cm) across,
borne in erect sprays in summer. Creamy-white
to bluish-violet. *Leaves* Basal, long, narrowly
linear, and keel-shaped. Bright green.
• NATIVE HABITAT Usually by streams, and
in damp meadows in western N. America.
• CULTIVATION Tolerates partial shade, but prefers
sun in rich, fertile, moist soil that is well-drained.
• PROPAGATION By seed as soon as ripe, or by
offsets in late summer.

☼ ◑

Z 3–10

HEIGHT
2–4½ft
(60–130cm)

SPREAD
8–12in
(20–30cm)

5in
(12cm)

Amaryllidaceae/ Liliaceae	

HYMENOCALLIS × *MACROSTEPHANA*

Habit Bulbous, perennial. *Flowers* Fragrant,
central cup with slender, spidery petals, 6–8in
(15–20cm) across, borne during spring or summer.
Greenish-white. *Leaves* Evergreen, basal,
strap-shaped, and semi-upright. Fresh green.
• NATIVE HABITAT Garden origin.
• CULTIVATION Grow as a house or conservatory
plant in cool climates. Use a mix of equal parts
loam, leaf mold, and sharp sand. Water freely
during growth, but keep bulb just moist in winter.
• PROPAGATION Offsets in spring to early summer.

☼ ◌

Z 7–10

HEIGHT
to 32in
(80cm)

SPREAD
12–18in
(30–45cm)

2–4in
(5–10cm)

Hyacinthaceae/ Liliaceae	GIANT PINEAPPLE LILY

EUCOMIS PALLIDIFLORA

Habit Bulbous, sturdy, slow-growing. *Flowers*
Small stars, in a dense spray with leaf-like bracts,
borne in summer. Greenish-white. *Leaves* Basal,
sword-shaped, and wavy-edged. Fresh green.
• NATIVE HABITAT Grasslands, southern Africa.
• CULTIVATION Needs fertile, well-drained soil
that stays moist throughout the growing season.
Give deep, dry, winter mulch.
• PROPAGATION By offsets in autumn, or by
seed as soon as ripe or in spring.
• OTHER NAME *E. punctata* var. *concolor*

☼ ◌

Z 8–10

HEIGHT
to 30in
(75cm)

SPREAD
12–24in
(30–60cm)

5in
(12cm)

Hyacinthaceae/Liliaceae	

CAMASSIA LEICHTLINII 'Semiplena'

Habit Tuft-forming, bulbous, perennial.
Flowers Semi-double, star-shaped, 1½–3in
(4–8cm) across, with many slender petals. Borne
in dense, upright spikes on leafless stems during
summer. Creamy-white. **Leaves** Basal, long,
narrowly linear, and keel-shaped. Bright green.
• NATIVE HABITAT Usually grows by streams and
in damp meadows of western N. America, from
British Columbia to California.
• CULTIVATION Tolerates partial or dappled shade,
but grows best in a sunny site. Needs a fertile,

moist but well-drained soil that is rich in organic
matter. This cultivar, and the species, may be
naturalized in damp grass or in open woodland
glades. In poorer soils, smaller, more delicate
flower spikes will be produced. This cultivar
is considered to be superior to the species for
general garden use and is certainly more suited
for growing as a showpiece in an herbaceous
border. The flowers are ideal for cutting and
will last quite well in water.
• PROPAGATION By offsets in late summer.

☼ ◊

Z 3–10

HEIGHT
3–5ft
(1–1.5m)

SPREAD
8–12in
(20–30cm)

5in
(12cm)

Araceae	

ZANTEDESCHIA AETHIOPICA
'Green Goddess'

Habit Tuberous, perennial. *Flowers* Cowl-like spathes, borne in summer. Pale green, each with a white- and green-splashed throat. *Leaves* Arrow-shaped, evergreen, and glossy. Deep green.
• NATIVE HABITAT Garden origin.
• CULTIVATION Needs fertile, moist but well-drained soil that is enriched with organic matter. May also be used as a waterside plant in up to 12in (30cm) of water. Deciduous in cold climates.
• PROPAGATION By suckers or division in spring.

☀ ◑

Z 8–10

HEIGHT
18–36in
(45cm–1m)

SPREAD
18–24in
(45–60cm)

4in
(10cm)

Iridaceae	

IRIS MAGNIFICA

Habit Upright, bulbous, perennial. *Flowers* Spanning 2½–3in (6–8cm), borne in leaf axils on upper stem in late spring. Pale lilac with yellow-stained falls. *Leaves* Scattered up the stem, channelled, lance-shaped, and glossy. Mid-green.
• NATIVE HABITAT Limestone, central Asia.
• CULTIVATION Suitable for growing in a warm, sunny border or raised bed. Grows best in deep, moderately fertile and sharply drained soil.
• PROPAGATION Separate young bulbs carefully in late summer. Avoid damaging the fleshy roots.

☀ ◔

Z 6–9

HEIGHT
1–2ft
(30–60cm)

SPREAD
6in (15cm)

2in
(5cm)

Liliaceae	GIANT LILY

CARDIOCRINUM GIGANTEUM

Habit Robust, bulbous, perennial. *Flowers* Fragrant, trumpet-shaped, 6in (15cm) across, borne on stout stems in summer. White, flushed maroon-purple at throat. *Leaves* Basal, broadly oval, and glossy, becoming smaller up the stem. Dark green.
• NATIVE HABITAT Damp woodland, Himalaya.
• CULTIVATION Needs fertile, leaf-rich soil that is enriched with organic matter. Protect from slugs.
• PROPAGATION By offsets in autumn or by ripe seed. Takes about 7 years to flower from seed.
• OTHER NAMES *Lilium giganteum.*

☀ ◑

Z 7–9

HEIGHT
5–12ft
(1.5–4m)

SPREAD
30in
(75cm)

Nose
level

Hyacinthaceae/ Liliaceae	PINEAPPLE LILY

EUCOMIS COMOSA

Habit Clump-forming, bulbous, perennial. *Flowers* Small stars, borne in a spike capped by bracts in summer. White to greenish-white, often flushed pink. *Leaves* Strap-shaped and wavy-margined. Green, with purple-spotted underside.
• NATIVE HABITAT Grasslands, S. Africa.
• CULTIVATION Needs fertile, well-drained soil that is moist during growing season. Provide a deep, dry, winter mulch in cold climates.
• PROPAGATION By offsets in autumn, or by seed as soon as ripe or in spring.

☀ ◔

Z 8–10

HEIGHT
to 28in
(70cm)

SPREAD
12–24in
(30–60cm)

5in
(12cm)

Amaryllidaceae/Liliaceae	

CRINUM MOOREI

Habit Robust, bulbous, perennial. *Flowers* Fragrant, long-tubed funnels, borne in clusters of 6–12 on leafless stems, in summer. White, often flushed pink, or shades of pink. *Leaves* Strap-shaped and semi-erect. Bright green.

• NATIVE HABITAT Forests of Natal, S. Africa.

• CULTIVATION If given a deep, dry mulch and the shelter of a warm, sunny wall, this species may survive temperatures below 32°F (0°C) for short periods. Elsewhere, it is ideal for growing in a cool greenhouse or conservatory. Plant in deep, fertile, moist but well-drained soil that is enriched with organic matter. Young leaves under glass should be shaded from hot sun. Water freely when in growth, but keep just moist during winter.

• PROPAGATION Separate small offsets in spring, taking care not to damage the fleshy roots. Sow seed as soon as it is ripe, or in spring. Flowers may appear by the third or fourth year.

• OTHER NAMES *C. colensoi* of gardens, *C. mackenii* of gardens, *C. makoyanum* of gardens, and *C. natalense* of gardens.

☼ ◊

Z 8–10

HEIGHT
20–48in
(50–120cm)

SPREAD
18in (45cm)

Neck above

Liliaceae/Liliaceae	

NOMOCHARIS PARDANTHINA

Habit Upright, bulbous, perennial. **Flowers** Drooping, flattened, butterfly-like, with fringed inner segments, borne on wiry stems in summer. White to pale pink, purple-spotted with a purple eye. **Leaves** Lance-shaped, in whorls. Mid-green.
• NATIVE HABITAT Mountains, western China.
• CULTIVATION Flowers best in cool summers. Suits peat bed or woodland garden, sheltered from winds. Needs leaf-rich, moist but well-drained soil.
• PROPAGATION Sow seed in late winter.
• OTHER NAME *N. mairei.*

☀ ◐ pH

Z 7–9

HEIGHT
to 3ft (1m)

SPREAD
5–6in
(12–15cm)

4in
(10cm)

Amaryllidaceae/ Liliaceae	

CRINUM × POWELLII

Habit Sturdy, perennial. **Flowers** Large, fragrant, widely funnel-shaped, borne in sprays of up to 10 on leafless stems, in late summer or autumn. Pale to mid-pink. **Leaves** Long, strap-shaped, and semi-upright. Fresh green.
• NATIVE HABITAT Garden origin.
• CULTIVATION Prefers to be sited in the shelter of a warm, sunny wall in fertile, moist but well-drained soil, that is enriched with organic matter. Needs a deep, dry winter mulch in colder areas.
• PROPAGATION Separate small offsets in spring.

☀ ◐

Z 7–10

HEIGHT
to 3ft (1m)

SPREAD
2ft (60cm)

Nose
level

Alliaceae/Liliaceae	

NECTAROSCORDUM SICULUM subsp. BULGARICUM

Habit Slender, upright, bulbous. **Flowers** Small, drooping, bell-shaped, borne in sprays in summer. White, shaded pink and green. **Leaves** Strap-shaped, dying back after flowering. Mid-green.
• NATIVE HABITAT Woods, Turkey and Bulgaria.
• CULTIVATION May be naturalized in woodland. Invasive, so site with care. Grow in moist but well-drained soil. Deadhead to prevent seeding.
• PROPAGATION By seed, when ripe or in spring.
• OTHER NAME *N. dioscoridis.*

☀ ◐

Z 6–10

HEIGHT
to 4ft
(1.2m)

SPREAD
12–18in
(30–45cm)

2in
(5cm)

GLADIOLUS

Gladiolus species are excellent for a mixed border. Cultivars are more commonly grown for exhibition and cutting. Plant corms 4–6in (10–15cm) deep, in spring, in a sunny, sheltered site with well-drained, fertile soil. Set corms on a layer of sharp sand to ensure good drainage. To achieve maximum flowering, apply high-potash fertilizer every 10–14 days as the spikes reach one-third of their height. Lift corms of gladiolus as the leaves wither in autumn. Dry off, separate new corms from the old ones, treat with fungicide, and store in dry, frost-free conditions. Species raised from seed take 2 to 3 years to reach flowering size; cultivars will not come true. Separate cormlets when dormant and grow on (see p. 174).

G. 'Ice Cap'
Habit Upright, cormous, perennial.
Flowers Ruffled petals, each 5½in (14cm) across, formally arranged in spikes, with 10 open at any one time. Borne in late summer. Pure white.
Leaves Narrow, sword-shaped. Mid-green.
• TIPS Suitable for arranging and cutting.
• HEIGHT 5½ft (1.7m).
• SPREAD 10in (25cm).

G. 'Ice Cap'

☼ ◊   Z 8–10

G. TRISTIS
Habit Upright, cormous, perennial.
Flowers Scented funnels, 2⅜in (6cm) long, borne on wiry stems in spring. Pale creamy-yellow.
Leaves Linear, twisted at the tips. Mid-green.
• TIPS Grows best in a cool greenhouse.
• HEIGHT 1½–5ft (45–150cm).
• SPREAD 2in (5cm).

G. tristis

☼ ◊   Z 8–10

G. 'The Bride'
Habit Upright, cormous, perennial.
Flowers Funnel-shaped, borne in slender spikes in spring and early summer. White, streaked yellow.
Leaves Narrow, sword-shaped. Mid-green.
• TIPS Good for planting in borders or containers.
• OTHER NAME
G. x *colvillei* 'The Bride'.
• HEIGHT 15in (40cm).
• SPREAD 2in (5cm).

G. 'The Bride'
(*G. cardinalis* hybrid)

☼ ◊   Z 8–10

G. 'Dancing Queen'
Habit Upright, cormous, perennial.
Flowers Silky, 4½–5½in (11–14cm) across, in formally arranged spikes, borne in late summer. Ivory-white, with claret-blotched throat.
Leaves Narrow, sword-shaped. Mid-green.
• TIPS Suitable for cutting and arranging.
• HEIGHT 4½ft (1.35m).
• SPREAD 10in (25cm).

G. 'Dancing Queen'

☼ ◊   Z 8–10

G. 'Nymph'
Habit Upright,
cormous, perennial.
Flowers Spanning 2in
(5cm), borne in loose,
slender spikes in early
summer. White, with
cream, red-rimmed lips.
Leaves Narrow, sword-
shaped. Mid-green.
• TIPS Ideal for cutting
and excellent for use in
decorative arrangements.
• HEIGHT 28in (70cm).
• SPREAD to 4in (10cm).

G. 'Nymph'

☼ ◊   Z 8–10

G. CALLIANTHUS
Habit Upright,
cormous, perennial.
Flowers Fragrant,
long-tubed, borne in
late summer. White,
with purple-red throat.
Leaves Linear. Green.
• TIPS Ideal for planting
in borders and cutting.
• OTHER NAMES
Acidanthera bicolor var.
murielae, A. murielae.
• HEIGHT to 3ft (1m).
• SPREAD 2in (5cm).

G. callianthus

☼ ◊   Z 8–10

G. 'Rose Supreme'
Habit Upright,
cormous, perennial.
Flowers Spanning 5½in
(14cm) or more, borne in
formally arranged spikes
in late summer. Rose-
pink, with darker streaks
and cream throat.
Leaves Narrow, sword-
shaped. Mid-green.
• TIPS Suitable for
cutting and arranging.
• HEIGHT 5½ft (1.7m).
• SPREAD 10in (25cm).

G. 'Rose Supreme'

☼ ◊   Z 8–10

G. PAPILIO
Habit Erect, clumping,
cormous, perennial.
Flowers Hooded bells,
borne in late summer.
Yellow, with purple
blotches on lower petals.
Leaves Sword-shaped.
Mid-green.
• TIPS Spreads by
underground runners.
• OTHER NAME
G. purpureoauratus.
• HEIGHT to 3ft (90cm).
• SPREAD 3in (8cm).

G. papilio

☼ ◊   Z 8–10

G. 'Amanda Mahy'
Habit Upright,
cormous, perennial.
Flowers Borne in loose,
slender spikes, 2in (5cm)
span, in early summer.
Salmon-pink, with white-
and violet-flecked lips.
Leaves Narrow, sword-
shaped. Mid-green.
• TIPS Ideal for cutting
and arranging, especially
for corsages.
• HEIGHT 20in (50cm).
• SPREAD to 4in (10cm).

G. 'Amanda Mahy'

☼ ◊   Z 8–10

G. 'Miss America'
Habit Upright,
cormous, perennial.
Flowers Strongly ruffled
petals, 3½–4½in (9–11cm)
span, borne in formally
arranged spikes in late
summer. Deep pink.
Leaves Narrow, sword-
shaped. Mid-green.
• TIPS Ideal specimen
for exhibition and
suitable for cut flowers.
• HEIGHT 5ft (1.5m).
• SPREAD 10in (25cm).

G. 'Miss America'

☼ ◊   Z 8–10

G. 'Deliverance'
Habit Upright, cormous, perennial.
Flowers Ruffled petals, 5½in (14cm) or more across, borne in formally arranged spikes in late summer. Salmon-pink, overlaid with orange.
Leaves Narrow, sword-shaped. Mid-green.
• TIPS Suitable for cutting and arranging.
• HEIGHT 5½ft (1.7m).
• SPREAD 10in (25cm).

G. 'Deliverance'

☼ ◊   Z 8–10

G. 'Mexicali Rose'
Habit Upright, cormous, perennial.
Flowers Spanning up to 4½in (14cm), with ruffled petals, formally arranged in spikes, borne in late summer. Deep rose-pink, silver-white margins.
Leaves Narrow, sword-shaped. Mid-green.
• TIPS Suitable for cutting and arranging.
• HEIGHT 5ft (1.5m).
• SPREAD 12in (30cm).

G. 'Mexicali Rose'

☼ ◊   Z 8–10

G. 'Inca Queen'
Habit Upright, cormous, perennial.
Flowers Waxy, ruffled petals, to 5½in (14cm) span, formally arranged, borne in late summer. Deep salmon-pink, with lemon-yellow throat.
Leaves Narrow, sword-shaped. Mid-green.
• TIPS Suitable for cutting or exhibition.
• HEIGHT 5ft (1.5m).
• SPREAD 10in (25cm).

G. 'Inca Queen'

☼ ◊   Z 8–10

G. ITALICUS
Habit Upright, cormous, perennial.
Flowers Narrow, funnel-shaped, borne in early summer. Pink-purple, with paler-marked lips.
Leaves Sword-shaped. Mid-green.
• TIPS Good for planting in borders and cutting.
• OTHER NAME G. segetum.
• HEIGHT to 3ft (90cm).
• SPREAD 3in (8cm).

G. italicus

☼ ◊   Z 8–10

G. 'Gigi'
Habit Upright, cormous, perennial.
Flowers Ruffled petals, 2½–3½in (6–9cm) across, in formally arranged spikes, borne in late summer. Deep pink, with white throat.
Leaves Narrow, sword-shaped. Mid-green.
• TIPS Good for planting in borders and cutting.
• HEIGHT 3ft (1m).
• SPREAD 6in (15cm).

G. 'Gigi'

☼ ◊   Z 8–10

G. COMMUNIS subsp. BYZANTINUS
Habit Upright, cormous, perennial.
Flowers Funnel-shaped, in loose spikes, borne in late spring. Magenta, with paler marks on lips.
Leaves Linear. Green.
• TIPS Good for planting in borders and cutting.
• OTHER NAME G. byzantinus.
• HEIGHT to 3ft (1m).
• SPREAD 3in (8cm).

G. communis subsp. byzantinus

☼ ◊   Z 8–10

G. 'Drama'
Habit Upright, cormous, perennial.
Flowers Slightly ruffled, formally arranged spikes, borne in late summer. Deep pink, with red-flecked yellow throat.
Leaves Narrow, sword-shaped. Mid-green.
• TIPS Ideal as cut flowers and suitable specimen for exhibition.
• HEIGHT 5½ft (1.7m).
• SPREAD 10in (25cm).

G. 'Drama'

☼ ◊   Z 8–10

G. 'Robin'
Habit Upright, cormous, perennial.
Flowers Hooded, 1½–3in (3.5–7cm) across, in semi-formal, ladder-like arrangement, borne in spikes in late summer. Deep rose-purple.
Leaves Narrow, sword-shaped. Mid-green.
• TIPS Suitable for cutting and arranging.
• HEIGHT 4ft (1.2m).
• SPREAD 8in (20cm).

G. 'Robin'

☼ ◊   Z 8–10

G. 'Pink Lady'
Habit Upright, cormous, perennial.
Flowers Slightly ruffled, up to 5½in (14cm) across, formally arranged in spikes, borne in late summer. Deep rose-pink, with white throat.
Leaves Narrow, sword-shaped. Mid-green.
• TIPS Suitable for cutting and arranging.
• HEIGHT 5ft (1.5m).
• SPREAD 10in (25cm).

G. 'Pink Lady'

☼ ◊   Z 8–10

G. CARDINALIS
Habit Upright, cormous, perennial.
Flowers Widely funnel-shaped, 2in (5cm) across, borne on arching stems, in summer. Bright red, with white-marked lips.
Leaves Sword-shaped. Mid-green.
• TIPS Good for cutting and in borders as a filler between plants.
• HEIGHT to 3ft (90cm).
• SPREAD 3in (8cm).

G. cardinalis

☼ ◊   Z 8–10

G. 'Black Lash'
Habit Upright, cormous, perennial.
Flowers Pointed, slightly reflexed, ruffled, up to 3½in (9cm) span, borne in formally arranged spikes, from late summer to early autumn. Deep rose-red.
Leaves Narrow, sword-shaped. Mid-green.
• TIPS Suitable for cutting and arranging.
• HEIGHT 4½ft (1.35m).
• SPREAD 6in (15cm).

G. 'Black Lash'

☼ ◊   Z 8–10

G. 'Renegade'
Habit Upright, cormous, perennial.
Flowers Neatly ruffled, 4½–5½in (11–14cm) span, in formally arranged spikes, 7–8 open at one time, borne in late summer. Rich, dark red.
Leaves Narrow, sword-shaped. Mid-green.
• TIPS Suitable for cutting and arranging.
• HEIGHT 5ft (1.5m).
• SPREAD 10in (25cm).

G. 'Renegade'

☼ ◊   Z 8–10

G. 'Rutherford'
Habit Upright, cormous, perennial.
Flowers Hooded, 1½–3in (3.5–7cm) across, in spikes with a semi-formal, ladder-like arrangement, borne in late summer. Deep red, splashed with cream.
Leaves Narrow, sword-shaped. Mid-green.
• TIPS Suitable for cutting and arranging.
• HEIGHT 3ft (1m).
• SPREAD 6in (15cm).

G. 'Rutherford'

☀ ◊   Z 8–10

G. 'Moon Mirage'
Habit Upright, cormous, perennial.
Flowers Ruffled, from 5½in (14cm) span, borne in formally arranged spikes in late summer. Canary-yellow, with dark yellow lips. **Leaves** Narrow, sword-shaped. Mid-green.
• TIPS Suitable for cutting and arranging.
• HEIGHT 5½ft (1.7m).
• SPREAD 1ft (30cm).

G. 'Moon Mirage'

☀ ◊   Z 8–10

G. 'Victor Borge'
Habit Upright, cormous, perennial.
Flowers Up to 5½in (14cm) across, formally arranged in spikes, borne in late summer. Rich, deep vermilion, with white-marked throat.
Leaves Narrow, sword-shaped. Mid-green.
• TIPS Suitable for cutting and arranging.
• HEIGHT 5½ft (1.7m).
• SPREAD 12in (30cm).

G. 'Victor Borge'

☀ ◊   Z 8–10

G. 'Green Woodpecker'
Habit Upright, cormous, perennial.
Flowers Ruffled petals, 3½–4½in (9–11cm) across, in formal spikes, borne in late summer. Lime-yellow, with claret throat.
Leaves Narrow, sword-shaped. Mid-green.
• TIPS Good specimen for exhibition.
• HEIGHT 5ft (1.5m).
• SPREAD 12in (30cm).

G. 'Green Woodpecker'

☀ ◊   Z 8–10

G. 'Tesoro'
Habit Upright, cormous, perennial.
Flowers Silky, slightly ruffled, spanning 3½–4½in (9–11cm), in formally arranged spikes, borne during early autumn. Lustrous, rich yellow.
Leaves Lance-shaped to oval, toothed. Mid-green.
• TIPS Ideal specimen for exhibition.
• HEIGHT 5ft (1.5m).
• SPREAD 10in (25cm).

G. 'Tesoro'

☀ ◊   Z 8–10

G. 'Christabel'
Habit Upright, cormous, perennial.
Flowers Fragrant, flared funnels, 3–4in (8–10cm) span, borne in loose spikes of 6–10 in spring. Primrose-yellow, with purple-brown veins.
Leaves Very narrow. Mid-green.
• TIPS Grows best in a cool greenhouse.
• HEIGHT 18in (45cm).
• SPREAD 3in (8cm).

G. 'Christabel'
(G. tristis hybrid)

☀ ◊   Z 8–10

G. 'Little Darling'
Habit Upright, cormous, perennial.
Flowers Borne in loose spikes, 1⅜in (3.5cm) span, in mid-summer. Rose- to salmon-pink, with lemon lips.
Leaves Narrow, sword-shaped. Mid-green.
• TIPS Suitable for cut flowers and ideal specimen for arranging.
• HEIGHT 3½ft (1.1m).
• SPREAD to 4in (10cm).

G. 'Little Darling'

☼ ◊   Z 8–10

G. 'Café au Lait'
Habit Upright, cormous, perennial.
Flowers Hooded, up to 3in (7cm) span, arranged semi-formally, ladder-like, in spikes, borne in late summer. Pale coffee, with beige throat.
Leaves Narrow, sword-shaped. Mid-green.
• TIPS Suitable for cutting and arranging.
• HEIGHT 3½ft (1.1m).
• SPREAD to 8in (20cm).

G. 'Café au Lait'

☼ ◊   Z 8–10

G. 'Melodie'
Habit Upright, cormous, perennial.
Flowers Spanning 2½–3½in (6–9cm), semi-formally arranged, ladder-like, in spikes, borne in late summer. Salmon-rose, with flame throat.
Leaves Narrow, sword-shaped. Mid-green.
• TIPS Suitable for cutting and arranging.
• HEIGHT 4ft (1.2m).
• SPREAD to 8in (20cm).

G. 'Melodie'

☼ ◊   Z 8–10

G. 'Peter Pears'
Habit Upright, cormous, perennial.
Flowers Up to 5½in (14cm) across, formally arranged in spikes, borne in late summer. Salmon-apricot, with red throat.
Leaves Narrow, sword-shaped. Mid-green.
• TIPS Ideal specimen for cutting, arranging, and exhibition.
• HEIGHT 5½ft (1.7m).
• SPREAD 14in (35cm).

G. 'Peter Pears'

☼ ◊   Z 8–10

G. 'Carioca'
Habit Upright, cormous, perennial.
Flowers Ruffled petals, 3½–4½in (9–11cm) across, in formally arranged spikes, borne in mid-summer. Clear orange, with red throat.
Leaves Narrow, sword-shaped. Mid-green.
• TIPS Suitable for cutting and arranging.
• HEIGHT 4½ft (1.35m).
• SPREAD to 1ft (30cm).

G. 'Carioca'

☼ ◊   Z 8–10

Iridaceae	FAIRY FISHING POLES

DIERAMA PULCHERRIMUM

Habit Erect, cormous, perennial. **Flowers** Small,
silky, funnel-shaped, with slender stalks. Borne in
spikes on arching stems, in summer. Pale to deep
pink, with silvery outer petals. **Leaves** Evergreen,
stiff, and linear. Grayish-green.
• NATIVE HABITAT Damp grassland, S. Africa.
• CULTIVATION Needs deep, fertile, moist but
well-drained soil, enriched with organic matter.
Good for waterside plantings (above the waterline).
• PROPAGATION Separate offsets after flowering,
or sow seed as soon as ripe. May self-seed.

☀ ◑

Z 8–10

HEIGHT
3–5ft
(1–1.5m)

SPREAD
2ft (60cm)

3–4in
(8–10cm)

Liliaceae	

NOTHOLIRION CAMPANULATUM

Habit Tufted, bulbous, perennial. **Flowers**
Drooping, funnel-shaped, borne in spikes of
10–40 on leafy stems, in summer. Deep lavender-
pink, tipped with green. **Leaves** Tufted, basal,
and narrowly lance-shaped. Fresh green.
• NATIVE HABITAT Grassy slopes, Tibet, Burma.
• CULTIVATION Prefers cool summers. Needs light,
moist but well-drained soil that is rich in organic
matter. Best grown in partial or dappled shade.
• PROPAGATION Separate bulblets or sow seed,
both in early spring.

☀ ◌

Z 7–10

HEIGHT
to 3ft (1m)

SPREAD
3–4in
(8–10cm)

3in
(7.5cm)

Iridaceae	

WATSONIA BORBONICA

Habit Robust, cormous, perennial. **Flowers**
Slightly scented, widely flared, irregularly
funnel-shaped, borne in branched spikes in
summer. Salmon-pink. **Leaves** Narrowly sword-
shaped, produced in two ranks. Mid-green.
• NATIVE HABITAT Hilly terrain, S. Africa.
• CULTIVATION In cooler areas, lift as foliage
starts to wither and store in frost-free conditions.
• PROPAGATION Separate cormels when dormant.
Sow seed in spring. Flowers appear in third year.
• OTHER NAMES W. pyramidata, W. rosea.

☀ ◌

Z 8–10

HEIGHT
3–5ft
(1–1.5m)

SPREAD
18in (45cm)

3–4in
(8–10cm)

Iridaceae	

WATSONIA PILLANSII

Habit Sturdy, cormous, rather slow-growing.
Flowers Irregularly tubular, borne in branched
spikes in late summer. Bright orange-red.
Leaves Evergreen, rigid, and linear. Mid-green.
• NATIVE HABITAT Open grasslands, S. Africa.
• CULTIVATION Ideal for a cool greenhouse or
conservatory in cold areas. Needs soil-based mix
with added sharp sand and leaf mold.
• PROPAGATION Separate cormels when dormant.
Sow seed in spring. Flowers appear in third year.
• OTHER NAME *W. beatricis.*

Amaryllidaceae/ Liliaceae	

PHAEDRANASSA CARNIOLI

Habit Upright, bulbous, perennial. **Flowers**
Drooping, tubular, in clusters of 6–10, on arching
stalks. Borne on leafless stems from spring to early
summer. Rich crimson, tipped green. **Leaves**
Basal, erect, and lance-shaped. Bluish-green.
• NATIVE HABITAT Andes, Peru.
• CULTIVATION Grow in a cool greenhouse or
conservatory in colder areas; elsewhere, use in
borders. Water moderately and apply a high-potash
fertilizer in summer. Keep barely moist in winter.
• PROPAGATION By offsets when dormant.

☼ ◊

Z 8–10

HEIGHT
20–30in
(50–70cm)

SPREAD
12in (30cm)

2–3in
(5–8cm)

☼ ◊

Z 8–10

HEIGHT
to 3ft (1m)

SPREAD
12–18in
(30–45cm)

3–4in
(8–10cm)

Cannaceae	

CANNA 'Rosemond Coles'

Habit Vigorous, rhizomatous, perennial. **Flowers**
Borne in spikes from mid-summer. Scarlet, with
yellow throat and edges, and golden petal reverse.
Leaves Large and broadly lance-shaped. Green.
• NATIVE HABITAT Garden origin.
• CULTIVATION Ideal for mixed borders in warm
areas. Elsewhere, grow as a house or conservatory
plant, or use in summer beds, lifting rhizome in
autumn. Needs fertile soil, rich in organic matter.
• PROPAGATION Divide dormant rhizomes in late
winter to early spring.

☼ ◗

Z 8–10

HEIGHT
5ft (1.5m)

SPREAD
20in (50cm)

4–6in
(9–15cm)

Iridaceae	

CROCOSMIA 'Lucifer'

Habit Vigorous, clump-forming, cormous, perennial. *Flowers* Funnel-shaped, 2–3in (6–8cm) long, borne in dense, arching, sparsely branched spikes in mid-summer. Brilliant tomato-red. *Leaves* Basal, sword-shaped, erect, and pleated. Brilliant green.
• NATIVE HABITAT Garden origin.
• CULTIVATION One of the most vigorous and strongly colored crocosmias, this tall cultivar is ideal for mixed and herbaceous borders, especially where a "hot" color theme is used. The flowers are excellent for cutting and last well in water. It tolerates sun or light, dappled shade and grows best in fertile, moist but well-drained soil that is rich in organic matter, although it will cope with drier conditions as the summer progresses. Apply a deep, dry winter mulch in very cold areas. To maintain vigor and flower production, lift and divide congested clumps every third or fourth year.
• PROPAGATION Divide the corm in spring, or separate cormels when dormant, just before the start of new growth.

☼ ◊

Z 5–9

HEIGHT
3–4ft
(1–1.2m)

SPREAD
8–10in
(20–25cm)

3–4in
(8–10cm)

Araceae	DRAGON ARUM

DRACUNCULUS VULGARIS

Habit Upright, tuberous, perennial. **Flowers** Foul-smelling, cowl-like, 14–36in (35–90cm) long, borne in spring or summer. Maroon-purple spathe, with a black-purple spike. **Leaves** Lobed and roughly triangular. Green, stained purple-brown.
• NATIVE HABITAT Rocky hillsides, Mediterranean.
• CULTIVATION Needs fertile soil and dry, winter mulch. Lift and divide every 3–4 years.
• PROPAGATION Separate offsets in autumn or spring, or sow seed in autumn.
• OTHER NAME *Arum dracunculus*.

☼ ◊

Z 8–10

HEIGHT
to 5ft
(1.5m)

SPREAD
18–24in
(45–60cm)

6in
(15cm)

Iridaceae	

CROCOSMIA 'Bressingham Blaze'

Habit Robust, clump-forming, cormous, perennial. **Flowers** Funnel-shaped, borne in branching spikes during late summer. Fiery orange-red, with yellow throat. **Leaves** Erect, sword-shaped, and pleated. Bright green.
• NATIVE HABITAT Garden origin.
• CULTIVATION Suitable for growing in borders. Needs fertile, moist but well-drained soil enriched with organic matter, and a deep, dry winter mulch.
• PROPAGATION By corm division or by separation of offsets in spring.

☼ ◊

Z 5–9

HEIGHT
30–36in
(75–90cm)

SPREAD
6–8in
(15–20cm)

3–4in
(8–10cm)

Colchicaceae/Liliaceae	

GLORIOSA SUPERBA 'Rothschildiana'

Habit Tuberous, perennial, tendril climber. **Flowers** Large, axillary, with 6 strongly reflexed petals, borne in summer. Rich red with scalloped, yellow edges. **Leaves** Scattered, broadly lance-shaped, and glossy. Bright green.
• NATIVE HABITAT Scrubland, S. Africa.
• CULTIVATION Needs gritty, soil-based mix. Water freely and apply liquid fertilizer every 2 weeks in summer. Keep tuber dry in winter. Grow in a house or conservatory in colder areas.
• PROPAGATION Divide in spring.

☼ ◊

Z 10–11

HEIGHT
to 6ft (2m)

SPREAD
12–18in
(30–45cm)

2in
(5cm)

Cannaceae	

CANNA 'Assaut'

Habit Vigorous, rhizomatous, perennial. **Flowers** Gladiolus-like, borne in spikes in summer. Rich scarlet, with purple bracts. **Leaves** Large and paddle-shaped. Purple-green.
• NATIVE HABITAT Garden origin.
• CULTIVATION Ideal for mixed borders in warmer areas. Elsewhere, grow indoors or use in summer beds, lifting bulb in autumn. Needs fertile soil enriched with organic matter.
• PROPAGATION Split in late winter to early spring.
• OTHER NAME *C.* × *generalis* 'Assault'.

☼ ◐

Z 8–10

HEIGHT
to 4ft
(1.2m)

SPREAD
18–24in
(45–60cm)

4–6in
(9–15cm)

Iridaceae	

CROCOSMIA MASONIORUM

Habit Sturdy, cormous, perennial. *Flowers* Semi-erect, funnel-shaped, borne on arching, almost horizontal stems in late summer. Bright vermilion. *Leaves* Erect, basal, and pleated. Dark green.
• NATIVE HABITAT Southeastern coast, S. Africa.
• CULTIVATION Needs fertile, moist but well-drained soil enriched with organic matter. Provide a deep, dry mulch in winter. Suitable for growing in borders, and excellent for coastal gardens.
• PROPAGATION Divide or separate cormels in spring. Sow seed as soon as ripe.

☼ ◊

Z 7–9

HEIGHT
4–5ft
(1.2–1.5m)

SPREAD
12–18in
(30–45cm)

3–4in
(8–10cm)

Alliaceae/Liliaceae	

ALLIUM STIPITATUM

Habit Sturdy, bulbous, perennial. *Flowers* Tiny, star-shaped, scarcely onion-scented. Borne in globular heads of up to 50 on leafless stems, in early summer. Purplish-pink. *Leaves* Basal, semi-upright, and strap-shaped. Mid-green.
• NATIVE HABITAT Central Asia.
• CULTIVATION Grow in fertile, well-drained soil, in a mixed or herbaceous border. Ideal for cut or dried flowers. Leaves die back at flowering time.
• PROPAGATION Sow seed when ripe, or divide established colonies in spring.

☼ ◊

Z 4–9

HEIGHT
3–5ft
(1–1.5m)

SPREAD
6–8in
(15–20cm)

3–4in
(8–10cm)

Amaryllidaceae/ Liliaceae	BLOOD FLOWER

SCADOXUS MULTIFLORUS subsp. KATHERINAE

Habit Sturdy, clump-forming, bulbous, perennial. *Flowers* Small stars, borne in heads of up to 200 in summer. Red. *Leaves* Lance-shaped and wavy-edged. Mid-green.
• NATIVE HABITAT Grasslands, southern Africa.
• CULTIVATION Grow as a house or conservatory plant in cold areas. Water moderately in growth, and keep barely moist during winter.
• PROPAGATION By seed or offsets in spring.
• OTHER NAME *Haemanthus katherinae*.

☼ ◊

Z 10–11

HEIGHT
to 4ft
(1.2m)

SPREAD
12–18in
(30–45cm)

 Nose
level

Iridaceae	

DIERAMA PENDULUM

Habit Arching, clumping, cormous, perennial. *Flowers* Small, silky funnels, with slender stalks, borne in loose heads in late summer. Purplish-pink, with silvery outer petals. *Leaves* Evergreen, arching, and linear. Grayish-green.
• NATIVE HABITAT Eastern coast, S. Africa.
• CULTIVATION Best in deep, fertile, moist but well-drained soil. Good for waterside plantings (above the waterline). May self-seed.
• PROPAGATION Separate offsets after flowering, or sow seed as soon as ripe.

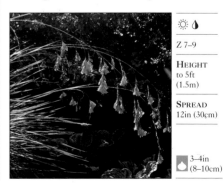

☼ ◊

Z 7–9

HEIGHT
to 5ft
(1.5m)

SPREAD
12in (30cm)

3–4in
(8–10cm)

Alliaceae/Liliaceae	GIANT ONION

ALLIUM GIGANTEUM

Habit Robust, bulbous, perennial. **Flowers** Small, star-shaped, borne in dense, spherical heads of 50 or more, spanning 4–6in (10–15cm), in summer. Lilac-blue, occasionally white.
Leaves Basal, semi-upright, and strap-shaped, dying back at flowering. Gray-green.
• NATIVE HABITAT Foothills, central Asia.
• CULTIVATION Grow in fertile, well-drained soil in an herbaceous border. Ideal as dried flowers.
• PROPAGATION By seed when ripe, or by offsets in late summer, when dormant.

☼ ◊

Z 6–10

HEIGHT
5–6ft
(1.5–2m)

SPREAD
12–14in
(30–35cm)

3–4in
(8–10cm)

Alliaceae/Liliaceae	

ALLIUM HOLLANDICUM

Habit Robust, bulbous, perennial. **Flowers** Small, star-shaped, in tight, spherical heads, 4in (10cm) span, borne in summer. Violet-purple. **Leaves** Basal, semi-erect, and strap-shaped, dying back at flowering. Grayish-green.
• NATIVE HABITAT Foothills, central Asia.
• CULTIVATION Grow in fertile, well-drained soil in an herbaceous border. Ideal as dried flowers.
• PROPAGATION By seed when ripe, or by offsets in late summer when dormant. May self-seed.
• OTHER NAME *A. aflatunense* of gardens.

☼ ◊

Z 4–10

HEIGHT
to 30in
(75cm)

SPREAD
6–8in
(15–20cm)

3–4in
(8–10cm)

Alliaceae/Liliaceae	

DICHELOSTEMMA CONGESTUM

Habit Upright, cormous, perennial. **Flowers** Small, tubular, borne on leafless stems in dense clusters, 2in (5cm) span, in early summer. Lilac-blue. **Leaves** Long and grass-like. Mid-green.
• NATIVE HABITAT Grasslands, western N. America.
• CULTIVATION Needs good drainage and a warm, sheltered site. Protect from excess wet in summer.
• PROPAGATION Sow seed as soon as ripe, or separate offsets in late summer.
• OTHER NAME *Brodiaea congesta.*

☼ ◊

Z 6–10

HEIGHT
16–36in
(40–90cm)

SPREAD
3–4in
(8–10cm)

4in
(10cm)

Iridaceae	

ARISTEA MAJOR

Habit Clump-forming, rhizomatous, perennial. **Flowers** Small, saucer-shaped, borne successively in loose spikes in summer. Purple-blue. **Leaves** Evergreen, upright, and sword-shaped. Mid-green.
• NATIVE HABITAT Cape Peninsula, S. Africa.
• CULTIVATION Needs good drainage and warm shelter. May survive to freezing, but prefers cool greenhouse in cold areas. Water sparingly in winter. Do not disturb roots when potting on.
• PROPAGATION By seed, when ripe or in spring.
• OTHER NAME *A. thyrsiflora.*

☼ ◊

Z 9–10

HEIGHT
to 3ft (1m)

SPREAD
18–24in
(45–60cm)

1in
(2–3cm)

Iridaceae	

NEOMARICA CAERULEA

Habit Rhizomatous, perennial. **Flowers** Fragrant, flattened, iris-like, short-lived, borne in succession in summer. Blue. **Leaves** Evergreen, upright, and sword-shaped, forming basal fan. Mid-green.
• NATIVE HABITAT Brazilian mountains.
• CULTIVATION In cool areas, grow in a greenhouse or conservatory. Needs fertile, moist but well-drained soil that is rich in organic matter. Water moderately during growth, but sparingly in winter.
• PROPAGATION Divide in spring or summer, or sow seed in spring.

☼ ◐

Z 10–11

HEIGHT
to 3ft (1m)

SPREAD
3ft (1m)

Nose level

Hyacinthaceae/	
Liliaceae	

GALTONIA VIRIDIFLORA

Habit Robust, upright, bulbous, perennial. **Flowers** Short-tubed, fragrant, drooping funnels, borne in slim spikes of up to 30 in late summer. Pale green. **Leaves** Long, fleshy, semi-upright, and strap-shaped. Gray-green.
• NATIVE HABITAT Grassland, southern Africa.
• CULTIVATION Ideal for growing in a sheltered, herbaceous border in sun with fertile, moist but well-drained soil. Resents disturbance.
• PROPAGATION By seed in spring, or by offsets in autumn or spring.

☼ ○

Z 7–9

HEIGHT
3–4ft
(1–1.2m)

SPREAD
7–9in
(18–23cm)

6in
(15cm)

Araceae	

ARISAEMA CONSANGUINEUM

Habit Robust, tuberous, perennial. **Flowers** Cowl-like spathes borne in summer. Pale green, brown-tinged, striped palest-purple or white. **Leaves** Solitary, umbrella-like, divided into 11–20 leaflets. Mid-green.
• NATIVE HABITAT Forests, central China.
• CULTIVATION Tolerates part-day sun. Grow in moist but well-drained, leaf-rich, neutral to acid soils. Mulch with leaf-mold each autumn.
• PROPAGATION Sow seed as soon as ripe. Separate offsets in late summer.

☼ ○

Z 7–9

HEIGHT
3ft (1m)

SPREAD
12–18in
(30–45cm)

10in
(25cm)

Iridaceae	

DIETES BICOLOR

Habit Tuft-forming, rhizomatous, perennial.
Flowers Flattened, iris-like, 1½in (4cm) span,
on branching stems. Short-lived, but bloom in
succession from spring through to summer. Pale
to deep yellow, with brown stain on lower petals.
Leaves Evergreen, upright, basal, narrowly
strap-shaped, and leathery. Pale to mid-green.
• NATIVE HABITAT Eastern Cape, S. Africa.
• CULTIVATION Excellent for growing in a sunny
border, either mixed or herbaceous, in cool areas.
Outdoors, it tolerates poor, dry soil and light,
dappled shade, but grows best in moderately
fertile, moist but well-drained soil in full sun.
In colder regions, grow in a conservatory or a cool
greenhouse that has good ventilation and full light.
Water freely and apply a balanced, liquid fertilizer
every 2 weeks during full growth. Watering
should be reduced after flowering, taking care
to keep soil barely moist in winter.
• PROPAGATION Sow seed in autumn or spring.
Rhizomes can be divided carefully after
flowering, but might prove slow to re-establish.

☼ ◊

Z 9–10

HEIGHT
to 3ft (1m)

SPREAD
1–2ft
(30–60cm)

Nose
level

Iridaceae	

CROCOSMIA 'Golden Fleece'

Habit Moderately vigorous, clump-forming, cormous, perennial. *Flowers* Funnel-shaped, 2–3in (5–8cm) long, borne in dense, slightly arching, well-branched spikes in late summer. Soft, warm, golden-yellow. *Leaves* Basal, sword-shaped, upright, and pleated. Bright green.
• NATIVE HABITAT Garden origin.
• CULTIVATION Grow in fertile, well-drained soil. Needs ample moisture in spring and early summer, but will bear drier conditions as the summer progresses. Tolerant of sun or light,

dappled shade. Where cold is severe or long-lasting, provide a deep, dry mulch in winter. To keep the plant vigorous, lift and divide congested clumps every third or fourth year. The flowers are suitable for cutting.
• PROPAGATION By division in spring, or by separation of offsets, when dormant, just before the start of new growth.
• OTHER NAMES Both *C.* 'George Davison' and *C.* 'Citronella' are sometimes wrongly applied to this cultivar.

☀ ◊

Z 6–9

HEIGHT
24–30in
(60–75cm)

SPREAD
6–8in
(15–20cm)

2in
(5cm)

Iridaceae	

MORAEA HUTTONII

Habit Upright, cormous, perennial. *Flowers* Sturdy-stemmed, iris-like, 2–3in (5–7cm) across, short-lived, but borne in succession throughout summer. Rich yellow, with brown markings. *Leaves* Basal, flat, and linear. Mid-green.
• NATIVE HABITAT By the sides of streams in southern Africa.
• CULTIVATION Prefers a warm, sheltered site in sun, with well-drained soil.
• PROPAGATION By seed in spring, or by separation of cormels when dormant.

☀ ◔

Z 9–10

HEIGHT
30–36in
(75cm–1m)

SPREAD
6–10in
(15–25cm)

2in
(5cm)

Araceae	GOLDEN ARUM LILY

ZANTEDESCHIA ELLIOTTIANA

Habit Tuberous, perennial. *Flowers* Cowl-like spathes, 6in (15cm) long, borne in summer. Yellow. *Leaves* Evergreen and heart-shaped. Deep green, with silver-translucent marks.
• NATIVE HABITAT Uncertain, possibly a hybrid.
• CULTIVATION Grow as a conservatory or house plant in cold areas. Needs fertile, moist but well-drained soil enriched with organic matter. Apply balanced liquid fertilizer every 2 weeks when in growth. Keep the tuber just moist during winter.
• PROPAGATION By suckers or by division in spring.

☀ ◔

Z 10–11

HEIGHT
2–3ft
(60cm–1m)

SPREAD
18–24in
(45–60cm)

4in
(10cm)

Colchicaceae/Liliaceae	

LITTONIA MODESTA

Habit Climbing, tuberous, perennial. *Flowers* Drooping bells, 1½–2in (4–5cm) across, borne from the leaf axils in summer. Golden-yellow. *Leaves* Lance-shaped, with tendrils at tip. Brilliant green.
• NATIVE HABITAT Scrubland and forests in southern Africa.
• CULTIVATION Grow as a house or conservatory plant in cold areas. Needs support and fertile soil. Keep tubers barely moist and frost-free in winter.
• PROPAGATION Sow seed in spring, or divide tubers when dormant.

☀ ◔

Z 10–11

HEIGHT
3–6ft
(1–2m)

SPREAD
4–6in
(10–15cm)

2in
(5cm)

Cannaceae	

CANNA IRIDIFLORA

Habit Vigorous, rhizomatous, perennial. *Flowers* Trumpet-shaped, borne in drooping clusters from mid-summer to autumn. Red-pink or orange. *Leaves* Broadly oval, up to 3ft (1m). Bluish-green.
• NATIVE HABITAT Moist forest clearings, Peru.
• CULTIVATION Suits mixed borders in warm, frost-free areas. Grow as a house or conservatory plant in cold areas, or use in summer beds, lifting the rhizome in autumn. Needs fertile, rich soil.
• PROPAGATION Divide dormant rhizomes, or sow presoaked seed during late winter to early spring.

☀ ◕

Z 8–10

HEIGHT
to 10ft (3m)

SPREAD
20in (50cm)

6in
(15cm)

LILIES

Lilies (*Lilium*) are grown for their elegant, colorful, and often fragrant flowers with pollen-rich stamens. Most of them thrive in well-drained, fertile soil that is neutral to acid, although some varieties prefer alkaline conditions. Lilies need their heads in sun, but some shade at their roots. Plant most bulbs at 2 to 3 times their own depth, spaced at 3 times the bulb's diameter. Stem-rooting types are planted at 3 times their own depth. Species take 2 to 4 years to flower when raised from seed and the species come true. Lilies can be increased by scales (see p. 178), offsets, bulblets, or by stem and leaf axil bulbils if produced. Divide established clumps every 3 to 4 years to relieve overcrowding. Flowers will appear after 1 to 2 years.

L. 'Casa Blanca'
Habit Upright, with stout stems, bulbous.
Flowers Large, fragrant, bowl-shaped, borne in sprays from mid- to late summer. Pure white.
Leaves Lance-shaped, alternate. Mid-green.
• TIPS Good for growing in mixed borders or for planting in large, patio containers. Flowers are suitable for cutting.
• HEIGHT 4ft (1.2m).

L. 'Casa Blanca'

☼ ◊   Z 4–8

L. REGALE
Habit Erect or arching, bulbous, stem-rooting.
Flowers Very fragrant, trumpet-shaped, borne in sprays of up to 25 in mid-summer. White, with purple underside.
Leaves Scattered, linear, and shiny. Dark green.
• TIPS Good for planting in mixed borders, except in very alkaline soil.
• HEIGHT 2–6ft (0.6–2m).

L. regale
Regal lily

☼ ◊   Z 4–9

L. CANDIDUM
Habit Upright, bulbous.
Flowers Very fragrant, broadly trumpet-shaped, borne in sprays of 5–20, in mid-summer. White.
Leaves Lance-shaped, basal, and scattered. Shiny, bright green.
• TIPS Ideal for growing in borders. Plant bulb nose at soil level. Needs neutral to alkaline soil.
• HEIGHT 3–5ft (1–1.8m).

L. candidum
Madonna lily

☼ ◊   Z 4–8

L. MARTAGON var. ALBUM
Habit Stem-rooting, clumping, bulbous.
Flowers Nodding turkscaps, borne in sprays of up to 50, during early and mid-summer. White.
Leaves Lance-shaped, in whorls. Bright green.
• TIPS Thrives in any well-drained soil, in sun or dappled shade.
• HEIGHT 3–6ft (0.9–2m).

L. martagon var. album

☼ ◊   Z 4–8

L. LONGIFLORUM
Habit Vigorous, bulbous, stem-rooting.
Flowers Scented, outward-facing trumpets, borne in short sprays, in mid-summer. White.
Leaves Lance-shaped. Dark green.
• TIPS Tolerant of lime and needs a partially shaded site. Usually grown under glass.
• HEIGHT 16in–3ft (40cm–1m).

L. longiflorum
Easter lily

◐ ◊   Z 6–8

L. Olympic Group
Habit Upright, bulbous.
Flowers Large, scented trumpets, borne in mid- to late summer. Pink, white, yellow, or cream, purple or pink outside and yellow throat.
Leaves Oval to linear. Mid-green.
• TIPS Suitable for planting in late summer flowering borders.
• HEIGHT 4–6ft (1.2–2m).

L. Olympic Group

☼ ◊   Z 4–8

L. 'Black Magic'
Habit Vigorous, bulbous.
Flowers Large, scented, trumpet-shaped, borne in sprays from mid- to late summer. Maroon outside, and lustrous white inside.
Leaves Oval to linear. Mid-green.
• TIPS Good for planting in mixed and herbaceous borders, and for cutting.
• HEIGHT 5–6ft (1.5–2m).

L. 'Black Magic'

☼ ◊   Z 4–8

L. DUCHARTREI
Habit Stem-rooting, bulbous, with rhizomes.
Flowers Nodding turkscaps, borne in sprays of up to 12, in summer. White, purple-spotted inner and -flushed outer.
Leaves Lance-shaped, stalkless, and scattered. Mid-green.
• TIPS Good for planting in moist, mixed borders.
• HEIGHT 2–3ft (60–100cm).

L. duchartrei

☼ ◊   Z 4–8

L. AURATUM var. PLATYPHYLLUM
Habit Vigorous, strong-stemmed, bulbous.
Flowers Fragrant, bowl-shaped, borne in late summer and autumn. White, each with a yellow central band.
Leaves Broadly lance-shaped and scattered. Dark green.
• TIPS Good for planting in a mixed border.
• HEIGHT to 5ft (1.5m).

L. auratum var.
platyphyllum
Gold-band lily

☼ ◊   Z 5–8

L. 'Mont Blanc'
Habit Low-growing, bulbous.
Flowers Large, bowl-shaped, borne in sprays, during early and mid-summer. Creamy-white, spotted with brown.
Leaves Narrowly oval and alternate. Mid-green.
• TIPS Good for planting at the front of borders or in containers.
• HEIGHT 24–28in (60–70cm).

L. 'Mont Blanc'

☼ ◊   Z 5–8

L. 'Sterling Star'
Habit Vigorous, bulbous.
Flowers Large, slightly scented, cup-shaped, borne in sprays, in early to mid-summer. Creamy-white, speckled brown.
Leaves Narrowly oval and alternate. Mid-green.
• TIPS Good for planting in tubs or mixed borders, and ideal as cut flowers.
• HEIGHT 3–4ft (1–1.2m).

L. 'Sterling Star'

☼ ◊   Z 5–8

L. 'Bright Star'
Habit Robust, bulbous.
Flowers Large, scented, strongly recurved, borne in mid- to late summer. Creamy-white, with orange central band.
Leaves Oval to linear. Mid-green.
• TIPS Good for growing in borders and large tubs, and for cutting. Will tolerate lime.
• HEIGHT 3–5ft (1–1.5m).

L. 'Bright Star'

☼ ◊   Z 4–8

L. 'Imperial Gold'
Habit Robust, bulbous.
Flowers Fragrant, star-shaped, recurved at tips, borne in sprays, during mid- to late summer. Glistening white, with a yellow central stripe.
Leaves Lance-shaped and alternate. Mid-green.
• TIPS Suitable for adding height to the back of a herbaceous or mixed border.
• HEIGHT 6ft (1.8–2m).

L. 'Imperial Gold'

☼ ◊   Z 4–8

L. 'Corsage'
Habit Vigorous, bulbous.
Flowers Shallowly star-shaped, recurved, borne in mid-summer. Pale pink, with a white, maroon-speckled center, flushed yellow outside.
Leaves Narrowly oval and alternate. Mid-green.
• TIPS Suitable for planting in borders or as cut flowers.
• HEIGHT 4ft (1.2m).

L. 'Corsage'

☼ ◊   Z 5–8

L. 'Magic Pink'
Habit Clump-forming, bulbous.
Flowers Semi-nodding, slightly fragrant, bowl-shaped, borne in sprays during mid-summer. Clear pink.
Leaves Lance-shaped and alternate. Mid-green.
• TIPS Ideal as cut flowers, or for mixed and herbaceous borders and large containers.
• HEIGHT 4ft (1.2m).

L. 'Magic Pink'

☀ ◊   Z 4–8

L. 'Bronwen North'
Habit Clump-forming, bulbous.
Flowers Drooping turkscaps, slightly fragrant, borne in sprays during early summer. Mauve-pink, with pale pink throat, spotted and lined purple.
Leaves Narrowly oval and alternate. Mid-green.
• TIPS Suitable for borders and large tubs.
• HEIGHT to 3ft (1m).

L. 'Bronwen North'

☀ ◊   Z 5–8

L. MARTAGON
Habit Vigorous, stem-rooting, bulbous, clump-forming.
Flowers Foul-smelling, nodding turkscaps, borne in sprays in mid-summer. Pink to red-purple.
Leaves Lance-shaped, in whorls. Bright green.
• TIPS Thrives in any well-drained soil, in sun or dappled shade.
• HEIGHT 3–6ft (0.9–2m).

L. martagon
Turkscap lily

☀ ◊   Z 4–8

L. RUBELLUM
Habit Bulbous, stem-rooting.
Flowers Funnel-shaped, fragrant, appearing from upper leaf axils in early summer. Clear pink, with maroon-spotted center.
Leaves Narrowly oval and scattered. Mid-green.
• TIPS Suitable for planting in a woodland garden.
• HEIGHT 12–32in (30–80cm).

L. rubellum

◐ ◊ pH   Z 4–8

L. MACKLINIAE
Habit Bulbous, stem-rooting.
Flowers Nodding, bowl-shaped, borne in sprays in early and mid-summer. Pink, flushed purple.
Leaves Narrowly lance-shaped, scattered, and whorled. Dark green.
• TIPS Suitable for planting in a mixed or herbaceous border.
• HEIGHT 12–24in (30–60cm).

L. mackliniae

☀ ◊   Z 5–8

L. 'Montreux'
Habit Low-growing, bulbous.
Flowers Cup-shaped, borne in sprays in mid-summer. Pink, with brown-speckled centers and yellow-buff anthers.
Leaves Narrowly oval and alternate. Mid-green.
• TIPS Good for planting at the front of borders and in containers.
• HEIGHT 32–36in (80–100cm).

L. 'Montreux'

☀ ◊   Z 5–8

L. 'Star Gazer'
Habit Vigorous, bulbous.
Flowers Large, star-shaped, with recurved tips, borne in sprays during mid-summer. Red, with darker spots.
Leaves Lance-shaped and alternate. Mid-green.
• TIPS Good for borders and large tubs, and suits cutting and forcing.
• HEIGHT 3–5ft (1–1.5m).

L. 'Star Gazer'

☀ ◊   Z 4–8

L. 'Côte d'Azur'
Habit Strong-stemmed, bulbous.
Flowers Bowl-shaped, recurved tips, borne in sprays from early to mid-summer. Deep, clear pink, with pale center.
Leaves Narrowly oval and alternate. Mid-green.
• TIPS Good for planting at the front of borders or in large tubs.
• HEIGHT 28–39in (70–100cm).

L. 'Côte d'Azur'

☀ ◊   Z 5–8

L. 'Journey's End'
Habit Robust, bulbous.
Flowers Large
turkscaps, borne in late
summer. Deep pink,
spotted maroon, with
white margins and tips.
Leaves Lance-shaped
and alternate. Mid-green.
• TIPS Suitable for
planting in mixed and
herbaceous borders, or
large tubs. Flowers are
good for cutting.
• HEIGHT 3–6ft (1–2m).

L. 'Journey's End'

☼ ◊   Z 4–8

L. × DALHANSONII
Habit Bulbous,
stem-rooting.
Flowers Foul-smelling
turkscaps, borne in well-
spaced sprays during
early summer. Maroon,
with gold spots.
Leaves Lance-shaped
and whorled. Mid-green.
• TIPS Thrives in most
well-drained soils, and
will tolerate sun or
partial shade.
• OTHER NAME
L. martagon var. *cattaniae*
× *L. hansonii*
• HEIGHT 3–5ft
(1–1.5m).

L. × *dalhansonii*

☼ ◊   Z 5–8

L. SPECIOSUM var. RUBRUM
Habit Vigorous,
bulbous, stem-rooting.
Flowers Fragrant,
drooping turkscaps,
borne in sprays in late
summer and autumn.
Deep carmine-red.
Leaves Broadly lance-
shaped. Dark green.
• TIPS Good for planting
in a woodland garden.
• HEIGHT 3–5½ft
(1–1.7m).

L. *speciosum* var.
rubrum

☼ ◊ pH   Z 5–8

L. 'Black Beauty'
Habit Vigorous,
bulbous.
Flowers Turkscaps,
borne in sprays in mid-
summer. Dark red, with
green center and edges.
Leaves Lance-shaped
and alternate. Mid-green.
• TIPS Suitable for
planting in borders.
• HEIGHT 4½–6ft
(1.4–2m).

L. 'Black Beauty'

☼ ◊   Z 4–8

L. 'Angela North'
Habit Clump-forming,
bulbous.
Flowers Slightly
fragrant, drooping
turkscaps, borne in
sprays during mid-
summer. Claret-red.
Leaves Narrowly oval
and alternate. Mid-green.
• TIPS Good for planting
in mixed and herbaceous
borders, or large tubs.
• HEIGHT 28–48in
(70–120cm).

L. 'Angela North'

☼ ◊   Z 5–8

L. 'Lady Bowes Lyon'
Habit Robust, bulbous.
Flowers Turkscaps,
borne in sprays during
mid-summer. Vivid red,
spotted black.
Leaves Narrowly oval
and alternate. Mid-green.
• TIPS Suitable for
planting in mixed and
herbaceous borders, or
in large containers.
• HEIGHT 3–4ft
(1–1.2m).

L. 'Lady Bowes Lyon'

☼ ◊   Z 5–8

L. 'Karen North'
Habit Robust, bulbous.
Flowers Drooping,
turkscaps, borne in
loose sprays during
mid-summer. Deep
orange-pink, with
darker spots.
Leaves Narrowly oval
and alternate. Mid-green.
• TIPS Suitable for large
containers and borders,
or for cutting.
• HEIGHT 3–4½ft
(1–1.4m).

L. 'Karen North'

☀ ◊   Z 5–8

L. CHALCEDONICUM
Habit Bulbous,
stem-rooting.
Flowers Drooping
turkscaps, borne in
sprays during mid-
summer. Bright red.
Leaves Lance-shaped
and spiraled. Dark green
with silver-haired edges.
• TIPS Thrives in well-
drained soil and sun or
partial shade.
• HEIGHT 2–5ft
(0.6–1.5m).

L. chalcedonicum
Scarlet turkscap lily

☀ ◊   Z 5–8

L. PYRENAICUM var. RUBRUM
Habit Stem-rooting,
clumping, bulbous.
Flowers Drooping,
turkscaps, borne in sprays
from early to mid-
summer. Orange-red.
Leaves Narrow, lance-
shaped. Bright green.
• TIPS Needs neutral to
alkaline soil, in sun or
partial shade.
• HEIGHT 12–39in
(30–100cm).

L. pyrenaicum var.
rubrum

☀ ◊   Z 5–8

L. PARDALINUM
Habit Rhizomatous,
clump-forming.
Flowers Nodding
turkscaps, borne in
sprays in mid-summer.
Orange-red to crimson,
spotted red and yellow.
Leaves Linear and
scattered. Bright green.
• TIPS Needs moist,
well-drained soil, in sun
or partial shade.
• HEIGHT 5–8ft
(1.5–2.5m).

L. pardalinum
Leopard lily

☀ ◑   Z 5–8

L. NEPALENSE
Habit Stem-rooting,
bulbous, with rhizomes.
Flowers Large, drooping
funnels, borne from early
to mid-summer. Yellow
to palest green, with
maroon center.
Leaves Lance-shaped,
scattered. Dark green.
• TIPS Needs a cool
sheltered site and
a dry winter dormancy.
• HEIGHT 2–3ft
(0.6–1m).

L. nepalense

☀ ◑ pH   Z 5–8

L. 'Golden Splendor'
Habit Vigorous, strong-
stemmed, bulbous,
stem-rooting.
Flowers Large, fragrant,
shallowly funnel-shaped,
borne in mid- to late
summer. Rich yellow,
banded maroon outside.
Leaves Narrowly oval
to linear. Mid-green.
• TIPS Good for planting
in borders and cutting.
• HEIGHT 4–6ft
(1.2–2m).

L. 'Golden Splendor'

☀ ◊   Z 5–8

L. 'Roma'
Habit Vigorous, bulbous.
Flowers Shallowly star-shaped, recurved tips, opening from green buds in mid-summer. Cream to palest yellow-green.
Leaves Narrowly oval and alternate. Mid-green.
• TIPS Suitable for planting in mixed or herbaceous borders, and as cut flowers.
• HEIGHT 5ft (1.5m).

L. 'Roma'

☼ ◊   Z 5–8

L. 'Golden Clarion'
Habit Vigorous, strong-stemmed, stem-rooting, bulbous.
Flowers Large, fragrant trumpets, borne in early to mid-summer. Pale to deep golden-yellow, often flushed red outside.
Leaves Narrowly oval to linear. Mid-green.
• TIPS Good for planting in borders and cutting.
• HEIGHT 5–6ft (1.5–2m).

L. 'Golden Clarion'

☼ ◊   Z 5–8

L. 'Connecticut King'
Habit Vigorous, clump-forming, bulbous.
Flowers Star-shaped, recurved tips, borne in early to mid-summer. Rich deep yellow, with paler tips.
Leaves Narrowly oval and alternate. Mid-green.
• TIPS Suits flower borders and large tubs. Cut flowers last well.
• HEIGHT 3ft (1m).

L. 'Connecticut King'

☼ ◊   Z 5–8

L. 'Rosemary North'
Habit Clump-forming, bulbous.
Flowers Distinctive, faintly scented turkscaps, borne from early to mid-summer. Orange-ochre.
Leaves Narrowly oval and alternate. Mid-green.
• TIPS Suitable for planting in mixed and herbaceous borders or in large containers.
• HEIGHT 3ft (1m).

L. 'Rosemary North'

☼ ◊   Z 5–8

L. MONADELPHUM
Habit Clump-forming, bulbous.
Flowers Fragrant trumpets, borne in early summer. Yellow, with purple-red spots inside and purple petal tips.
Leaves Lance-shaped and scattered. Emerald.
• TIPS Suitable for a warm, sunny border in dry or heavy soils.
• HEIGHT 3–5ft (1–1.5m).

L. monadelphum

☼ ◊   Z 5–8

L. 'Destiny'
Habit Vigorous, clump-forming, bulbous.
Flowers Bowl-shaped, with recurved tips, borne in early summer. Yellow, with brown spots.
Leaves Narrowly oval and alternate. Mid-green.
• TIPS Good for growing in borders or large containers, and suitable as cut flowers.
• HEIGHT 3–4ft (1–1.2m).

L. 'Destiny'

☼ ◊   Z 5–8

L. 'Amber Gold'
Habit Clump-forming, bulbous.
Flowers Turkscaps, borne in sprays from early to mid-summer. Golden-amber, with maroon center.
Leaves Narrowly oval and alternate. Mid-green.
• TIPS Suitable for growing in herbaceous or mixed borders.
• HEIGHT 3–4ft (1–1.2m).

L. 'Amber Gold'

☼ ◊   Z 4–8

L. HANSONII
Habit Vigorous, bulbous, stem-rooting.
Flowers Fragrant, turkscaps, borne in sprays during early summer. Golden-orange, with purple-brown spots.
Leaves Lance-shaped and whorled. Pale green.
• TIPS Ideal for growing in woodland gardens or shady borders.
• HEIGHT 3–5ft (1–1.5m).

L. hansonii

☀ ◊   Z 5–8

L. SUPERBUM
Habit Stem-rooting, bulbous, with rhizomes.
Flowers Drooping turkscaps, borne in sprays from late summer to early autumn. Red, with green base and maroon spots.
Leaves Linear- to lance-shaped and whorled. Mid-green.
• TIPS Prefers a sunny or partially shaded site.
• HEIGHT 5–10ft (1.5–3m).

L. superbum
American Turkscap lily

☀ ◊ pH   Z 5–8

L. CANADENSE
Habit Bulbous, with rhizomes.
Flowers Faintly scented, slender, widely trumpet-shaped, with recurved tips, borne in mid- to late summer. Yellow, with maroon-spotted center.
Leaves Lance-shaped and whorled. Mid-green.
• TIPS Suits planting in borders or wild gardens.
• HEIGHT 3–5½ft (1–1.6m).

L. canadense
Meadow lily

☀ ◊ pH   Z 5–8

L. MEDEOLOIDES
Habit Stem-rooting, bulbous.
Flowers Drooping turkscaps, borne in mid-summer. Orange-red, with darker spots.
Leaves Stalkless, lance-shaped, in whorls and scattered. Mid-green.
• TIPS Suitable for woodland gardens or shady borders.
• HEIGHT 16–30in (40–75cm).

L. medeoloides
Wheel lily

☀ ◊ pH   Z 5–8

L. 'Apollo'
Habit Clump-forming, bulbous.
Flowers Turkscaps, borne during mid-summer. Pale golden-orange, with sparse, maroon flecking at the center.
Leaves Narrowly oval and alternate. Mid-green.
• TIPS Good for mixed or herbaceous borders, and for cutting.
• HEIGHT 4ft (1.2m).

L. 'Apollo'

☀ ◊   Z 5–8

L. LANCIFOLIUM var. SPLENDENS
Habit Bulbous, stem-rooting, clumping.
Flowers Turkscaps, borne in late summer. Flame-red, spotted black.
Leaves Lance-shaped, scattered. Mid-green.
• TIPS Tolerant of some lime.
• OTHER NAME *L. tigrinum* var. *splendens*
• HEIGHT 2–5ft (0.6–1.5m).

L. lancifolium var. *splendens*

☀ ◊   Z 4–8

L. PYRENAICUM
Habit Bulbous, stem-rooting, clump-forming.
Flowers Foul-smelling, drooping turkscaps, borne in early to mid-summer. Yellow, with maroon-spotted center.
Leaves Lance-shaped and scattered. Emerald.
• TIPS Needs neutral to alkaline soil, in sun or partial shade.
• HEIGHT 12–39in (30–100cm).

L. pyrenaicum

☀ ◊   Z 5–8

L. 'Brushmarks'
Habit Bulbous, clump-forming.
Flowers Cup-shaped, with recurved tips, borne in early to mid-summer. Rich orange, marked deep red at the base, with green center.
Leaves Narrowly oval and alternate. Mid-green.
• TIPS Good for planting in borders and large tubs, or for cutting.
• HEIGHT to 3ft (1m).

L. 'Brushmarks'

☀ ◊   Z 5–8

L. BULBIFERUM var. CROCEUM
Habit Bulbous, clump-forming.
Flowers Upright, bowl-shaped, borne in sprays from early to mid-summer. Pure golden-orange.
Leaves Lance-shaped and scattered. Mid-green.
• TIPS Thrives in acid or alkaline soils. Suitable for planting in herbaceous and mixed borders. Bulbils are present on the species, but absent on this variety.
• HEIGHT 16–60in (40–150cm).

L. bulbiferum var. *croceum*

☼ ◊   Z 5–8

L. 'Enchantment'
Habit Vigorous, bulbous, clump-forming.
Flowers Cups, borne in early summer. Rich, deep orange, with black spots.
Leaves Narrowly oval and alternate. Mid-green.
• TIPS Good for planting in borders, and excellent as cut flowers.
• HEIGHT 2–3ft (60cm–1m).

L. 'Enchantment'

☼ ◊   Z 5–8

L. TSINGTAUENSE
Habit Stem-rooting, bulbous.
Flowers Erect, shallowly trumpet-shaped, borne in sprays in mid-summer. Orange, spotted maroon.
Leaves Lance-shaped and whorled. Mid-green.
• TIPS Prefers acid soil but tolerates some lime.
• HEIGHT 28–39in (70–100cm).

L. tsingtauense

☼◑ ◐ pH   Z 5–8

L. 'Harmony'
Habit Vigorous, bulbous, clumping.
Flowers Cup-shaped, with recurved tips, borne during early summer. Orange, with maroon spots.
Leaves Narrowly oval and alternate. Mid-green.
• TIPS Good for planting in borders and large tubs, or as cut flowers.
• HEIGHT 20–39in (0.5–1m).

L. 'Harmony'

☼ ◊   Z 5–8

L. DAVIDII var. WILLMOTTIAE
Habit Arching, bulbous, with rhizomes.
Flowers Long-stalked turkscaps, borne during summer. Vermilion-red, with purple-black spots.
Leaves Linear and scattered. Dark green.
• TIPS Suitable for adding height to the back of mixed and herbaceous borders.
• HEIGHT to 6ft (2m).

L. davidii var, *willmottiae*

☼ ◊   Z 5–8

DAHLIAS

Dahlias (*Dahlia*) are classified according to the size and form of their flower heads (see below). Most varieties suit cutting and those raised for exhibition are best grown in prepared beds away from other plants. All dahlias, except for low-growing types, need staking (see p. 169). Grow in deep, fertile, moist but well-drained soil, in a sheltered site in full sun. Bedding dahlias can be increased by seed in early spring. Divide tubers so that each portion has a bud, or take basal cuttings from tubers started under glass, in late winter or early spring. Lift tubers after the first frost, dry off, dust with fungicide, and place in a box or tray of compost. Keep dry and store in airy, frost-proof conditions. For diseases, pests, and storage problems, see p. 183.

SINGLE
Each flower usually has between 8–10 broad petals which surround an open, central disk.

ANEMONE
Fully double flowers, with one or more rings of flattened ray petals around a dense group of short, tubular petals, usually longer than those of single dahlias.

COLLERETTE
Single flowers, each with 8–10 broad, outer petals and an inner "collar" of smaller petals around an open, central disk.

WATERLILY
Fully double flowers with large, generally sparse, ray petals that are flat or have slightly incurved or recurved margins, giving a flat appearance.

DECORATIVE
Fully double flowers each with broad, flat petals that incurve slightly at their margins and usually reflex to the stem.

BALL
Flattened to spherical, fully double flowers with densely packed petals that are almost tubular in shape.

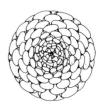

POMPON
Flattened to spherical, fully double flowers that are no more than 2in (5cm) across. A miniature form of ball flowers.

CACTUS
Fully double flowers with narrow, pointed petals that are straight or curl inward and have recurved edges for more than two-thirds of their length.

SEMI-CACTUS
Fully double flowers that are similar to cactus flowers but have broader-based petals, the edges of which are generally recurved toward their tips.

MISCELLANEOUS
A wide range of unclassified types of flower, including orchid-like (shown right), single, and double forms.

D. 'Angora'
Habit Clump-forming.
Flowers Small-flowered,
4in (10cm) across, with
split petal tips, borne in
mid-summer. Pure white.
Leaves Divided into
oval leaflets. Mid-green.
• TIPS Ideal for planting
in borders and cutting.
• HEIGHT 3½ft (1.1m).
• SPREAD 2ft (60cm).

D. 'Angora'
(Decorative)

☼ ◊   Z 9–10

D. 'Small World'
Habit Clump-forming.
Flowers Small-flowered,
2in (5cm) across, borne
during summer and
autumn. Pure white.
Leaves Divided into
oval leaflets. Glossy
and dark green.
• TIPS Excellent for
growing in borders, and
as cut flowers. Suitable
for exhibition.
• HEIGHT 3ft (1m).
• SPREAD 2ft (60cm).

D. 'Small World'
(Pompon)

☼ ◊   Z 9–10

D. 'Nina Chester'
Habit Clump-forming.
Flowers Spanning 4–6in
(10–15cm), borne on
strong stems, from late
summer onward. White,
with lilac-flushed tips.
Leaves Divided into
oval leaflets. Mid-green.
• TIPS Ideal for growing
in borders, and as cut
flowers. Good specimen
for exhibition.
• HEIGHT 3½ft (1.1m).
• SPREAD 2ft (60cm).

D. 'Nina Chester'
(Decorative)

☼ ◊   Z 9–10

D. 'Majestic Kerkrade'
Habit Clump-forming.
Flowers Spanning 4–6in
(10–15cm), borne during
summer and autumn.
Soft salmon-pink, with
yellow base.
Leaves Oval leaflets.
Glossy and dark green.
• TIPS Ideal for cutting
or borders, and good
specimen for exhibition.
• HEIGHT 4ft (1.2m).
• SPREAD 2ft (60cm).

D. 'Majestic Kerkrade'
(Cactus)

☼ ◊   Z 9–10

D. 'Easter Sunday'
Habit Clump-forming.
Flowers Borne in late
summer to autumn,
5in (12cm) across.
Creamy-white, with
golden-yellow centers.
Leaves Oval leaflets.
Glossy and dark green.
• TIPS Ideal for growing
in borders, and as cut
flowers. Good specimen
for exhibition.
• HEIGHT 3ft (1m).
• SPREAD 1½ft (45cm).

D. 'Easter Sunday'
(Collerette)

☼ ◊   Z 9–10

D. 'Rhonda'
Habit Clump-forming.
Flowers Spanning 2in
(5cm), borne during
summer and autumn.
White, with lilac flush
on margins.
Leaves Divided into
oval leaflets. Mid-green.
• TIPS Ideal for growing
in borders, and as cut
flowers. Good specimen
for exhibition.
• HEIGHT 3½ft (1.1m).
• SPREAD 2ft (60cm).

D. 'Rhonda'
(Pompon)

☼ ◊   Z 9–10

D. 'White Klankstad'
Habit Clump-forming.
Flowers Borne during
summer and autumn,
spanning 4–6in
(10–15cm). White.
Leaves Oval leaflets.
Glossy and dark green.
• TIPS Ideal for growing
in borders, and as cut
flowers. Good specimen
for exhibition.
• HEIGHT to 4ft (1.2m).
• SPREAD 2ft (60cm).

D. 'White Klankstad'
(Cactus)

☼ ◊   Z 9–10

D. 'Vicky Crutchfield'
Habit Clump-forming.
Flowers Slightly curled
petals, 4–6in (10–15cm)
across, borne in summer
and autumn. Shell-pink.
Leaves Oval leaflets.
Mid-green.
• TIPS Ideal for growing
in borders, and as cut
flowers. Good specimen
for exhibition.
• HEIGHT 3½ft (1.1m).
• SPREAD 2ft (60cm).

D. 'Vicky Crutchfield'
(Waterlily)

☼ ◊   Z 9–10

D. 'Monk Marc'
Habit Clump-forming.
Flowers Spanning 4–6in
(10–15cm), borne in
summer and autumn.
Pale pink.
Leaves Divided into
oval leaflets. Dark green.
• TIPS Ideal for growing
in borders, and as cut
flowers. Good specimen
for exhibition.
• HEIGHT 3ft (1m).
• SPREAD 2–3ft
(60cm–1m).

D. 'Monk Marc'
(Cactus)

☼ ◊   Z 9–10

D. 'Noreen'
Habit Clump-forming.
Flowers Borne in
summer and autumn, 2in
(5cm) across. Pale pink-
purple blends.
Leaves Divided into
oval leaflets. Mid-green.
• TIPS Ideal for cutting
or borders, and good
specimen for exhibition.
• HEIGHT 3ft (1m).
• SPREAD 1½ft (45cm).

D. 'Noreen'
(Pompon)

☼ ◊   Z 9–10

D. 'Pink Symbol'
Habit Clump-forming.
Flowers Borne from
summer onward, 6–8in
(15–20cm) span. Soft
pink, blending to yellow
at base of petal.
Leaves Divided into
oval leaflets. Mid-green.
• TIPS Good specimen
for exhibition.
• HEIGHT 4½ft (1.3m).
• SPREAD 2ft (60cm).

D. 'Pink Symbol'
(Semi-cactus)

☼ ◊   Z 9–10

D. 'Candy Keene'
Habit Clump-forming.
Flowers Borne during
summer and autumn,
spanning 8–10in
(10–25cm). Lilac-pink,
with white blends.
Leaves Divided into
oval leaflets. Mid-green.
• TIPS Good specimen
for exhibition.
• HEIGHT 4ft (1.2m).
• SPREAD 2ft (60cm).

D. 'Candy Keene'
(Semi-cactus)

☼ ◊   Z 9–10

D. 'Athalie'
Habit Clump-forming.
Flowers Up to 6in
(15cm) across, borne in
summer and autumn.
Deep pink, blending to
lemon at base of petal.
Leaves Divided into
oval leaflets. Glossy,
dark green.
• TIPS Suitable for
cutting or borders, and
good for exhibition.
• HEIGHT 4ft (1.2m).
• SPREAD 2ft (60cm).

D. 'Athalie'
(Cactus)

☼ ◊   Z 9–10

D. 'Gilt Edge'
Habit Clump-forming.
Flowers Freely borne, on strong stems, 6–8in (15–20cm) across, in summer and autumn. Lilac-pink, with faint, gold staining to tips of petals.
Leaves Divided into oval leaflets. Mid-green.
• TIPS Good for cutting and ideal for exhibition.
• HEIGHT 3½ft (1.1m).
• SPREAD 2ft (60cm).

D. 'Gilt Edge'
(Decorative)

 Z 9–10

D. 'Gay Princess'
Habit Clump-forming.
Flowers Strong-stemmed, 4–6in (10–15cm) across, held clear of the foliage, borne in summer and autumn. Rich lilac-pink.
Leaves Divided into oval leaflets. Mid-green.
• TIPS Suitable as cut flowers, and good specimen for exhibition.
• HEIGHT 5ft (1.5m).
• SPREAD 2½ft (75cm)

D. 'Gay Princess'
(Waterlily)

 Z 9–10

D. 'By the Cringe'
Habit Clump-forming
Flowers Spanning 5in (12cm), borne during summer and autumn. Lilac-pink.
Leaves Divided into oval leaflets. Mid-green.
• TIPS Ideal for planting in borders or cutting.
• HEIGHT 3½ft (1.1m).
• SPREAD 2ft (60cm).

D. 'By the Cringe'
(Cactus)

 Z 9–10

D. 'Wootton Cupid'
Habit Clump-forming.
Flowers Spanning 3–4in (8–10cm), borne clear of the foliage on strong stems, during summer and autumn. Clear salmon-pink.
Leaves Divided into oval leaflets. Mid-green.
• TIPS Good for planting in borders or cutting. A top exhibition variety.
• HEIGHT 3½ft (1.1m).
• SPREAD 2ft (60cm).

D. 'Wootton Cupid'
(Mini-ball)

 Z 9–10

D. 'Pontiac'
Habit Clump-forming.
Flowers Freely borne, 4–6in (10–15cm) across, in summer and autumn. Bright pink, with mauve shading at base.
Leaves Divided into oval leaflets. Glossy and dark green.
• TIPS Good for growing in borders, and suitable as cut flowers.
• HEIGHT 4ft (1.2m).
• SPREAD 2ft (60cm).

D. 'Pontiac'
(Cactus)

 Z 9–10

D. 'Fascination'
Habit Clump-forming.
Flowers Spanning 3–4in (8–10cm), borne from summer onward. Pale purplish-pink.
Leaves Oval leaflets. Glossy, dark bronze.
• TIPS Bred for bedding, but suitable for large containers or cutting.
• HEIGHT 2ft (60cm).
• SPREAD 18in (45cm).

D. 'Fascination'
(Miscellaneous, dwarf-bedding)

 Z 9–10

D. 'Jocondo'
Habit Clump-forming.
Flowers Spanning 12in (30cm) or more, borne on strong stems from mid-summer to autumn. Bright red-purple.
Leaves Divided into oval leaflets. Dark green.
• TIPS Good specimen for exhibition.
• HEIGHT 4ft (1.2m).
• SPREAD 2ft (60cm).

D. 'Jocondo'
(Decorative)

 Z 9–10

D. 'Betty Bowen'
Habit Clump-forming.
Flowers Neat and symmetrical, 4–6in (10–15cm) across, borne in summer and autumn. Rich purple.
Leaves Divided into oval leaflets. Glossy, dark green.
• TIPS Good as cut flowers and suitable for exhibition.
• HEIGHT 5ft (1.5m).
• SPREAD 2½ft (75cm).

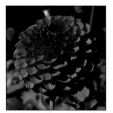

D. 'Betty Bowen'
(Decorative)

 Z 9–10

D. 'Whale's Rhonda'
Habit Clump-forming.
Flowers Borne in summer and autumn, 2in (5cm) across. Rich maroon, with silvery underside.
Leaves Divided into oval leaflets. Glossy, deep, dark green.
• TIPS Ideal for cutting or borders, and good specimen for exhibition.
• HEIGHT 3ft (1m).
• SPREAD 1½ft (45cm).

D. 'Whale's Rhonda'
(Pompon)

☼ ◊   Z 9–10

D. 'Comet'
Habit Clump-forming.
Flowers Velvet-textured, 4–6in (10–15cm) across, borne in summer and autumn. Rich dark red.
Leaves Divided into oval leaflets. Glossy, dark green.
• TIPS Good for borders and cutting.
• HEIGHT 3½ft (1.1m).
• SPREAD 2ft (60cm).

D. 'Comet'
(Anemone)

☼ ◊   Z 9–10

D. 'Brunton'
Habit Clump-forming.
Flowers Spanning 3–4in (8–10cm), borne in summer and autumn. Clear bright red.
Leaves Divided into oval leaflets. Dark green.
• TIPS Ideal for cutting or borders, and good specimen for exhibition.
• HEIGHT 3½ft (1.1m).
• SPREAD 2ft (60cm).

D. 'Brunton'
(Decorative)

☼ ◊   Z 9–10

D. 'Bishop of Llandaff'
Habit Clump-forming.
Flowers Peony-style, 4–5in (10–12cm) across, borne in summer and autumn. Rich dark red, with golden anthers.
Leaves Oval leaflets. Dark red-bronze.
• TIPS Good for use in bedding or borders, and suitable for cut flowers.
• HEIGHT 3½ft (1.1m).
• SPREAD 1½ft (45cm).

D. 'Bishop of Llandaff'
(Miscellaneous)

☼ ◊   Z 9–10

D. 'Corona'
Habit Clump-forming.
Flowers Borne on strong stems, 3–4in (8–10cm) across, in summer and autumn. Flame-red.
Leaves Oval leaflets. Glossy, dark green.
• TIPS Good for use in bedding and borders. Staking not needed.
• HEIGHT 1½–2ft (45–60cm).
• SPREAD 1½–2ft (45–60cm).

D. 'Corona'
(Semi-cactus, dwarf-bedding)

☼ ◊   Z 9–10

D. 'Scarlet Beauty'
Habit Clump-forming.
Flowers Uniform, 4–6in (10–15cm) across, borne in summer and autumn. Rich scarlet.
Leaves Divided into oval leaflets. Mid-green.
• TIPS Ideal for cutting or borders, and good specimen for exhibition.
• HEIGHT 3½ft (1.1m).
• SPREAD 2ft (60cm).

D. 'Scarlet Beauty'
(Waterlily)

☼ ◊   Z 9–10

D. 'Chimborazo'
Habit Clump-forming.
Flowers Freely borne, 4in (10cm) across, in summer and autumn. Rich maroon, with yellow inner petals and disc.
Leaves Oval leaflets. Glossy, dark green.
• TIPS Ideal for growing in borders, and as cut flowers. Good specimen for exhibition.
• HEIGHT 4ft (1.2m).
• SPREAD 2ft (60cm).

D. 'Chimborazo'
(Collerette)

☼ ◊   Z 9–10

D. 'Flutterby'
Habit Clump-forming.
Flowers Borne in summer and autumn, up to 4in (10cm) across. Yellow, suffused with red toward the petal tips.
Leaves Divided into oval leaflets. Mid-green.
•TIPS Suitable for planting in mixed and herbaceous borders, and good for cut flowers.
• HEIGHT 3ft (1m).
• SPREAD 18in (45cm).

D. 'Flutterby'
(Decorative)

☼ ◊   Z 9–10

D. 'Bassingbourne Beauty'
Habit Clump-forming.
Flowers Spanning 4–6in (10–15cm), borne in summer and autumn. Pale yellow, flushed orange-pink.
Leaves Divided into oval leaflets. Mid-green.
• TIPS Ideal for cutting or borders, and good specimen for exhibition.
• HEIGHT 4ft (1.2m).
• SPREAD 2ft (60cm).

D. 'Bassingbourne Beauty'
(Decorative)

☀ ◊   Z 9–10

D. 'Hamari Katrina'
Habit Clump-forming.
Flowers Borne during summer and autumn, 8–10in (20–25cm) across. Pale lemon-yellow.
Leaves Divided into oval leaflets. Mid-green.
• TIPS Good specimen for exhibition.
• HEIGHT 4½ft (1.3m).
• SPREAD 2ft (60cm).

D. 'Hamari Katrina'
(Semi-cactus)

☀ ◊   Z 9–10

D. 'Yellow Hammer'
Habit Clump-forming.
Flowers Borne clear of the foliage, 3in (8cm) across, from mid-summer to autumn. Rich yellow.
Leaves Divided into oval leaflets. Rich bronze.
• TIPS Good for planting in large containers, borders, or bedding, and suitable for cut flowers.
• HEIGHT 2ft (60cm).
• SPREAD 1½ft (45cm).

D. 'Yellow Hammer'
(Single, dwarf-bedding)

☀ ◊   Z 9–10

D. 'Clair de Lune'
Habit Clump-forming.
Flowers Borne from summer onwards, 3–4in (8–10cm) across. Lemon-yellow, creamy-yellow inner petals and golden anthers.
Leaves Divided into oval leaflets. Mid-green.
• TIPS Ideal for cutting or borders, and good specimen for exhibition.
• HEIGHT 3½ft (1.1m).
• SPREAD 2ft (60cm).

D. 'Clair de Lune'
(Collerette)

☀ ◊   Z 9–10

D. 'Butterball'
Habit Clump-forming.
Flowers Spanning 3–4in (8–10cm), borne in early summer. Clear, bright yellow.
Leaves Divided into oval leaflets. Mid-green.
• TIPS Ideal for planting in borders and cutting
• HEIGHT 3ft (1m).
• SPREAD 1½ft (45cm).

D. 'Butterball'
(Decorative, dwarf-bedding)

☀ ◊   Z 9–10

D. 'Early Bird'
Habit Clump-forming.
Flowers Borne during summer and autumn, 4–6in (10–15cm) across. Golden-yellow.
Leaves Divided into oval leaflets. Mid-green.
• TIPS Good for planting in borders and cutting.
• HEIGHT 4ft (1.2m).
• SPREAD 2ft (60cm).

D. 'Early Bird'
(Decorative)

☀ ◊   Z 9–10

D. 'Cortez Sovereign'
Habit Clump-forming.
Flowers Spanning 4–6in (10–15cm), borne in summer and autumn. Pale yellow.
Leaves Divided into oval leaflets. Mid-green.
• TIPS Good for planting in borders and suitable as cut flowers.
• HEIGHT 3–4ft (1–1.2m).
• SPREAD 2ft (60cm).

D. 'Cortez Sovereign'
(Semi-cactus)

☀ ◊   Z 9–10

D. 'Davenport Sunlight'

Habit Clump-forming.
Flowers Borne clear of the foliage, 6–8in (15–20cm) across, during summer and autumn. Bright yellow.
Leaves Divided into oval leaflets. Mid-green.
• TIPS Suitable for planting in borders and good for exhibition.
• HEIGHT 4ft (1.2m).
• SPREAD 2ft (60cm).

D. 'Davenport Sunlight'
(Semi-cactus)

☼ ◊   Z 9–10

D. 'Gay Mini'

Habit Clump-forming.
Flowers Borne in summer and autumn, 3–4in (8–10cm) across. Yellow, suffused with rich bronze-yellow.
Leaves Divided into oval leaflets. Mid-green.
• TIPS Good for planting in borders and cutting.
• HEIGHT 3ft (1m).
• SPREAD 1½ft (45cm).

D. 'Gay Mini'
(Decorative)

☼ ◊   Z 9–10

D. 'East Anglian'

Habit Clump-forming.
Flowers Spanning 4–6in (10–15cm), borne in summer and autumn. Soft golden-orange.
Leaves Divided into oval leaflets. Mid-green.
• TIPS Good for planting in borders and cutting.
• HEIGHT 3ft (1m).
• SPREAD 1½ft (45cm).

D. 'East Anglian'
(Decorative, dwarf-bedding)

☼ ◊   Z 9–10

D. 'So Dainty'

Habit Clump-forming.
Flowers Spanning 3–4in (8–10cm), borne on strong stems in summer and autumn. Golden-bronze, flushed apricot.
Leaves Divided into oval leaflets. Mid-green.
• TIPS Ideal for growing in borders, and as cut flowers. Good specimen for exhibition.
• HEIGHT 3½ft (1.1m).
• SPREAD 2ft (60cm).

D. 'So Dainty'
(Semi-cactus)

☼ ◊   Z 9–10

D. 'Shandy'

Habit Clump-forming.
Flowers Borne during summer and autumn, spanning 4–6in (10–15cm). Orange and light-pink blends.
Leaves Divided into oval leaflets. Mid-green.
• TIPS Good for planting in borders and cutting.
• HEIGHT 3ft (1m).
• SPREAD 1½ft (45cm).

D. 'Shandy'
(Semi-cactus)

☼ ◊   Z 9–10

D. 'Chinese Lantern'

Habit Clump-forming.
Flowers Borne from mid-summer to early autumn, 4–6in (10–15cm) across. Yellow, strongly infused with dark flame-orange.
Leaves Divided into oval leaflets. Mid-green.
• TIPS Good for planting in borders and cutting.
• HEIGHT 3½ft (1.1m).
• SPREAD 2ft (60cm).

D. 'Chinese Lantern'
(Decorative)

☼ ◊   Z 9–10

D. 'Corton Olympic'

Habit Clump-forming.
Flowers Strong-stemmed, 10–12in (25–30cm) across, borne in late summer. Rich bronze-orange.
Leaves Divided into oval leaflets. Dark green.
• TIPS Good specimen for exhibition.
• HEIGHT 4ft (1.2m).
• SPREAD 2ft (60cm).

D. 'Corton Olympic'
(Decorative)

☼ ◊   Z 9–10

D. 'Frank Hornsey'

Habit Clump-forming.
Flowers Borne on strong stems, 4–6in (10–15cm) across, from mid-summer to autumn. Apricot and bronze-yellow blends.
Leaves Divided into oval leaflets. Glossy, dark green.
• TIPS Ideal for cutting or borders, and good specimen for exhibition.
• HEIGHT 4ft (1.2m).
• SPREAD 2ft (60cm).

D. 'Frank Hornsey'
(Decorative)

☀ ◊　　　Z 9–10

D. 'Biddenham Sunset'

Habit Clump-forming.
Flowers Borne on strong stems, 4–5in (10–12cm) across, from mid-summer to autumn. Rich orange-red, with golden-yellow petal base.
Leaves Divided into oval leaflets. Dark green.
• TIPS Good for planting in borders and cutting.
• HEIGHT 4½ft (1.3m).
• SPREAD 2ft (60cm).

D. 'Biddenham Sunset'
(Decorative)

☀ ◊　　　Z 9–10

D. 'Paul Chester'

Habit Clump-forming.
Flowers Spanning 4–6in (10–15cm), borne in summer and autumn. Peachy orange-yellow.
Leaves Divided into oval leaflets. Mid-green.
• TIPS Ideal for cutting or borders, and good specimen for exhibition.
• HEIGHT 3ft (1m).
• SPREAD 1½ft (45cm).

D. 'Paul Chester'
(Cactus)

☀ ◊　　　Z 9–10

D. 'Quel Diable'

Habit Clump-forming.
Flowers Borne in summer and autumn, spanning 8–10in (20–25cm). Intense, flame red-orange.
Leaves Divided into oval leaflets. Dark green.
• TIPS Ideal for growing in borders, and as cut flowers. Good specimen for exhibition.
• HEIGHT 4ft (1.2m).
• SPREAD 2ft (60cm).

D. 'Quel Diable'
(Semi-cactus)

☀ ◊　　　Z 9–10

D. 'Highgate Torch'

Habit Clump-forming.
Flowers Spanning 6–8in (15–20cm), and borne on strong stems in summer and autumn. Rich flame-orange.
Leaves Lance-shaped to oval, toothed. Mid-green.
• TIPS Good for planting in borders and cutting.
• HEIGHT 3–4ft (1–1.2m).
• SPREAD 1½–2ft (45–60cm)

D. 'Highgate Torch'
(Semi-cactus)

☀ ◊　　　Z 9–10

Amaryllidaceae/Liliaceae	

AMARYLLIS BELLADONNA 'Hathor'

Habit Robust, bulbous, perennial. *Flowers* Fragrant, funnel-shaped, 4in (10cm) long, borne in sprays of 6 or more on stout stems, in autumn. White, with a yellow throat. *Leaves* Strap-shaped, fleshy, appearing after the flowers. Fresh green.
• NATIVE HABITAT Garden origin.
• CULTIVATION Best planted at the base of a warm, sunny wall, with deep, well-drained, preferably sandy soil. Needs adequate warmth to encourage flowering, and a wall base to ensure some protection from cold and excessive rainfall.

Where hard frost is expected, shield the bulbs and winter leaves with a dry mulch of straw, propped cloches, or horticultural fleece. Amaryllis eventually adjust to their preferred depths, but overcrowding may push the bulbs to the surface.
• PROPAGATION Separate offsets in spring.

☼ ◊

Z 7–10

HEIGHT
20–32in
(50–80cm)

SPREAD
12–18in
(30–45cm)

Nose
level

Amaryllidaceae/ Liliaceae	

× *AMARYGIA PARKERI*

Habit Robust, bulbous, perennial. *Flowers*
Frilled funnels, 4in (10cm) long, borne on stout
stems in early autumn. Pale pink, with yellow and
white throat. *Leaves* Basal, semi-erect, and strap-
shaped, appearing after the flowers. Mid-green.
• NATIVE HABITAT Garden origin.
• CULTIVATION Suitable for a cool greenhouse.
Overwintering foliage should be protected with
horticultural fleece from hard frost.
• PROPAGATION Separate offsets in spring.
• OTHER NAME × *Brunsdonna parkeri.*

☼ ◊

Z 9–10

HEIGHT
to 3ft (1m)

SPREAD
24in (60cm)

▯ Neck level

Amaryllidaceae/ Liliaceae	

× *AMARCRINUM MEMORIA-CORSII*

Habit Clump-forming, bulbous, perennial.
Flowers Scented funnels, 4in (10cm) long, in loose
sprays of 10, borne on stout stems in late summer.
Rose-pink. *Leaves* Evergreen (deciduous in cold
areas), strap-shaped, and semi-erect. Dark green.
• NATIVE HABITAT Garden origin.
• CULTIVATION Suitable for growing at the base
of a warm wall in sun. Excellent as a container-
grown plant in a cool greenhouse.
• PROPAGATION Separate offsets in early spring.
• OTHER NAMES × *A. howardii,* × *Crinodonna corsii.*

☼ ◊

Z 8–10

HEIGHT
3ft (1m)

SPREAD
24in (60cm)

▯ Nose level

Amaryllidaceae/ Liliaceae	BELLADONNA LILY

AMARYLLIS BELLADONNA

Habit Robust, bulbous, perennial. *Flowers*
Fragrant funnels, in sprays of 6, borne on purple-
green stems in autumn. Pink. *Leaves* Semi-erect,
strap-shaped, appearing after flowers. Dark green.
• NATIVE HABITAT By coasts and streams, S. Africa.
• CULTIVATION Plant at the base of a warm, sunny,
sheltered wall. Needs deep, fertile, well-drained
and preferably sandy soil enriched with organic
matter. Protect winter foliage from severe frosts
with horticultural fleece. Remove withered leaves.
• PROPAGATION Divide offsets, or sow ripe seed.

☼ ◊

Z 7–10

HEIGHT
20–32in
(50–80cm)

SPREAD
12–18in
(30–45cm)

▯ Nose level

Liliaceae	

ERYTHRONIUM OREGONUM

Habit Vigorous, clump-forming, bulbous, perennial. **Flowers** Drooping, with 6 petals that reflex as the flower opens fully. Borne in terminal clusters of up to 6 on naked stems, in spring. Creamy-white, yellow-eyed, with yellow stamens and orange-brown markings on petal base. **Leaves** Basal, semi-erect, oval and glossy, up to 6in (15cm) in length. Mid- to dark green, with paler mottling.
• NATIVE HABITAT Meadows, damp woods, and evergreen forests in N. America, from British Columbia to Oregon and northwestern California.

• CULTIVATION Excellent for naturalizing in drifts in a woodland garden. Equally good for planting beneath shrubs in a shrub border, or in a partially shaded site in a rock garden. Thrives in light, dappled, or partial shade. Provide fertile, moist but well-drained, leaf-rich soil that is enhanced with organic matter. Bulbs should not be allowed to dry out during storage or after planting.
• PROPAGATION By division of established clumps, or by separation of offsets (which are freely formed), after flowering.

☼ ◐ ◊

Z 3–9

HEIGHT
14in (35cm)

SPREAD
5in (12cm)

4–6in
(9–15cm)

Alliaceae/Liliaceae	

ALLIUM NEAPOLITANUM

Habit Slender, bulbous, perennial. *Flowers* Small stars in open sprays of 40, borne on slender stems in summer. White. *Leaves* Narrowly tapered and semi-erect, dying before the flowers. Mid-green.
• NATIVE HABITAT Southern Europe and N. Africa.
• CULTIVATION Needs well-drained, moderately fertile, and preferably sandy soil in full sun. Easy to grow, and spreads quickly.
• PROPAGATION By offsets in autumn, or by seed, as soon as it is ripe or in spring.
• OTHER NAME *A. cowanii.*

☼ ◌

Z 6–10

HEIGHT
8–20in
(20–50cm)

SPREAD
4–5in
(10–12cm)

3–4in
(8–10cm)

Amaryllidaceae	

PAMIANTHE PERUVIANA

Habit Elegant, bulbous, perennial. *Flowers* Fragrant, bell-shaped cups, with 6 spreading petals, borne in sprays of 2–4 in spring. Creamy-white. *Leaves* Strap-shaped, keeled, and semi-erect. Mid-green.
• NATIVE HABITAT Andes, Peru.
• CULTIVATION Grow as a house or conservatory plant in cold areas. Prefers fertile, rich soil. Water moderately during growth, but otherwise sparingly.
• PROPAGATION By offsets in autumn, or by seed as soon as it is ripe.

☼ ◌

Z 10–11

HEIGHT
20in (50cm)

SPREAD
18in (45cm)

3–4in
(8–10cm)

Liliaceae	GLOBE LILY

CALOCHORTUS ALBUS

Habit Slender, bulbous, perennial, with branched stems. *Flowers* Drooping, spherical to rounded, paper-thin bells, borne in spring to early summer. White. *Leaves* Linear. Grayish-green.
• NATIVE HABITAT Coastal foothills of California.
• CULTIVATION Prefers gritty, sharply drained soil and a warm, sheltered site. Dislikes winter moisture. Suitable for growing in a bulb frame or cool greenhouse. Dormant from July to November.
• PROPAGATION By seed when ripe, or by offsets in late summer.

☼ ◌

Z 4–10

HEIGHT
8–20in
(20–50cm)

SPREAD
2–4in
(5–10cm)

4–6in
(9–15cm)

Liliaceae/Liliaceae	

CALOCHORTUS VENUSTUS

Habit Slender, bulbous, perennial, with branching stems. *Flowers* Erect cups, borne in sprays during late spring to summer. White, marked maroon and yellow at petal base. *Leaves* Linear. Mid-green.
• NATIVE HABITAT Grassland, California.
• CULTIVATION Needs sandy, sharply drained soil in a warm, sheltered site. Dislikes winter moisture. Suitable for growing in a bulb frame or cold greenhouse. Dormant from July to November.
• PROPAGATION By seed when ripe, or by offsets in late summer.

☼ ◌

Z 6–10

HEIGHT
to 24in
(60cm)

SPREAD
2–4in
(5–10cm)

4–6in
(9–15cm)

Liliaceae	

ERYTHRONIUM CALIFORNICUM 'White Beauty'

Habit Very vigorous, clump-forming, bulbous, perennial. *Flowers* Drooping, in terminal clusters of 1–3, borne on slender, naked stems in spring. Each head bears 6 strongly reflexed petals, with rust-red markings at the base forming an attractive central ring. Creamy-white, with white anthers. *Leaves* Basal, oval, and glossy. Dark green, with sparse, pale-green mottling.

• NATIVE HABITAT Scrub, damp, shady woodland glades and mixed, evergreen forests in northern California, USA.

• CULTIVATION This robust cultivar is excellent for naturalizing in a woodland garden, or for planting beneath shrubs in a shrub border. It is easy to grow, and can be increased readily and quite quickly by offsets. Grow in light, dappled, or partial shade. Needs fertile, leaf-rich, moist but well-drained soil that is enhanced with organic matter. The bulbs should not be allowed to dry out during storage or after planting.

• PROPAGATION By division of established clumps, or by separation of offsets after flowering.

☼ ◊

Z 3–8

HEIGHT
8–12in
(20–30cm)

SPREAD
4–5in
(10–12cm)

4–6in
(9–15cm)

TULIPS

Tulips (*Tulipa*) offer a range of colors seldom found in other spring-flowering bulbs and are classified into 15 divisions:

Div. 1 Single early Single, cup-shaped.

Div. 2 Double early Double, last well.

Div. 3 Triumph Single, conical to rounded, sturdy-stemmed.

Div. 4 Darwin hybrids Single, large, strong-stemmed.

Div. 5 Single late Single, variable, usually with pointed petals.

Div. 6 Lily-flowered Single, long, with pointed petals, narrow waist, strong stems.

Div. 7 Fringed Fringed, similar to Div. 6.

Div. 8 Viridiflora Single, variable, with greenish petals.

Div. 9 Rembrandt (Mostly old cultivars). Striped or feathered, similar to Div. 6.

Div. 10 Parrot Single, large, variable, with frilled or fringed petals, often twisted.

Div. 11 Double late (peony-flowered) Double, bowl-shaped.

Div. 12 Kaufmanniana hybrids Single, with bicolored, mottled, or striped leaves.

Div. 13 Fosteriana hybrids Single, large, leaves are often mottled or striped.

Div. 14 Greigii hybrids Single, large, with mottled or striped, wavy-edged leaves.

Div. 15 Miscellaneous Other species and their varieties, cultivars, and hybrids.

Tulips need well-drained, fertile soil in a sunny site. Provide shelter from wind and protect plants from excessive moisture. Plant bulb 4–6in (10–15cm) deep. Bulbs may be lifted when the foliage dies. Store in a warm, dry spot to ripen, before replanting in autumn. Kaufmanniana hybrids and the species may be left *in situ* for several years; some may self-seed, and a few will spread to form colonies. Divide small offset bulbs, and grow on in a nursery bed. Propagate by seed, as soon as ripe or in a cold frame, in autumn. Flowers take 4–7 years to appear from seed.

T. 'White Triumphator'
Habit Bulbous, perennial.
Flowers Single, goblet-shaped, narrow petals with reflexed tips, borne in late spring. White.
Leaves Broadly lance-shaped. Grayish-green.
• TIPS Suitable for growing in a mixed or herbaceous border.
• HEIGHT 26–28in (65–70cm).

T. 'White Triumphator'
(Div. 6)

☼ ◊   Z 3–8

T. 'White Parrot'
Habit Bulbous, perennial.
Flowers Single, cup-shaped, with ruffled, fringed petals, borne in late spring. Pure white, flecked green at the base.
Leaves Broadly lance-shaped. Mid-green.
• TIPS Good for growing in a mixed or herbaceous border, and excellent for cut flowers.
• HEIGHT 22in (55cm).

T. 'White Parrot'
(Div. 10)

☼ ◊   Z 3–8

T. 'White Dream'
Habit Bulbous, perennial.
Flowers Single, cup-shaped, borne in mid-to late spring. Pure white, with yellow anthers.
Leaves Lance-shaped. Mid-green.
• TIPS Good for cut flowers and bedding.
• HEIGHT 16–18in (40–45cm).

T. 'White Dream'
(Div. 3)

☼ ◊   Z 3–8

T. BIFLORA
Habit Bulbous, perennial.
Flowers Scented, star-shaped, borne in early spring. Ivory-white, with yellow base, and flushed greenish-pink outside.
Leaves Linear and arching. Gray-green.
• TIPS Good for growing in a rock garden.
• OTHER NAME *T. polychroma*.
• HEIGHT 4in (10cm).

T. biflora
(Div. 15)

☼ ◊   Z 3–8

T. 'Spring Green'
Habit Bulbous, perennial.
Flowers Single, cup-shaped, borne in late spring. Ivory-white, with central, feathered, green stripe on reverse and light-green anthers.
Leaves Lance-shaped. Mid-green.
• TIPS Ideal for growing in a mixed border, and excellent for cutting and arranging.
• HEIGHT 16in (40cm).

T. 'Spring Green'
(Div. 8)

☼ ◊　　　　Z 3–8

T. *TURKESTANICA*
Habit Bulbous, perennial.
Flowers Foul-smelling, star-shaped, borne in early or mid-spring. White, with orange center stripe, flushed gray-pink on reverse.
Leaves Linear. Gray-green.
• TIPS Suitable for growing in a rock garden or sunny border.
• HEIGHT 12in (30cm).

T. turkestanica
(Div. 15)

☼ ◊　　　　Z 3–8

T. 'Purissima'
Habit Bulbous, perennial.
Flowers Cup-shaped, single, borne on strong stems in mid-spring. Pure white.
Leaves Broad and lance-shaped. Light grayish-green.
• TIPS Suits a border or large container.
• OTHER NAME
T. 'White Emperor'.
• HEIGHT 14in (35cm).

T. 'Purissima'
(Div. 13)

☼ ◊　　　　Z 3–8

T. 'Diana'
Habit Bulbous, perennial.
Flowers Cup-shaped, single, borne on strong stems in mid-spring. Ivory-white.
Leaves Lance-shaped. Mid-green.
• TIPS Suitable for growing in mixed borders and as bedding.
• HEIGHT 15in (38cm).

T. 'Diana'
(Div. 1)

☼ ◊　　　　Z 3–8

T. 'Carnaval de Nice'
Habit Bulbous, perennial.
Flowers Double, bowl-shaped, borne in late spring. White, with dark red feathering and markings.
Leaves Broadly lance-shaped. Grayish-green.
• TIPS Suitable for growing in borders and as bedding.
• HEIGHT 16in (40cm).

T. 'Carnaval de Nice'
(Div. 11)

☼ ◊　　　　Z 3–8

T. 'Angélique'
Habit Bulbous, perennial.
Flowers Double, bowl-shaped, slightly scented, borne in mid-spring. Pale pink with paler and deeper streaks, and paler pink petal margins.
Leaves Broadly lance-shaped. Mid-green.
• TIPS Good for use in borders and bedding.
• HEIGHT 16in (40cm).

T. 'Angélique'
(Div. 11)

☀ ◊   Z 3–8

T. 'Fancy Frills'
Habit Bulbous, perennial.
Flowers Single, cup-shaped, borne in late spring. Deep rose-pink, with paler petal edges.
Leaves Broadly lance-shaped. Mid-green.
• TIPS Suitable for growing in a mixed or herbaceous border, and excellent for arranging or as cut flowers.
• HEIGHT 18in (45cm).

T. 'Fancy Frills'
(Div. 7)

☀ ◊   Z 3–8

T. 'Groenland'
Habit Bulbous, perennial.
Flowers Single, cup-shaped, borne in late spring. Pale green, with broad, soft pink margins on petals.
Leaves Lance-shaped. Mid-green.
• TIPS Good for growing in mixed borders or as bedding. Suitable for cut flowers.
• HEIGHT 18in (45cm).

T. 'Groenland'
(Div. 8)

☀ ◊   Z 3–8

T. 'Menton'
Habit Robust, bulbous, perennial.
Flowers Single, cup-shaped, borne in late spring. Rose-pink, pale orange petal margins, and bright red inside with white veins.
Leaves Broadly lance-shaped. Grayish-green.
• TIPS Suitable for bedding and good as cut flowers.
• HEIGHT 24in (60cm).

T. 'Menton'
(Div. 5)

☀ ◊   Z 3–8

T. 'New Design'
Habit Bulbous, perennial.
Flowers Widely cup-shaped, borne in mid-spring. Pale yellow, with pale fuchsia-pink petal margins, stained apricot inside.
Leaves Lance-shaped. Mid-green, with cream, pink-tinted margins.
• TIPS Ideal for bedding and as cut flowers.
• HEIGHT 18in (45cm).

T. 'New Design'
(Div. 3)

☀ ◊   Z 3–8

T. 'Ballade'
Habit Bulbous, perennial.
Flowers Single, goblet-shaped, with elegantly reflexed petal tips, borne in late spring. Red-magenta, with white margins.
Leaves Lance-shaped. Grayish-green.
• TIPS Suitable for formal bedding.
• HEIGHT 20in (50cm).

T. 'Ballade'
(Div. 6)

☼ ◊   Z 3–8

T. 'China Pink'
Habit Bulbous, perennial.
Flowers Single, goblet-shaped, with slightly reflexed, pointed petals, borne in late spring. Pink, with white basal blotch inside.
Leaves Narrowly lance-shaped. Mid-green.
• TIPS Suitable for formal bedding and as cut flowers.
• HEIGHT 20in (50cm).

T. 'China Pink'
(Div. 6)

☼ ◊   Z 3–8

T. SAXATILIS
Habit Bulbous, perennial, with stolons.
Flowers Scented, star-shaped, borne singly or in clusters of 4 in mid-spring. Pink, with yellow, white-edged base.
Leaves Linear and glossy. Mid-green.
• TIPS Good for growing in a rock garden.
• OTHER NAME
T. bakeri.
• HEIGHT 6in (15cm).

T. saxatilis
(Div. 15)

☼ ◊   Z 6–8

T. 'Gordon Cooper'
Habit Bulbous, perennial.
Flowers Single, egg-shaped, borne in mid-spring. Red, fading to pink with red margins. Glossy red inside, with a black-and-yellow basal blotch and black anthers.
Leaves Lance-shaped. Mid-green.
• TIPS Suitable for bedding and cutting.
• HEIGHT 24in (60cm).

T. 'Gordon Cooper'
(Div. 4)

☼ ◊   Z 3–8

T. 'Page Polka'
Habit Bulbous, perennial.
Flowers Single, cup-shaped, borne in mid-spring. Dark red, with white veins and a white basal blotch.
Leaves Broadly lance-shaped. Mid-green.
• TIPS Good for bedding and as cut flowers.
• HEIGHT 16in (40cm).

T. 'Page Polka'
(Div. 3)

☼ ◊   Z 3–8

T. 'Peer Gynt'
Habit Bulbous, perennial.
Flowers Cup-shaped, borne in mid-spring. Rose-pink, fading to pale purple at petal margins, with white basal blotch inside, marked yellow.
Leaves Lance-shaped. Mid-green.
• TIPS Suitable for bedding, and good as cut flowers.
• HEIGHT 18in (45cm).

T. 'Peer Gynt'
(Div. 3)

☼ ◊   Z 3–8

T. 'Attila'
Habit Bulbous, perennial.
Flowers Single, cup-shaped, borne on strong stems in mid-spring. Pink-purple.
Leaves Broadly lance-shaped. Grayish-green.
• TIPS Good for bedding and as cut flowers. Also suitable for forcing.
• HEIGHT 16in (40cm).

T. 'Attila'
(Div. 3)

☼ ◊   Z 3–8

T. 'Don Quichotte'
Habit Bulbous, perennial.
Flowers Single, cup-shaped, borne on strong stems in late spring. Cherry-pink.
Leaves Lance-shaped. Grayish-green.
• TIPS Good for bedding. Flowers are long-lasting, both in the ground and as cut flowers.
• HEIGHT 16in (40cm).

T. 'Don Quichotte'
(Div. 3)

☼ ◊   Z 3–8

T. 'Dreamland'
Habit Bulbous, perennial.
Flowers Single, egg-shaped, borne in late spring. Red, faintly flamed cream, and pink-red inside with a white basal blotch.
Leaves Lance-shaped. Mid-green.
• TIPS Suitable for bedding, and good as cut flowers.
• HEIGHT 24in (60cm).

T. 'Dreamland'
(Div. 5)

☼ ◊   Z 3–8

T. CLUSIANA
Habit Bulbous, perennial.
Flowers Single, opening to star-shaped, borne in mid-spring. White, with deep pink stripes and red basal blotch inside.
Leaves Linear and glaucous. Gray-green.
• TIPS Good for growing in a rock garden.
• OTHER NAME T. aitchisonii.
• HEIGHT 12in (30cm).

T. clusiana
Lady tulip
(Div. 15)

☼ ◊   Z 3–8

T. 'Bird of Paradise'
Habit Bulbous, perennial.
Flowers Cup-shaped, borne in late spring. Cardinal-red, with white petal margins. Red inside, feathered darker red, with yellow base.
Leaves Lance-shaped. Mid-green.
• TIPS Suitable for growing in borders and as cut flowers.
• HEIGHT 22in (55cm).

T. 'Bird of Paradise'
(Div. 10)

☼ ◊   Z 3–8

T. 'Estella Rijnveld'
Habit Bulbous, perennial.
Flowers Single, cup-shaped, with deeply cut petals, borne in late spring. Red, flamed with white and green.
Leaves Lance-shaped. Mid-green.
• TIPS Ideal for growing in borders and cutting.
• OTHER NAME T. 'Gay Presto'.
• HEIGHT 22in (55cm).

T. 'Estella Rijnveld'
(Div. 10)

☼ ◊   Z 3–8

T. 'Union Jack'
Habit Bulbous, perennial.
Flowers Single, cup-shaped, borne in late spring. Ivory-white, flamed deep raspberry-red, with a bluish-edged, white basal blotch.
Leaves Lance-shaped. Mid-green.
• TIPS Good for use in bedding or borders, and as cut flowers.
• HEIGHT 24in (60cm).

T. 'Union Jack'
(Div. 5)

☀ ◊   Z 3–8

T. 'Garden Party'
Habit Bulbous, perennial.
Flowers Goblet-shaped, borne in mid- to late spring. White with broad, deep pink petal margins and inner feathering.
Leaves Lance-shaped. Mid-green.
• TIPS Good for bedding and cutting.
• HEIGHT 18in (45cm).

T. 'Garden Party'
(Div. 3)

☀ ◊   Z 3–8

T. 'Red Parrot'
Habit Bulbous, perennial.
Flowers Large, single, cup-shaped, with deeply cut petals, borne on strong stems in late spring. Raspberry-red.
Leaves Lance-shaped. Grayish-green.
• TIPS Good for borders and cutting.
• HEIGHT 22in (55cm).

T. 'Red Parrot'
(Div. 10)

☀ ◊   Z 3–8

T. 'Madame Lefeber'
Habit Bulbous, perennial.
Flowers Single, bowl-shaped, borne on strong stems in early spring. Glossy red.
Leaves Lance-shaped. Light green.
• TIPS Suits borders and large pots.
• OTHER NAME *T.* 'Red Emperor'.
• HEIGHT 14in (35cm).

T. 'Madame Lefeber'
(Div. 13)

☀ ◊   Z 3–8

T. LINIFOLIA
Habit Slender, bulbous, perennial.
Flowers Bowl-shaped, rounded base, borne in early or mid-spring. Glossy red, with black base. Cream or yellow margins often present.
Leaves Linear and curved. Gray-green, with red wavy margins.
• TIPS Good for growing in a rock garden.
• HEIGHT 8in (20cm).

T. linifolia
(Div. 15)

☀ ◊   Z 3–8

T. HAGERI 'Splendens'
Habit Bulbous, perennial.
Flowers Star-shaped, borne in mid-spring. Dull red, with a black basal blotch and buff-tinted reverse.
Leaves Lance-shaped. Pale green, often with purple margins.
• TIPS Good for growing in a rock garden.
• HEIGHT 12in (30cm).

T. hageri 'Splendens'
(Div. 15)

☀ ◊   Z 3–8

T. SPRENGERI
Habit Bulbous, perennial.
Flowers Solitary, goblet-shaped, borne in early summer. Red or orange-red, with buff base.
Leaves Linear, erect, and glossy. Mid-green.
• TIPS Good for a woodland garden, or for naturalizing in turf. Prefers partial shade, and peaty, fertile soil.
• HEIGHT 20in (50cm).

T. sprengeri
(Div. 15)

☀ ◊   Z 3–8

T. 'Bing Crosby'

Habit Bulbous, perennial.
Flowers Single, cup-shaped, borne on strong stems in mid-spring. Rich scarlet.
Leaves Lance-shaped. Mid-green.
• TIPS Suitable for bedding or borders, and as cut flowers.
• HEIGHT 16in (40cm).

T. 'Bing Crosby'
(Div. 3)

☼ ◊   Z 3–8

T. 'Lustige Witwe'

Habit Bulbous, perennial.
Flowers Cup-shaped, single, borne on strong stems in mid-spring. Dark red, edged white.
Leaves Lance-shaped. Grayish-green.
• TIPS Suitable for borders or bedding, and as cut flowers.
• OTHER NAME
T. 'Merry Widow'.
• HEIGHT 16in (40cm).

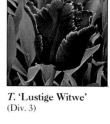

T. 'Lustige Witwe'
(Div. 3)

☼ ◊   Z 3–8

T. 'Uncle Tom'

Habit Bulbous, perennial.
Flowers Double, bowl-shaped, peony-like, borne on strong stems in late spring. Rich maroon-red.
Leaves Broadly lance-shaped. Grayish-green.
• TIPS Good for use in borders or bedding.
• HEIGHT 20in (50cm).

T. 'Uncle Tom'
(Div. 11)

☼ ◊   Z 3–8

T. 'Balalaika'

Habit Bulbous, perennial.
Flowers Single, egg- to cup-shaped, borne in late spring. Bright red, with a yellow basal blotch and black stamens.
Leaves Lance-shaped. Grayish-green.
• TIPS Good for borders or bedding, and cutting.
• HEIGHT 22in (55cm).

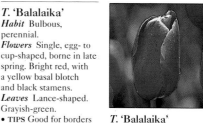

T. 'Balalaika'
(Div. 5)

☼ ◊   Z 3–8

T. 'Kingsblood'

Habit Bulbous, perennial.
Flowers Single, cup-shaped, borne in late spring. Bright cherry-red, with scarlet margins.
Leaves Broadly lance-shaped. Grayish-green.
• TIPS Ideal for bedding or borders, and suitable as cut flowers.
• HEIGHT 24in (60cm).

T. 'Kingsblood'
(Div. 5)

☼ ◊   Z 3–8

T. PRAESTANS 'Unicum'

Habit Bulbous, perennial.
Flowers Single, bowl-shaped, in clusters of up to 5, borne in early or mid-spring. Bright red.
Leaves Oblong-lance-shaped. Gray-green, with creamy-white margins.
• TIPS Easy to grow and suitable for planting in a rock garden.
• HEIGHT 12in (30cm).

T. praestans 'Unicum'
(Div. 15)

☼ ◊   Z 3–8

T. 'Oranje Nassau'

Habit Bulbous, perennial.
Flowers Double, bowl-shaped, borne in mid-spring. Blood-red, flushed hot-orange.
Leaves Lance-shaped to oval, toothed. Mid-green.
• TIPS Good for bedding and suitable for planting in containers.
• HEIGHT 12in (30cm).

T. 'Oranje Nassau'
(Div. 2)

☼ ◊   Z 3–8

T. UNDULATIFOLIA

Habit Bulbous, perennial.
Flowers Narrowly bowl-shaped, borne in early and mid-spring. Orange-red, with buff reverse.
Leaves Linear and crimped. Gray-green.
• TIPS Good for growing in a rock garden.
• OTHER NAME
T. eichleri.
• HEIGHT 6–20in (15–50cm).

T. undulatifolia
(Div. 15)

☼ ◊   Z 3–8

T. 'Red Riding Hood'

Habit Bulbous, perennial.
Flowers Single, narrowly bowl-shaped, borne on sturdy stems in early spring. Vivid scarlet.
Leaves Broadly lance-shaped, spreading. Blue-green, marked purple.
• TIPS Good for a rock garden, border, and containers.
• HEIGHT 8in (20cm).

T. 'Red Riding Hood'
(Div. 14)

☼ ◊   Z 3–8

T. 'Plaisir'

Habit Bulbous, perennial.
Flowers Broadly urn-shaped, borne in early spring. Deep carmine, with pale yellow margins.
Leaves Broadly lance-shaped and spreading. Blue-green, marked red.
• TIPS Ideal for a rock garden or the front of a border, and for planting in containers.
• HEIGHT 6in (15cm).

T. 'Plaisir'
(Div. 14)

☼ ◊   Z 3–8

T. 'Margot Fonteyn'

Habit Bulbous, perennial.
Flowers Single, neatly cup-shaped, borne in mid-spring. Bright red, with yellow margins, yellow basal blotch inside, and black anthers.
Leaves Lance-shaped. Grayish-green.
• TIPS Suitable for bedding and good as cut flowers.
• HEIGHT 16in (40cm).

T. 'Margot Fonteyn'
(Div. 3)

☼ ◊   Z 3–8

T. 'Fringed Beauty'

Habit Bulbous perennial.
Flowers Double, bowl-shaped, borne on sturdy stems in late spring. Bright vermilion, with rich gold fringes.
Leaves Lance-shaped. Grayish-green.
• TIPS Good for cutting and borders. Excellent for forcing.
• HEIGHT 14in (35cm).

T. 'Fringed Beauty'
(Div. 7)

☼ ◊   Z 3–8

T. 'Keizerskroon'
Habit Bulbous, perennial.
Flowers Single, cup-shaped, borne in mid-spring. Rich scarlet, with broad, yellow margins.
Leaves Lance-shaped. Mid-green.
• TIPS Suitable for bedding, mixed borders and containers.
• OTHER NAME
T. 'Grand Duc'.
• HEIGHT 12in (30cm).

T. 'Keizerskroon'
(Div. 1)

☼ ◊   Z 3–8

T. ACUMINATA
Habit Bulbous, perennial.
Flowers Solitary, round at the base, with slender, pointed petals, borne in mid-spring. Light red or yellow, often tinted dark red or green outside.
Leaves Linear to lance-shaped. Gray-green.
• TIPS Suitable for growing in an alpine house or rock garden.
• HEIGHT 18in (45cm).

T. acuminata
(Div. 15)

☼ ◊   Z 3–8

T. 'Juan'
Habit Bulbous, perennial.
Flowers Single, bowl-shaped, borne in mid-spring. Deep orange-red, tinted pink, with golden-yellow petal base.
Leaves Broadly lance-shaped. Mid-green, with red-brown stripes.
• TIPS Good for borders or containers.
• HEIGHT 10in (25cm).

T. 'Juan'
(Div. 13)

☼ ◊   Z 3–8

T. 'Apeldoorn's Elite'
Habit Bulbous, perennial.
Flowers Single, egg-shaped, borne in mid-spring. Buttercup-yellow, feathered cherry-red and flushed green at the base, with black anthers.
Leaves Broadly lance-shaped. Grayish-green.
• TIPS Good for bedding and cutting.
• HEIGHT 24in (60cm).

T. 'Apeldoorn's Elite'
(Div. 4)

☼ ◊   Z 3–8

T. MARJOLLETTII
Habit Bulbous, perennial.
Flowers Solitary, bowl-shaped, borne in early or mid-spring. Creamy-white, with dark pink margins and flushed purple outside.
Leaves Oval to lance-shaped. Gray-green.
• TIPS Suitable specimen for planting in borders.
• HEIGHT 18in (45cm).

T. marjollettii
(Div. 15)

☼ ◊   Z 3–8

T. 'Dreaming Maid'
Habit Bulbous, perennial.
Flowers Single, cup-shaped, borne in mid-spring. Violet with white-margined petals.
Leaves Lance-shaped. Mid-green.
• TIPS Good for bedding and cutting.
• HEIGHT 20in (50cm).

T. 'Dreaming Maid'
(Div. 3)

☼ ◊   Z 3–8

T. HUMILIS
Violacea Group
Habit Bulbous,
perennial.
Flowers Star-shaped,
borne in early or mid-
spring. Purple, with
a yellow basal blotch.
Leaves Linear, glaucous,
channeled. Gray-green.
• TIPS Good for a rock
garden or raised bed.
• OTHER NAME
T. violacea.
• HEIGHT 10in (25cm).

T. humilis Violacea
Group
(Div. 15)

☼ ◊   Z 3–8

T. HUMILIS
Habit Variable,
bulbous, perennial.
Flowers Star-shaped,
borne in early or mid-
spring. Purple, often
with a gray-green tinted
reverse, and a yellow-
green or blue-black
basal blotch.
Leaves Linear, glaucous,
channeled. Gray-green.
• TIPS Good for planting
in a rock garden.
• HEIGHT 10in (25cm).

T. humilis
(Div. 15)

☼ ◊   Z 3–8

T. 'Greuze'
Habit Bulbous,
perennial.
Flowers Single,
cup-shaped, borne on
strong stems in late
spring. Violet-purple.
Leaves Lance-shaped.
Mid-green.
• TIPS Good for
bedding and cutting.
• HEIGHT 22in (55cm).

T. 'Blue Parrot'
Habit Bulbous,
perennial.
Flowers Very large, with
frilled and twisted, satiny
petals, borne on strong
stems in late spring.
Bright violet-blue,
often bronzed within.
Leaves Lance-shaped.
Mid-green.
• TIPS Suitable for
growing in borders,
and as cut flowers.
• HEIGHT 24in (60cm).

T. 'Blue Parrot'
(Div. 10)

☼ ◊   Z 3–8

T. 'Queen of Night'
Habit Robust,
bulbous, perennial.
Flowers Single, cup-
shaped, satin-textured,
borne in late spring.
Deep maroon-purple.
Leaves Broadly lance-
shaped. Grayish-green.
• TIPS Suitable for
growing in mixed
borders alongside gray-
leaved plants. Good
for cut flowers.
• HEIGHT 24in (60cm).

T. 'Queen of Night'
(Div. 5)

☼ ◊   Z 3–8

T. 'Greuze'
(Div. 5)

☼ ◊   Z 3–8

T. LINIFOLIA
Batalinii Group
Habit Bulbous, perennial.
Flowers Solitary, bowl-shaped, rounded base, borne in early or mid-spring. Pale yellow.
Leaves Linear and curved. Gray-green.
• TIPS Good for growing in a rock garden.
• OTHER NAME *T. batalinii*.
• HEIGHT 12in (30cm).

T. linifolia
Batalinii Group
(Div. 15)

☼ ◊   Z 3–8

T. KAUFMANNIANA
Habit Bulbous, perennial.
Flowers Bowl-shaped, solitary or in clusters of up to 5, borne in early spring. Cream or yellow, flushed pink or gray outside.
Leaves Lance-shaped and slightly wavy-margined. Gray-green.
• TIPS Good for planting in a rock garden.
• HEIGHT 10in (25cm).

T. kaufmanniana
Waterlily tulip (Div. 15)

☼ ◊   Z 3–8

T. TARDA
Habit Bulbous, perennial.
Flowers Star-shaped, borne in clusters of 4–6, in early or mid-spring. White, with yellow base and red outer flush.
Leaves Lance-shaped. Shiny, bright green.
• TIPS Grows best in peat-rich, fertile soil.
• OTHER NAME *Tulipa dasystemon* of gardens.
• HEIGHT 6in (15cm).

T. tarda
(Div. 15)

☼ ◊   Z 3–8

T. 'Maja'
Habit Bulbous, perennial.
Flowers Single, cup-shaped, with neatly fringed petals, borne in late spring. Pale yellow and bronze-yellow base.
Leaves Lance-shaped. Mid-green.
• TIPS Good for borders and cutting.
• HEIGHT 20in (50cm).

T. 'Maja'
(Div. 7)

☼ ◊   Z 3–8

T. 'Bellona'
Habit Bulbous, perennial.
Flowers Scented, single, egg-shaped, borne on strong stems in mid-spring. Clear golden-yellow.
Leaves Lance-shaped. Mid-green.
• TIPS Good for bedding and cutting.
• HEIGHT 16in (40cm).

T. 'Bellona'
(Div. 1)

☼ ◊   Z 3–8

T. 'West Point'
Habit Bulbous, perennial.
Flowers Single, goblet-shaped, with reflexed tips, borne in late spring. Primrose-yellow.
Leaves Lance-shaped. Mid-green.
• TIPS Suitable for planting in borders and as formal bedding.
• HEIGHT 20in (50cm).

T. 'West Point'
(Div. 6)

☼ ◊   Z 3–8

T. SYLVESTRIS
Habit Bulbous, perennial.
Flowers Star-shaped, scented, nodding in bud, later erect, borne in mid- or late spring. Yellow, with green basal flush.
Leaves Linear, glaucous, channeled. Light green.
• TIPS Suitable for naturalizing in turf.
• OTHER NAME *T. australis*.
• HEIGHT 18in (45cm).

T. sylvestris
(Div. 15)

☼ ◊   Z 3–8

T. URUMIENSIS
Habit Bulbous, perennial.
Flowers Star-shaped, borne singly or in pairs, in early spring. Yellow, with lilac or red-brown flush outside.
Leaves Linear, glaucous, forming basal rosettes. Mid-green.
• TIPS Suitable for growing in a raised bed or rock garden.
• HEIGHT 6in (15cm).

T. urumiensis
(Div. 15)

☼ ◊   Z 3–8

T. 'Yokahama'

Habit Bulbous, perennial.
Flowers Single, pointed to egg-shaped, borne in early spring. Rich yellow.
Leaves Lance-shaped. Mid-green.
• TIPS Good for growing in containers, mixed borders, and bedding.
• HEIGHT 12in (30cm).

T. 'Yokahama'
(Div. 1)

☼ ◊   Z 3–8

T. 'Golden Artist'

Habit Bulbous, perennial.
Flowers Cup-shaped, single, with crimped petal margins, borne in late spring. Yellow, with green stripes.
Leaves Lance-shaped. Mid-green.
• TIPS Suitable for growing in a mixed border, and for cutting and arranging.
• HEIGHT 18in (45cm).

T. 'Golden Artist'
(Div. 8)

☼ ◊   Z 3–8

T. CLUSIANA var. CHRYSANTHA

Habit Bulbous, perennial.
Flowers Bowl- then star-shaped, borne in trios from early to mid-spring. Yellow, tinted red-brown.
Leaves Linear and glaucous. Gray-green.
• TIPS Suitable for a raised bed or rock garden.
• OTHER NAME *T. chrysantha.*
• HEIGHT 12in (30cm).

T. clusiana var. *chrysantha*
(Div. 15)

☼ ◊   Z 3–8

T. 'Candela'

Habit Bulbous, perennial.
Flowers Large, single, oblong bowl-shaped, borne on sturdy stems from early through to mid-spring. Deep pure yellow, with black anthers.
Leaves Lance-shaped. Gray-green.
• TIPS Suitable for growing in borders.
• HEIGHT 14in (35cm).

T. 'Candela'
(Div. 13)

☼ ◊   Z 3–8

T. 'Golden Apeldoorn'

Habit Bulbous, perennial.
Flowers Single, egg-shaped, borne in mid-spring. Golden-yellow, with black anthers and a black, bronze-edged, basal blotch in the shape of a star.
Leaves Lance-shaped. Mid-green.
• TIPS Good for bedding and cutting.
• HEIGHT 24in (60cm).

T. 'Golden Apeldoorn'
(Div. 4)

☼ ◊   Z 3–8

T. 'Cape Cod'
Habit Bulbous, perennial.
Flowers Single, bowl-shaped, borne in mid-spring. Yellow, with broad, red stripes.
Leaves Broadly lance-shaped, with wavy margins. Blue-gray, marked maroon.
• TIPS Suitable for growing in a rock garden or border.
• HEIGHT 8in (20cm).

T. 'Cape Cod'
(Div. 14)

☼ ◊   Z 3–8

T. 'Artist'
Habit Bulbous, perennial.
Flowers Cup-shaped, single, with crimped petal margins, borne in late spring. Salmon-red, striped green outside.
Leaves Lance-shaped. Mid-green.
• TIPS Suitable for growing in a mixed border, and for cutting and arranging.
• HEIGHT 18in (45cm).

T. 'Artist'
(Div. 8)

☼ ◊   Z 3–8

T. 'Apricot Beauty'
Habit Bulbous, perennial.
Flowers Cup-shaped, borne in early and mid-spring. Soft salmon-pink, with faint orange-red petal margins.
Leaves Lance-shaped. Mid-green.
• TIPS Suitable for planting in beds or mixed borders, and good for forcing.
• HEIGHT 15in (38cm).

T. 'Apricot Beauty'
(Div. 1)

☼ ◊   Z 3–8

T. 'Dillenberg'
Habit Bulbous, perennial.
Flowers Neatly cup-shaped, borne on strong stems in late spring. Brick-red.
Leaves Lance-shaped. Mid-green.
• TIPS Ideal for bedding, and good as cut flowers.
• HEIGHT 26in (65cm).

T. 'Dillenberg'
(Div. 5)

☼ ◊   Z 3–8

T. 'Dreamboat'
Habit Bulbous, perennial.
Flowers Single, urn-shaped, borne in mid-spring. Amber-yellow, strongly tinted red, with green-bronze base inside.
Leaves Lance-shaped and wavy-margined. Blue-gray, marked red.
• TIPS Good for growing in a rock garden or border.
• HEIGHT 8in (20cm).

T. 'Dreamboat'
(Div. 14)

☼ ◊   Z 3–8

T. 'Prinses Irene'
Habit Bulbous, perennial.
Flowers Cup-shaped, single, borne in early spring. Orange, with a pale purple stripe.
Leaves Lance-shaped. Grayish-green.
• TIPS Suitable for bedding or mixed borders, and cutting.
• HEIGHT 14in (35cm).

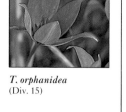

T. 'Prinses Irene'
(Div. 1)

☼ ◊   Z 3–8

T. 'Shakespeare'
Habit Bulbous, perennial.
Flowers Single, bowl-shaped, borne in early spring. Deep carmine-red, edged salmon-pink, with a yellow base.
Leaves Lance-shaped. Mid-green.
• TIPS Suitable for a rock garden or border.
• HEIGHT 10in (25cm).

T. 'Shakespeare'
(Div. 12)

☼ ◊   Z 3–8

T. PRAESTANS 'Van Tubergen's Variety'
Habit Bulbous, perennial.
Flowers Large, bowl-shaped, borne in clusters of up to 3 in early or mid-spring. Flame-red.
Leaves Oblong to lance-shaped. Gray-green.
• TIPS Suits a rock garden or border.
• HEIGHT 8in (20cm).

T. praestans 'Van Tubergen's Variety'
(Div. 15)

☼ ◊   Z 3–8

T. ORPHANIDEA
Habit Bulbous, perennial.
Flowers Star-shaped, borne singly or in clusters of up to 3 in mid- or late spring. Bright orange-brown to orange-red, tinted buff-green outside.
Leaves Lance-shaped. Mid-green, edged red.
• TIPS Suitable for planting in a rock garden.
• HEIGHT 12in (30cm).

T. orphanidea
(Div. 15)

☼ ◊   Z 3–8

T. ORPHANIDEA Whittallii Group
Habit Bulbous, perennial.
Flowers Single, star-shaped, with pointed petals, borne in early or mid-spring. Burnt orange, with buff-tinted outside and a black basal blotch.
Leaves Lance-shaped. Mid-green.
• TIPS Good for growing in a rock garden.
• OTHER NAME
T. whittallii.
• HEIGHT 14in (35cm).

T. orphanidea Whittallii Group
(Div. 15)

☼ ◊   Z 3–8

Liliaceae

ERYTHRONIUM HENDERSONII

Habit Robust, clump-forming, bulbous, perennial.
Flowers Drooping, delicate, with 6 reflexed
petals, borne in terminal clusters of up to 10,
on slender, naked stems, in spring. Pale pinkish-
lilac, deeper purple at base, occasionally with a
central yellow ring, and purple anthers. **Leaves**
Basal, oval, and wavy-margined. Dark green,
with light-brown mottling.
• NATIVE HABITAT Open glades in the
coniferous forests of southwest Oregon
and northwest California.

• CULTIVATION Suitable for naturalizing in
open glades in a woodland garden, or for planting
beneath shrubs in a shrub border. This species
prefers soils that are moist in winter and spring
but dry out during the summer months. Grow in
light, dappled, or partial shade in fertile, freely
draining, sandy soil that is rich in organic matter.
• PROPAGATION By division of established clumps,
or by separation of offsets after flowering. It may
also be raised from seed that is sown in seed-
starting mix as soon as ripe.

☀ ◊

Z 3–9

HEIGHT
6–14in
(15–35cm)

SPREAD
4–5in
(10–12cm)

4–6in
(9–15cm)

Alliaceae/Liliaceae	

ALLIUM UNIFOLIUM

Habit Bulbous, perennial. *Flowers* Small, open bells, borne in domed heads of up to 20, in late spring. Purple-pink. *Leaves* Basal, linear, with one leaf per bulb, dying back at flowering. Gray-green.
• NATIVE HABITAT Evergreen forests in coastal mountain ranges, Oregon and California, USA.
• CULTIVATION Needs well-drained soil that is rich in organic matter and a warm, sheltered site.
• PROPAGATION By seed when ripe or in spring, or by offsets in autumn.
• OTHER NAME *A. murrayanum*.

☼ ◊

Z 4–10

HEIGHT
to 12in
(30cm)

SPREAD
3–4in
(8–10cm)

3–4in
(8–10cm)

Amaryllidaceae	AZTEC LILY, JACOBEAN LILY

SPREKELIA FORMOSISSIMA

Habit Clump-forming, bulbous, perennial. *Flowers* Solitary, loosely star-shaped, to 5in (12cm) across, borne in spring. Scarlet to dark crimson. *Leaves* Strap-shaped. Mid-green.
• NATIVE HABITAT Rocky mountain slopes of Mexico and Guatemala.
• CULTIVATION Suitable for a sunny border, or in cold areas, as a house or conservatory plant. Needs fertile, well-drained soil mix. Under glass, the bulb should be kept almost dry when dormant.
• PROPAGATION By offsets in early autumn.

☼ ◊

Z 8–10

HEIGHT
6–14in
(15–35cm)

SPREAD
5–6in
(12–15cm)

Neck
above

Araceae	MONARCH OF THE EAST, VOODOO LILY

SAUROMATUM VENOSUM

Habit Tuberous, perennial. *Flowers* Long, fleshy, acrid spike, with large spathe, borne in late spring to early summer. Lime, mottled red, with purplish-green spike. *Leaves* Single and rounded, appearing after the flowers. Glossy green.
• NATIVE HABITAT River valleys, Himalaya.
• CULTIVATION Grow as a house or conservatory plant in cold areas. Can also be flowered in water under glass. Elsewhere, plant tuber in leaf-rich soil.
• PROPAGATION By offsets in winter.
• OTHER NAME *S. guttatum*.

☼ ◊ pH

Z 10–11

HEIGHT
to 18in
(45cm)

SPREAD
6in (15cm)

6in
(15cm)

Ranunculaceae	

ANEMONE PAVONINA

Habit Tuberous, perennial. *Flowers* Solitary, shallowly cup-shaped, borne in early spring. Red, purple or blue, with dark center. *Leaves* Lobed, rounded, and dissected. Mid- to dark green.
• NATIVE HABITAT Fields and hills, Mediterranean.
• CULTIVATION Needs light, sandy, well-drained soil and a warm, sunny, sheltered site. Lift in autumn where winters are severe; otherwise, protect *in situ* with a deep, dry, winter mulch.
• PROPAGATION Separate tubers when dormant in late summer.

☼ ◊

Z 8–10

HEIGHT
12in (30cm)

SPREAD
8in (20cm)

2–3in
(5–8cm)

Hyacinthaceae/Liliaceae	

MUSCARI LATIFOLIUM

Habit Bulbous, perennial. **Flowers** Tiny bells, constricted at the mouth, borne in dense, erect spikes in spring. Lower florets are deep black-purple; upper ones are smaller and paler. **Leaves** Single and broadly lance-shaped. Grayish-green.
• NATIVE HABITAT Mountain pine forests, Turkey.
• CULTIVATION Needs a warm, sheltered site in freely draining soil. Excellent for growing at the front of a border or in a rock garden. May self-seed.
• PROPAGATION Divide established colonies during late summer, or sow seed as soon as ripe.

☼ ◊

Z 2–10

HEIGHT
to 10in
(25cm)

SPREAD
2in (5cm)

3in
(7.5cm)

Alliaceae/Liliaceae	GLORY-OF-THE-SUN

LEUCOCORYNE IXIOIDES

Habit Bulbous, perennial. **Flowers** Fragrant, small, star-shaped, borne in loose, wiry-stemmed sprays of up to 10, in spring. Clear, soft blue, with a white eye. **Leaves** Linear and grass-like, dying back before the flowers. Mid-green.
• NATIVE HABITAT Chile.
• CULTIVATION Grow in a cool greenhouse in colder areas, keeping plant warm and dry when dormant in summer. Elsewhere, grow in a warm, sunny border. Needs freely draining soil.
• PROPAGATION By seed or offsets in autumn.

☼ ◊

Z 9–10

HEIGHT
12–16in
(30–40cm)

SPREAD
3–4in
(8–10cm)

1–2in
(3–5cm)

Hyacinthaceae/Liliaceae	ENGLISH BLUEBELL

HYACINTHOIDES NON-SCRIPTA

Habit Vigorous, clumping, bulbous, perennial. **Flowers** Scented, narrowly bell-shaped, borne in arching, one-sided spikes in late spring. Blue, pink, or white. **Leaves** Linear and glossy. Rich green.
• NATIVE HABITAT Woods, western Europe.
• CULTIVATION Ideal for naturalizing in a wild or woodland garden. Needs moist, well-drained soil.
• PROPAGATION By seed as soon as ripe, or by offsets in summer.
• OTHER NAMES *Endymion non-scriptus, Scilla non-scripta.*

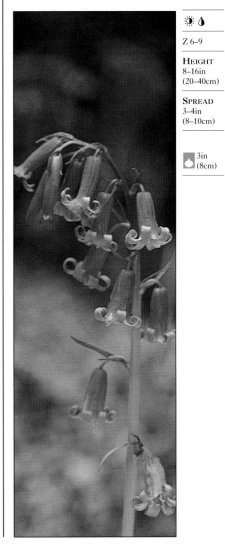

☼ ◊

Z 6–9

HEIGHT
8–16in
(20–40cm)

SPREAD
3–4in
(8–10cm)

3in
(8cm)

Hyacinthaceae/Liliaceae	SPANISH BLUEBELL

HYACINTHOIDES HISPANICA 'Excelsior'

Habit Robust, clump-forming, bulbous, perennial.
Flowers Bell-shaped with reflexed petal tips, borne in upright clusters during late spring. Blue-violet, with paler blue stripes. *Leaves* Strap-shaped and glossy. Rich green.
• NATIVE HABITAT Woodland and shady, rocky places in Portugal, Spain, and N. Africa.
• CULTIVATION Most cultivars of the species are hybrids with *H. non-scripta* and have drooping flowers. The true species is distinguished by its upright clusters of erect flowers. Grow in fertile,

moist but well-drained soil. Sufficiently robust to withstand being placed at the front of a mixed, shrub, or herbaceous border. Also suitable for naturalizing in a wild or woodland garden. Will self-seed unless deadheaded.
• PROPAGATION By seed as soon as ripe (only the species comes true), or by offsets in summer.
• OTHER NAMES *Endymion hispanicus, Scilla campanulata, S. hispanica.*

☀ ◐

Z 4–9

HEIGHT
20–22in
(50–55cm)

SPREAD
4–6in
(10–15cm)

3in
(8cm)

Amaryllidaceae/ Ixioliriaceae	

IXIOLIRION TATARICUM

Habit Bulbous, perennial. **Flowers** Funnel-shaped, borne in loose sprays of up to 10, in late spring to early summer. Blue or blue-violet. **Leaves** Basal and narrowly lance-shaped. Mid-green.
• NATIVE HABITAT Grasslands, from southwest and central Asia to Kashmir.
• CULTIVATION Needs good drainage. Must be kept warm and dry during summer dormancy.
• PROPAGATION By seed as soon as ripe, or by offsets after flowering.
• OTHER NAMES *I. montanum, I. pallasii.*

☼ ◌

Z 7–10

HEIGHT
to 16in
(40cm)

SPREAD
3–4in
(8–10cm)

6in
(15cm)

Iridaceae	

IXIA VIRIDIFLORA

Habit Cormous, perennial. **Flowers** Open, star-shaped, borne in upright spikes in spring or early summer. Pale blue-green, red-rimmed, with black-purple eye. **Leaves** Erect and linear. Rich green.
• NATIVE HABITAT Grasslands of western Cape, S. Africa.
• CULTIVATION Needs moderately fertile, freely draining soil and a warm, sheltered site. Lift corms in autumn and store in a dry, frost-free place.
• PROPAGATION By offsets in late summer, or by seed as soon as ripe.

☼ ◌

Z 9–10

HEIGHT
12–24in
(30–60cm)

SPREAD
2in (5cm)

4–6in
(9–15cm)

Iridaceae	WIDOW IRIS

HERMODACTYLUS TUBEROSUS

Habit Upright, tuberous, perennial. **Flowers** Scented, single, borne on erect stems in spring. Yellow-green inner petals, with velvety black-brown tips. **Leaves** Linear. Blue- or gray-green.
• NATIVE HABITAT Dry, rocky slopes, from southern Europe to N. Africa, Turkey, and Israel.
• CULTIVATION Needs sharply drained, alkaline soil and a warm, sunny site. Can be grown in an alpine house to protect blooms from bad weather.
• PROPAGATION Divide in early summer.
• OTHER NAME *Iris tuberosa.*

☼ ◌

Z 7–9

HEIGHT
8–16in
(20–40cm)

SPREAD
2–3in
(5–8cm)

4in
(10cm)

Iridaceae	

FERRARIA CRISPA

Habit Cormous, perennial. **Flowers** Upward-facing, wavy-edged, borne in late winter to early spring. Brown or yellow-brown, with dark-brown lines and stains inside. **Leaves** Narrow, lance-shaped, and stem-clasping. Fresh green.
• NATIVE HABITAT Dry, sandy areas, S. Africa.
• CULTIVATION Grow under glass in cool areas, planted in deep pots and sharply drained compost.
• PROPAGATION Separate offsets in late summer, or sow seed as soon as ripe.
• OTHER NAME *F. undulata.*

☼ ◌

Z 9–10

HEIGHT
8–16in
(20–40cm)

SPREAD
3–4in
(8–10cm)

6in
(15cm)

Araceae	

ARUM CRETICUM

Habit Tuberous, perennial. *Flowers* Sweet-scented, slender, cowl-like, recurves at the tip when mature to reveal pencil-like, scented, deep-yellow spike in spring. Cream or deep yellow. *Leaves* Arrow-shaped, glossy. Dark green.
• NATIVE HABITAT Stony hillsides on Greek islands of Crete, Samos, Rhodes, and Karpathos.
• CULTIVATION Grow in well-drained, moderately fertile soil, enriched with organic matter, in a warm, sheltered site in sun. Prefers to be kept dry during dormant period in summer. Also suitable for a cool greenhouse or conservatory, where it can either be grown in deep pots, or planted directly into the greenhouse border in soilless potting mix with added grit. Water moderately and apply a balanced liquid fertilizer each month during growth. Reduce water when the leaves start to wither; keep bulb dry when dormant.
• PROPAGATION Divide after flowering. Sow seed as soon as ripe. The flesh from the berries can be caustic, therefore it should be removed carefully with gloved hands.

☼ ◌

Z 8–10

HEIGHT
12–20in
(30–50cm)

SPREAD
8–12in
(20–30cm)

4–6in
(9–15cm)

DAFFODILS

Daffodils (*Narcissus*) are classified in 12 divisions, which are illustrated below except for Division 10 (species and wild forms of daffodils and wild hybrids) and Division 12 (miscellaneous). Most daffodils need a dry period of dormancy in summer, and those bearing delicate flowers in winter or early spring need to be grown in an alpine house or bulb frame, in gritty, soil-based potting mix. Plant in early autumn, at two and a half times the bulb's depth. Daffodils need fertile, well-drained soil that stays moist during growth, but they will tolerate either dappled shade or full sun. Propagate by ripe seed, twin scaling, chipping, or offsets (see pp. 173–182). Offsets will flower within 1 to 2 years, while flowers raised from seed take 3 to 5 years. For common flowering and storage problems see p. 183.

DIV. 1 TRUMPET
Usually solitary flowers, each with a trumpet that is as long as, or longer, than the petals. Early to late spring-flowering.

DIV. 2 LARGE-CUPPED
Solitary flowers, each with a cup that is at least one-third the length of, but shorter than, the petals. Spring-flowering.

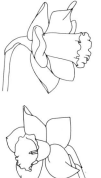

DIV. 3 SMALL-CUPPED
Flowers are often borne singly, each with a cup that is not more than one-third the length of the petals. Spring- or early summer-flowering.

DIV. 4 DOUBLE
Solitary, large, fully or semi-double flowers, with the cup and petals, or just the cup replaced by petaloid structures. Some have small flowers in clusters of 4 or more. Spring- or early summer-flowering.

DIV. 5 TRIANDRUS
Nodding flowers, with short, often straight-sided cups and narrow, reflexed petals that are borne 2–6 per stem. Spring-flowering.

DIV. 6 CYCLAMINEUS
Flowers are borne 1 or 2 per stem. Cups are often flanged and longer than Div. 5 types. Petals are reflexed. narrow, and pointed. Early to mid-spring-flowering.

DIV. 7 JONQUILLA
Sweetly scented flowers that are borne usually 2 or more per stem. Cups are short, sometimes flanged, and petals are often flat, fairly broad, and rounded. Spring-flowering.

DIV. 8 TAZETTA
Flowers are borne in clusters of either 12 or more small, fragrant flowers per stem, or 3–4 large ones. Cups are small and often have straight sides, with broad and mostly pointed petals. Flowering in late autumn to mid-spring.

DIV. 9 POETICUS
Flowers each have a small, colored cup and glistening white petals. They are borne singly or sometimes 2 per stem and may be sweetly fragrant. Late spring- or early summer-flowering.

DIV. 11 SPLIT-CUPPED
Usually solitary flowers, with cups that are typically split for more than half of their length. Cup segments lie back on the petals and may be ruffled. Spring-flowering.

N. WATIERI
Habit Tiny,
bulbous, perennial.
Flowers Solitary, ½in
(1.5cm) across, with flat
petals and a broadly
funnel-shaped cup, borne
in mid-spring. White.
Leaves Strap-shaped,
keeled, and upright.
Gray-green.
• TIPS Best grown
in an alpine house.
• HEIGHT 4in (10cm).
• SPREAD 2–3in (5–8cm).

N. *watieri*
(Div. 10)

☼ ◊   Z 9–10

N. 'Portrush'
Habit Bulbous,
perennial.
Flowers Overlapping
petals, 3in (8cm) across,
with a small, flat, green-
eyed cup, borne in
mid-spring. Pure white.
Leaves Narrowly strap-
shaped. Mid-green.
• TIPS Suitable for
a mixed border and
for naturalizing in turf.
• HEIGHT 18in (45cm).
• SPREAD 6in (15cm).

N. 'Portrush'
(Div. 3)

☼ ◊   Z 3–8

N. 'Thalia'
Habit Slender,
bulbous, perennial.
Flowers Spanning
2in (5cm), with slightly
twisted petals and
funnel-shaped cups,
usually 2 per stem, borne
in mid-spring. White.
Leaves Narrowly strap-
shaped. Grayish-green.
• TIPS Ideal for planting
in a mixed border.
• HEIGHT 14in (35cm).
• SPREAD 3in (8cm).

N. 'Thalia'
(Div. 5)

☼ ◊   Z 3–8

N. 'Dover Cliffs'
Habit Bulbous,
perennial.
Flowers Spanning
4⅓in (11cm), petals
lean forward over the
cup, borne in mid-
spring. Pure white.
Leaves Narrow and
strap-shaped. Mid-green.
• TIPS Good for growing
in a mixed border or for
naturalizing in turf.
• HEIGHT 16in (40cm).
• SPREAD 6in (15cm).

N. 'Dover Cliffs'
(Div. 2)

☼ ◊   Z 3–8

N. 'Panache'
Habit Bulbous,
perennial.
Flowers Spanning 4½in
(11.5cm), with
overlapping petals and
a green-based cup, borne
in mid-spring. White.
Leaves Narrow and
strap-shaped. Mid-green.
• TIPS Suitable for
growing in borders or
for naturalizing in turf.
• HEIGHT 16in (40cm).
• SPREAD 6in (15cm).

N. 'Panache'
(Div. 1)

☼ ◊   Z 3–8

N. 'Cool Crystal'
Habit Bulbous,
perennial.
Flowers Spanning 4¼in
(10.5cm), with
a green-eyed, bowl-
shaped cup, borne in
mid-spring. White.
Leaves Narrow and
strap-shaped. Mid-green.
• TIPS Suitable for
using in a border and
massed plantings.
• HEIGHT 20in (50cm).
• SPREAD 6in (15cm).

N. 'Cool Crystal'
(Div. 3)

☼ ◊   Z 3–8

N. 'Mount Hood'
Habit Bulbous,
perennial.
Flowers Overlapping
petals, 4in (10cm) across,
borne in mid-spring.
White, with a creamy-
white trumpet.
Leaves Narrow and
strap-shaped. Mid-green.
• TIPS Suitable for
growing in borders and
for naturalizing.
• HEIGHT 18in (45cm).
• SPREAD 6in (15cm).

N. 'Mount Hood'
(Div. 1)

☼ ◊   Z 3–8

N. 'Irene Copeland'

Habit Bulbous, perennial.
Flowers Double, 3¼in (8.5cm) across, borne in mid-spring. White petaloids interspersed with creamy-yellow ones.
Leaves Narrow and strap-shaped. Mid-green.
• TIPS Suitable as cut flowers.
• HEIGHT 16in (40cm).
• SPREAD 6in (15cm).

N. 'Irene Copeland'
(Div. 4)

☼ ◊   Z 3–8

N. 'Trousseau'

Habit Bulbous, perennial.
Flowers Spanning 5in (12cm), satin-textured, borne in mid-spring. White petals, with a soft yellow trumpet, later buff-pink.
Leaves Narrow and strap-shaped. Mid-green.
• TIPS Good for borders and cutting.
• HEIGHT 18in (45cm).
• SPREAD 5in (12cm).

N. 'Trousseau'
(Div. 1)

☼ ◊   Z 3–8

N. 'Silver Chimes'

Habit Sturdy, bulbous, perennial.
Flowers Nodding, fragrant, 2in (5cm) across, in clusters of 10, borne in mid- to late spring. Creamy-white, with primrose-yellow cup.
Leaves Narrow and strap-shaped. Mid-green.
• TIPS Suitable as cut flowers.
• HEIGHT 12in (30cm).
• SPREAD 3in (8cm).

N. 'Silver Chimes'
(Div. 8)

☼ ◊   Z 3–8

N. 'Empress of Ireland'

Habit Bulbous, perennial.
Flowers Spanning 4½in (11cm), with triangular petals and a narrow, flanged trumpet, borne in mid-spring. White.
Leaves Narrow and strap-shaped. Mid-green.
• TIPS Good for borders and cutting.
• HEIGHT 16in (40cm).
• SPREAD 5in (12cm).

N. 'Empress of Ireland'
(Div. 1)

☼ ◊   Z 3–8

N. 'Aircastle'

Habit Bulbous, perennial.
Flowers Spanning 3½in (9cm), borne in mid-spring. White petals, later tinted green, with lemon-yellow cup.
Leaves Narrow and strap-shaped. Mid-green.
• TIPS Suitable for growing in borders and as cut flowers.
• HEIGHT 16in (40cm).
• SPREAD 6in (15cm).

N. 'Aircastle'
(Div. 3)

☼ ◊   Z 3–8

N. 'Ice Follies'

Habit Bulbous, perennial.
Flowers Spanning 3¾in (9.5cm), with wide, frilled cup, borne in mid-spring. Creamy-white petals and lemon-yellow cup, fading to white.
Leaves Narrow and strap-shaped. Mid-green.
• TIPS Good in borders or naturalized.
• HEIGHT 16in (40cm).
• SPREAD 6in (15cm).

N. 'Ice Follies'
(Div. 2)

☼ ◊   Z 3–8

N. 'Cheerfulness'

Habit Bulbous, perennial.
Flowers Sweetly scented, double, 2½in (5.5cm) across, in clusters of 4 or more, borne in mid-spring. White, with cream center.
Leaves Narrow and strap-shaped. Mid-green.
• TIPS Suitable as cut flowers.
• HEIGHT 16in (40cm).
• SPREAD 6in (15cm).

N. 'Cheerfulness'
(Div. 4)

☼ ◊   Z 3–8

N. 'Passionale'
Habit Bulbous, perennial.
Flowers Spanning 4in (10cm), borne in mid-spring. White petals and slightly frilled, rose-pink cup.
Leaves Narrow and strap-shaped. Mid-green.
• TIPS Good for borders, and suitable for cutting and arranging.
• HEIGHT 16in (40cm).
• SPREAD 6in (15cm).

N. 'Passionale'
(Div. 2)

☼ ◊   Z 3–8

N. 'Actaea'
Habit Bulbous, perennial.
Flowers Scented, 3¼in (8.5cm) across, with wavy petals and flat, bowl-shaped cup, borne in late spring. White, with yellow, red-rimmed cup.
Leaves Narrow and strap-shaped. Mid-green.
• TIPS Suitable for naturalizing and borders.
• HEIGHT 18in (45cm).
• SPREAD 6in (15cm).

N. 'Actaea'
(Div. 9)

☼ ◊   Z 3–8

N. 'Satin Pink'
Habit Bulbous, perennial.
Flowers Up to 5in (12cm) across, with overlapping petals, borne in mid-spring. White, with pale pink cup and a yellow-green eye.
Leaves Narrow and strap-shaped. Mid-green.
• TIPS Good for borders and cutting.
• HEIGHT 18in (45cm).
• SPREAD 6in (15cm).

N. 'Satin Pink'
(Div. 2)

☼ ◊   Z 3–8

N. 'Merlin'
Habit Bulbous, perennial.
Flowers Spanning 3in (7.5cm), borne in mid-spring. Pure white, with a flat, pale yellow, red-rimmed cup.
Leaves Narrow and strap-shaped. Mid-green.
• TIPS Suitable for cut flowers, and for naturalizing or borders.
• HEIGHT 14in (35cm).
• SPREAD 6in (15cm).

N. 'Merlin'
(Div. 3)

☼ ◊   Z 3–8

N. POETICUS var. RECURVUS
Habit Bulbous, perennial.
Flowers Recurved, 1½in (4cm) span, borne in late spring. White, with a red-rimmed, yellow cup.
Leaves Erect, narrow, strap-shaped, and channeled. Mid-green.
• TIPS Suitable for naturalizing in turf.
• HEIGHT 14in (35cm).
• SPREAD 4in (10cm).

N. poeticus var. *recurvus*
Old pheasant's eye
(Div. 10)

☼ ◊   Z 3–8

N. 'Pride of Cornwall'

Habit Bulbous, perennial.
Flowers Scented, 2½in (6cm) across, borne in mid-spring. White, with red-rimmed, orange-yellow cup.
Leaves Narrow and strap-shaped. Mid-green.
• TIPS Ideal for planting in borders and cutting.
• HEIGHT 16in (40cm).
• SPREAD 38in (8cm).

N. 'Pride of Cornwall'
(Div. 8)

☼ ◊   Z 3–8

N. 'Bridal Crown'

Habit Bulbous, perennial.
Flowers Fragrant, double, 1⅛in (4cm) span, borne in early spring. White, with clustered, soft orange center.
Leaves Narrow and strap-shaped. Mid-green.
• TIPS Suitable as cut flowers and good for growing in borders.
• HEIGHT 16in (40cm).
• SPREAD 6in (15cm).

N. 'Bridal Crown'
(Div. 4)

☼ ◊   Z 3–8

N. 'Kilworth'

Habit Bulbous, perennial.
Flowers Spanning 4½in (11cm), with bowl-shaped cup, borne in mid-spring. White, with bright red-orange cup.
Leaves Narrow and strap-shaped. Mid-green.
• TIPS Suitable as cut flowers, and for naturalizing or borders.
• HEIGHT 18in (45cm).
• SPREAD 6in (15cm).

N. 'Kilworth'
(Div. 2)

☼ ◊   Z 3–8

N. 'Acropolis'

Habit Bulbous, perennial.
Flowers Scented, double, 4½in (11cm) across, with clustered center, borne in mid-spring. White, with white and orange center.
Leaves Narrow and strap-shaped. Mid-green.
• TIPS Ideal for planting in borders and cutting.
• HEIGHT 18in (45cm).
• SPREAD 6in (15cm).

N. 'Acropolis'
(Div. 4)

☼ ◊   Z 3–8

N. 'Salome'

Habit Bulbous, perennial.
Flowers Spanning 3½in (9cm), with waxy petals, borne in mid-spring. Creamy-white, with large, peach-pink cup.
Leaves Narrow and strap-shaped. Mid-green.
• TIPS Good for borders, and suitable for cutting and arranging.
• HEIGHT 18in (45cm).
• SPREAD 6in (15cm).

N. 'Salome'
(Div. 2)

☼ ◊   Z 3–8

N. 'Rainbow'
Habit Vigorous,
bulbous, perennial.
Flowers Spanning 4in
(10cm), borne during
mid-spring. White, with
white cup and copper-
pink band at the mouth.
Leaves Narrow and
strap-shaped. Mid-green.
• TIPS Suitable as
cut flowers.
• HEIGHT 18in (45cm).
• SPREAD 6in (15cm).

N. 'Rainbow'
(Div. 2)

☼ ◊   Z 3–8

N. 'Broadway Star'
Habit Bulbous,
perennial.
Flowers Spanning 3in
(8cm), with flat, split
central petals, borne in
mid-spring. White, with
an orange, central stripe.
Leaves Narrow and
strap-shaped. Mid-green.
• TIPS Good for planting
in borders and suitable
as cut flowers.
• HEIGHT 16in (40cm).
• SPREAD 6in (15cm).

N. 'Broadway Star'
(Div. 11)

☼ ◊   Z 3–8

N. 'Woodland Star'
Habit Bulbous,
perennial.
Flowers Spanning
3½in (9.5cm), with
a bowl-shaped cup,
borne in mid-spring.
White, with a dark
orange-red cup.
Leaves Narrow and
strap-shaped. Mid-green.
• TIPS Suitable for
naturalizing and cutting.
• HEIGHT 20in (50cm).
• SPREAD 6in (15cm).

N. 'Woodland Star'
(Div. 3)

☼ ◊   Z 3–8

N. 'Rockall'
Habit Bulbous,
perennial.
Flowers Overlapping
petals, 4⅓in (11cm)
span, with saucer-shaped,
fluted cups, borne in
mid-spring. White, with
red-orange cup.
Leaves Narrow and
strap-shaped. Mid-green.
• TIPS Good for borders,
naturalizing and cutting.
• HEIGHT 20in (50cm).
• SPREAD 6in (15cm).

N. 'Rockall'
(Div. 3)

☼ ◊   Z 3–8

N. POETICUS 'Praecox'
Habit Bulbous,
perennial.
Flowers Fragrant,
to 3in (7cm) across,
borne in mid-spring.
White, with yellow,
red-rimmed cup.
Leaves Narrowly strap-
shaped. Mid-green.
• TIPS Suitable for
naturalizing in turf.
• HEIGHT 17in (42cm).
• SPREAD 6in (15cm).

N. poeticus 'Praecox'
(Div. 9)

☼ ◊   Z 3–8

N. 'Dove Wings'

Habit Bulbous,
perennial.
Flowers Backswept
petals, 3¼in (8.5cm)
across, borne in early
spring. Creamy-white,
with lemon-yellow cup.
Leaves Narrow and
strap-shaped. Mid-green.
• TIPS Suitable for
borders and rock gardens,
or for naturalizing.
• HEIGHT 12in (30cm).
• SPREAD 3in (8cm).

N. 'Dove Wings'
(Div. 6)

☼ ◊   Z 3–8

N. 'Avalanche'

Habit Bulbous,
perennial.
Flowers Scented, 1½in
(3.5cm) across, in clusters
of 10 or more, borne in
mid-spring. Pure white,
with lemon-yellow cup.
Leaves Narrow and
strap-shaped. Mid-green.
• TIPS Suitable as cut
flowers and last well
in water.
• HEIGHT 14in (35cm).
• SPREAD 3in (8cm).

N. 'Avalanche'
(Div. 8)

☼ ◊   Z 3–8

N. 'February Silver'

Habit Robust,
bulbous, perennial.
Flowers Spanning
3in (7.5cm), with slightly
reflexed petals and large
cup, borne in early
spring. White, with
lemon-yellow cup.
Leaves Narrow and
strap-shaped. Mid-green.
• TIPS Suitable for a
border or rock garden.
• HEIGHT 12in (30cm).
• SPREAD 3in (8cm).

N. 'February Silver'
(Div. 6)

☼ ◊   Z 3–8

N. 'Little Beauty'

Habit Dwarf, sturdy,
bulbous, perennial.
Flowers Spanning 1¼in
(3cm), borne during
early spring. Creamy-
white, with clear
yellow trumpet.
Leaves Narrow and
strap-shaped. Mid-green.
• TIPS Suitable for
growing in a rock garden
or border.
• HEIGHT 5½in (14cm).
• SPREAD 3in (8cm).

N. 'Little Beauty'
(Div. 1)

☼ ◊   Z 3–8

N. TAZETTA 'Canaliculatus'

Habit Bulbous,
perennial.
Flowers Scented, 1½in
(4cm) across, borne in
mid-spring. White, with
a deep yellow cup.
Leaves Mid-green.
• TIPS Suitable as
cut flowers.
• OTHER NAME
N. tazetta subsp. *lacticolor.*
• HEIGHT 9in (23cm).
• SPREAD 3in (8cm).

N. tazetta
'Canaliculatus'
(Div. 8)

☼ ◊   Z 7–9

N. TRIANDRUS

Habit Bulbous,
perennial.
Flowers Nodding, round
cup and reflexed petals,
2½in (6cm) span, borne
in mid-spring. Cream.
Leaves Erect or arching,
flat or channeled, and
strap-shaped. Mid-green.
• TIPS Good for growing
in a rock garden.
• HEIGHT 4–10in
(10–25cm).
• SPREAD 4in (10cm).

N. triandrus
Angel's tears
(Div. 10)

☼ ◊   Z 3–8

N. 'Jack Snipe'

Habit Vigorous,
bulbous, perennial.
Flowers Reflexed petals,
1½in (4cm) across, borne
in early to mid-spring.
White, with a short,
lemon-yellow cup.
Leaves Narrow and
strap-shaped. Mid-green.
• TIPS Suitable for
planting in a rock garden
or containers.
• HEIGHT 8in (20cm).
• SPREAD 3in (8cm).

N. 'Jack Snipe'
(Div. 6)

☼ ◊   Z 3–8

N. 'Lemon Glow'

Habit Bulbous,
perennial.
Flowers Large, trumpet-
shaped cup, 3in (8cm)
span, borne in mid-
spring. Sulfur-yellow,
slightly darker toward
the lip.
Leaves Narrowly strap-
shaped. Mid-green.
• TIPS Good for planting
in borders and cutting.
• HEIGHT 18in (45cm).
• SPREAD 6in (15cm).

N. 'Lemon Glow'
(Div. 1)

☼ ◊   Z 3–8

N. ROMIEUXII
Habit Bulbous,
perennial.
Flowers Funnel-shaped,
with pointed petals, 1½in
(3.5cm) span,
borne in early spring.
Pale primrose-yellow.
Leaves Semi-cylindrical.
Deep green.
• TIPS Best grown in
an alpine house.
• HEIGHT to 4in (10cm).
• SPREAD 2in (5cm).

N. romieuxii
(Div. 10)

☼ ◊   Z 7–9

N. 'Cassata'
Habit Bulbous,
perennial.
Flowers Spanning 4in
(10cm), with a broad, flat
center, borne in mid-
spring. Pure white, with
lemon-yellow center,
fading to white.
Leaves Narrow and
strap-shaped. Mid-green.
• TIPS Good for planting
in borders and cutting.
• HEIGHT 16in (40cm).
• SPREAD 6in (15cm).

N. 'Cassata'
(Div. 11)

☼ ◊   Z 3–8

N. 'Daydream'
Habit Bulbous,
perennial.
Flowers Flared cup, 3in
(8cm) span, borne in mid-
spring. Sulfur-yellow,
with lemon-yellow cup,
fading to white, and a
white basal halo.
Leaves Narrow and
strap-shaped. Mid-green.
• TIPS Good for planting
in borders and cutting.
• HEIGHT 14in (35cm).
• SPREAD 6in (15cm).

N. 'Daydream'
(Div. 2)

☼ ◊   Z 3–8

N. 'Pipit'
Habit Bulbous,
perennial.
Flowers Scented, 3in
(7cm) span, borne in
mid- to late spring.
Lemon-yellow, with
the cup fading to
cream at maturity.
Leaves Narrow and
strap-shaped. Mid-green.
• TIPS Good for growing
in a rock garden or at the
front of a border.
• HEIGHT 10in (25cm).
• SPREAD 3in (8cm).

N. 'Pipit'
(Div. 7)

☼ ◊   Z 3–8

N. 'Yellow Cheerfulness'

Habit Bulbous, perennial.
Flowers Sweetly scented, double, ¾in (2cm) across, in clusters of 3–4, borne in mid-spring. Golden-yellow.
Leaves Narrow and strap-shaped. Mid-green.
• TIPS Suitable for cut flowers.
• HEIGHT 18in (45cm).
• SPREAD 6in (15cm).

N. 'Yellow Cheerfulness'
(Div. 4)

☼ ◊   Z 3–8

N. BULBOCODIUM

Habit Bulbous, perennial.
Flowers Spanning 1½in (3.5cm), funnel-shaped, fine-textured, with slender, pointed petals, borne in mid-spring. Deep yellow.
Leaves Semi-cylindrical. Dark green.
• TIPS Suitable for naturalizing in fine turf.
• HEIGHT to 6in (15cm) .
• SPREAD 2in (5cm).

N. bulbocodium
Hoop-petticoat daffodil
(Div. 10)

☼ ◊   Z 3–8

N. PSEUDONARCISSUS

Habit Bulbous, perennial.
Flowers Up to 3in (7cm) span, with slender, twisted petals, borne in early spring. Cream, with yellow trumpet.
Leaves Strap-shaped and glaucous. Mid-green.
• TIPS Suitable for naturalizing in turf.
• HEIGHT 6–14in (15–35cm).
• SPREAD to 6in (15cm).

N. pseudonarcissus
Lent lily, Wild daffodil
(Div. 10)

☼ ◊   Z 3–8

N. 'Binkie'
Habit Robust, bulbous, perennial.
Flowers Spanning 4in (10cm), borne in mid-spring. Lemon-yellow, with cup fading to cream at maturity.
Leaves Narrow and strap-shaped. Mid-green.
• TIPS Suitable for borders and naturalizing, and good as cut flowers.
• HEIGHT 14in (35cm).
• SPREAD 6in (15cm).

N. 'Binkie'
(Div. 2)

☼ ◊   Z 3–8

N. 'Liberty Bells'
Habit Robust, bulbous, perennial.
Flowers Nodding, 3½in (9cm) across, borne in pairs in mid-spring. Clear lemon-yellow.
Leaves Narrow and strap-shaped. Mid-green.
• TIPS Good for planting in a rock garden or at the front of a border. Suitable for cutting.
• HEIGHT 12in (30cm).
• SPREAD 3in (8cm).

N. 'Liberty Bells'
(Div. 5)

☼ ◊   Z 3–8

N. 'Hawera'
Habit Multi-stemmed, bulbous, perennial.
Flowers Spanning 1¼–2in (3–5cm), with reflexed petals, borne in clusters of 5 in late spring. Canary-yellow.
Leaves Very narrow and strap-shaped. Mid-green.
• TIPS Suitable for planting in a rock garden or containers.
• HEIGHT 7in (18cm).
• SPREAD 3in (8cm).

N. 'Hawera'
(Div. 5)

☼ ◊   Z 3–8

N. 'Charity May'
Habit Bulbous, perennial.
Flowers Long-cupped, 3½in (9cm) across, with broadly reflexed petals, borne in early spring. Lemon-yellow.
Leaves Narrow and strap-shaped. Mid-green.
• TIPS Suitable for planting in a rock garden or border.
• HEIGHT 12in (30cm).
• SPREAD 3in (8cm).

N. 'Charity May'
(Div. 6)

☼ ◊   Z 3–8

N. JONQUILLA
Habit Slender, bulbous, perennial.
Flowers Scented, spanning 1¼in (3cm), with a flat cup and pointed petals, borne in heads of up to 5, in late spring. Golden-yellow.
Leaves Narrow, semi-cylindrical. Mid-green.
• TIPS Suitable as cut flowers.
• HEIGHT 12in (30cm).
• SPREAD 3in (8cm).

N. jonquilla
Wild jonquil
(Div. 10)

☼ ◊   Z 3–8

N. 'Fortune'
Habit Bulbous, perennial.
Flowers Spanning 4¼in (11cm), borne in mid-spring. Butter-yellow, with soft orange cup and darker mouth.
Leaves Narrow and strap-shaped. Mid-green.
• TIPS Good as cut flowers, or for borders and naturalizing.
• HEIGHT 18in (45cm).
• SPREAD 6in (15cm).

N. 'Fortune'
(Div. 2)

☼ ◊   Z 3–8

N. × ODORUS 'Rugulosus'
Habit Robust, bulbous, perennial.
Flowers Scented, 2¼in (5.5cm) across, in heads of up to 4, borne in early spring. Orange-yellow.
Leaves Strap-shaped and keeled. Mid-green.
• TIPS Good for borders, naturalizing in turf, and as cut flowers.
• HEIGHT 12in (30cm).
• SPREAD 3in (8cm).

N. × *odorus* 'Rugulosus'
(Div. 10)

☼ ◊   Z 3–8

N. 'Rip van Winkle'
Habit Bulbous, perennial.
Flowers Double, 2in (5cm) across, borne in spring. Sulfur-yellow.
Leaves Narrow and strap-shaped. Mid-green.
• TIPS Good for planting in a rock garden or at the front of a border.
• OTHER NAME *N. pumilus* 'Plenus'.
• HEIGHT 5½in (14cm).
• SPREAD 3in (8cm).

N. 'Rip van Winkle'
(Div. 4)

☼ ◊   Z 3–8

N. RUPICOLA
Habit Bulbous, perennial.
Flowers Rounded, with 6-lobed cups, 1¼in (3cm) across, borne in mid-spring. Golden-yellow.
Leaves Erect, keeled, cylindrical. Gray-green.
• TIPS Best in an alpine house or bulb frame. Needs to be kept dry in summer dormancy.
• HEIGHT 6in (15cm).
• SPREAD 2in (5cm).

N. rupicola
(Div. 10)

☼ ◊   Z 3–8

N. CYCLAMINEUS
Habit Robust, bulbous, perennial.
Flowers Solitary, 1¾in (4.5cm) long, with a narrow trumpet and reflexed petals, borne in early spring. Rich yellow.
Leaves Narrow and keeled. Bright green.
• TIPS Suitable for growing in a rock garden, woodland, or fine turf.
• HEIGHT to 8in (20cm).
• SPREAD 3in (8cm).

N. cyclamineus
(Div. 10)

☼ ◊   Z 3–8

N. MINOR
Habit Bulbous, perennial.
Flowers Borne in early spring, 1¼in (3cm) across. Clear yellow.
Leaves Erect and flat or channeled. Gray-green.
• TIPS Tends to increase rapidly.
• OTHER NAME *N. nanus* of gardens.
• HEIGHT 4–6in (10–15cm).
• SPREAD 3in (8cm).

N. minor (Div. 10)

☼ ◊   Z 3–8

N. 'Pencrebar'
Habit Bulbous, perennial.
Flowers Fragrant, rounded, double, 1¼in (3cm) across, sometimes 2 per stem, borne in mid-spring. Golden-yellow.
Leaves Narrow and strap-shaped. Mid-green.
• TIPS Good for planting in a rock garden, or at the front of a border.
• HEIGHT 7in (18cm).
• SPREAD 3in (8cm).

N. 'Pencrebar'
(Div. 4)

☼ ◊   Z 3–8

N. 'Tête-à-Tête'
Habit Robust, bulbous, perennial.
Flowers Slightly reflexed petals, 2½in (6.5cm) across, borne in early spring. Golden-yellow, with yellow-orange cup.
Leaves Very narrow and strap-shaped. Mid-green.
• TIPS Suitable for a rock garden or containers.
• HEIGHT 6in (15cm).
• SPREAD 2in (5cm).

N. 'Tête-à-Tête'
(Div. 12)

☼ ◊   Z 3–8

N. 'Jumblie'
Habit Multi-stemmed, bulbous, perennial.
Flowers Spanning 1¼in (3cm), with reflexed petals, borne in early spring. Golden-yellow, with orange cup.
Leaves Very narrow and strap-shaped. Mid-green.
• TIPS Suitable for growing in a rock garden.
• HEIGHT 7in (17cm).
• SPREAD 3in (8cm).

N. 'Jumblie'
(Div. 12)

☼ ◊   Z 3–8

N. 'Sweetness'
Habit Robust, bulbous, perennial.
Flowers Strongly scented, 1½in (4cm) across, borne on stiff stems in mid-spring. Golden-yellow.
Leaves Narrow and strap-shaped. Mid-green.
• TIPS Suitable for growing in borders and for cut flowers.
• HEIGHT 16in (40cm).
• SPREAD 3in (8cm).

N. 'Sweetness'
(Div. 7)

☼ ◊   Z 3–8

N. 'Bob Minor'
Habit Bulbous, perennial.
Flowers Stiff-stemmed, 2½in (6.5cm) across, with twisted petals and long trumpet, borne in mid-spring. Golden-yellow.
Leaves Narrow and strap-shaped. Mid-green.
• TIPS Suitable for growing in a border or rock garden.
• HEIGHT 8in (20cm).
• SPREAD 4in (10cm).

N. 'Bob Minor'
(Div. 1)

☼ ◊   Z 3–8

N. 'February Gold'

Habit Vigorous, bulbous, perennial.
Flowers Slightly reflexed petals, 3in (7.5cm) across, borne in early spring. Golden-yellow, with slightly darker yellow trumpet.
Leaves Narrow and strap-shaped. Mid-green.
• TIPS Suitable for a border or rock garden.
• HEIGHT 12in (30cm).
• SPREAD 3in (8cm).

N. 'February Gold'
(Div. 6)

☼ ◊   Z 3–8

N. 'St. Keverne'

Habit Vigorous, bulbous, perennial.
Flowers Large, flared cup, 4in (10cm) across, borne in mid-spring. Rich golden-yellow.
Leaves Narrow and strap-shaped. Mid-green.
• TIPS Ideal as cut flowers, and suitable for planting in borders or naturalizing.
• HEIGHT 18in (45cm).
• SPREAD 6in (15cm).

N. 'St. Keverne'
(Div. 2)

☼ ◊   Z 3–8

N. 'Tahiti'

Habit Bulbous, perennial.
Flowers Double, 4½in (11cm) across, borne in mid spring. Yellow, with bright red-orange center.
Leaves Narrow and strap-shaped. Mid-green.
• TIPS Good for planting in borders and cutting.
• HEIGHT 18in (45cm).
• SPREAD 6in (15cm).

N. 'Tahiti'
(Div. 4)

☼ ◊   Z 3–8

N. 'Golden Ducat'

Habit Bulbous, perennial.
Flowers Strongly double, 4½in (11cm) across, with neatly symmetrical, pointed segments, borne in mid-spring. Golden-yellow.
Leaves Narrow and strap-shaped. Mid-green.
• TIPS Suitable for borders and cutting.
• HEIGHT 14in (35cm).
• SPREAD 4in (10cm).

N. 'Golden Ducat'
(Div. 4)

☼ ◊   Z 3–8

N. 'Bartley'

Habit Bulbous, perennial.
Flowers Spanning 2½in (6cm), reflexed petals and slender trumpet, borne in early spring. Golden-yellow.
Leaves Narrow and strap-shaped. Mid-green.
• TIPS Suitable for growing in borders, or naturalizing.
• HEIGHT 16in (40cm).
• SPREAD 3in (8cm).

N. 'Bartley'
(Div. 6)

☼ ◊   Z 3–8

N. 'Stratosphere'

Habit Strong-stemmed, bulbous, perennial.
Flowers Scented, 2½in (6.5cm) across, borne in mid-spring. Golden-yellow, with small, deep gold cup.
Leaves Narrow and strap-shaped. Mid-green.
• TIPS Good for planting in borders and cutting.
• HEIGHT 16in (40cm).
• SPREAD 4in (10cm).

N. 'Stratosphere'
(Div. 7)

☼ ◊   Z 3–8

N. 'Kingscourt'

Habit Robust, bulbous, perennial.
Flowers Well proportioned, spans 4½in (11cm), with trumpet slightly flared at mouth, borne during mid-spring. Golden-yellow.
Leaves Narrow and strap-shaped. Mid-green.
• TIPS Good for planting in borders and cutting.
• HEIGHT 18in (45cm).
• SPREAD 6in (15cm).

N. 'Kingscourt'
(Div. 1)

☀ ◊   Z 3–8

N. 'Chanterelle'

Habit Bulbous, perennial.
Flowers Up to 4in (10cm) across, with broad, flat center, borne in mid-spring. Creamy-white, with golden-yellow center.
Leaves Narrow and strap-shaped. Mid-green.
• TIPS Good for planting in borders and cutting.
• HEIGHT 16in (40cm).
• SPREAD 6in (15cm).

N. 'Chanterelle'
(Div. 11)

☀ ◊   Z 3–8

N. 'Ambergate'

Habit Bulbous, perennial.
Flowers Spanning 3¾in (9.5cm), borne in mid-spring. Pale tangerine, with deep red-orange cup.
Leaves Narrow and strap-shaped. Mid-green.
• TIPS Suitable for planting in borders, and as cut flowers.
• HEIGHT 16in (40cm).
• SPREAD 6in (15cm).

N. 'Ambergate'
(Div. 2)

☀ ◊   Z 3–8

N. 'Suzy'

Habit Bulbous, perennial.
Flowers Scented, 2⅜in (6cm) across, borne in mid-spring. Primrose-yellow, with deep orange cup.
Leaves Narrow and strap-shaped. Mid-green.
• TIPS Suitable for growing in borders and for cut flowers.
• HEIGHT 16in (40cm).
• SPREAD 3in (8cm).

N. 'Suzy'
(Div. 7)

☀ ◊   Z 3–8

N. 'Sealing Wax'

Habit Bulbous, perennial.
Flowers Broad, rounded petals, 3½in (9cm) across, borne in mid-spring. Golden-yellow, with small, red-orange cup.
Leaves Narrow and strap-shaped. Mid-green.
• TIPS Suitable for growing in borders, and as cut flowers.
• HEIGHT 20in (50cm).
• SPREAD 6in (15cm).

N. 'Sealing Wax'
(Div. 2)

☀ ◊   Z 3–8

N. 'Home Fires'

Habit Bulbous, perennial.
Flowers Neat, pointed petals and short cup, 4⅜in (11cm) across, borne in mid-spring. Yellow, with bright orange cup.
Leaves Narrow and strap-shaped. Mid-green.
• TIPS Suitable for growing in borders and as cut flowers.
• HEIGHT 18in (45cm).
• SPREAD 6in (15cm).

N. 'Home Fires'
(Div. 2)

☀ ◊   Z 3–8

N. 'Scarlet Gem'

Habit Bulbous, perennial.
Flowers Scented, 2in (5cm) across, borne in clusters in mid-spring. Yellow, with red cup.
Leaves Narrow and strap-shaped. Mid-green.
• TIPS Good for planting in borders and cutting.
• HEIGHT 14in (35cm).
• SPREAD 3in (8cm).

N. 'Scarlet Gem'
(Div. 8)

☀ ◊   Z 3–8

N. 'Altruist'

Habit Bulbous, perennial.
Flowers Up to 3⅜in (8.5cm) across, with pointed petals and fluted cup, borne in mid-spring. Apricot-yellow, with orange-red cup.
Leaves Narrow and strap-shaped. Mid-green.
• TIPS Good for planting in borders and cutting.
• HEIGHT 18in (45cm).
• SPREAD 6in (15cm).

N. 'Altruist'
(Div. 3)

☀ ◊   Z 3–8

Iridaceae	

IRIS ORCHIOIDES of gardens

Habit Vigorous, perennial, with fleshy roots.
Flowers Borne in late spring, 1½–2½in (4–6cm)
across, up to 6 per stem, emerging from the upper
leaf axils. White to pale or deep golden-yellow,
with a yellow mark on the falls. *Leaves* Narrowly
lance-shaped, channeled, and glossy. Fresh green.
• NATIVE HABITAT Stony and grassy hillsides,
from northeast Afghanistan to central Asia.
• CULTIVATION This bulb is one of the easiest
irises to grow. It is suitable for a rock garden or
sunny, raised bed. Needs light, well-drained,
moderately fertile, soil that is neutral to slightly
acid and enriched with organic matter. Best grown
in a warm, sheltered site in full sun. Take care
when transplanting not to damage the thick but
fragile, fleshy storage roots.
• PROPAGATION Divide or separate offsets
carefully in mid-summer after the foliage dies
down, and replant immediately.
• OTHER NAME *I. bucharica*.

☼ ◊

Z 4–9

HEIGHT
8–16in
(20–40cm)

SPREAD
5in (12cm)

2in
(5cm)

Liliaceae	YELLOW MARIPOSA

CALOCHORTUS LUTEUS

Habit Slender, bulbous, perennial, with branching stems. **Flowers** Erect, open, bell-shaped, borne in spring. Clear yellow, lined and marked red-brown at center. **Leaves** Linear and upright. Mid-green.
• NATIVE HABITAT Grasslands and mixed evergreen forests in California.
• CULTIVATION Needs sandy, sharply drained soil and a warm, sheltered site. Dislikes winter moisture, but suits a bulb frame or cold greenhouse.
• PROPAGATION By seed when ripe, or by offsets in late summer.

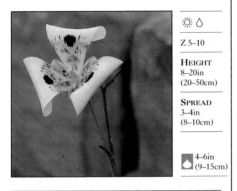

☀ ◊

Z 5–10

HEIGHT
8–20in
(20–50cm)

SPREAD
3–4in
(8–10cm)

4–6in
(9–15cm)

Liliaceae	

ERYTHRONIUM 'Pagoda'

Habit Very vigorous, bulbous, perennial. **Flowers** Drooping, borne in clusters of up to 10, in spring. Pale sulfur-yellow, with deep-yellow anthers and a brown, central ring. **Leaves** Basal, oval, and glossy. Dark green, with bronze mottling.
• NATIVE HABITAT Garden origin.
• CULTIVATION Grow in light, dappled shade in moist but well-drained soil that is rich in organic matter. Do not allow bulbs to dry out in storage.
• PROPAGATION By division of established clumps, or by separation of offsets after flowering.

☀ ◊

Z 4–9

HEIGHT
6–14in
(15–35cm)

SPREAD
6–8in
(15–20cm)

4–6in
(9–15cm)

Amaryllidaceae/ Liliaceae	

STENOMESSON VARIEGATUM

Habit Clump-forming, bulbous, perennial. **Flowers** Drooping, tubular, borne in sprays, in early spring. White, yellow, pink, or scarlet, with green-marked lobes. **Leaves** Strap-shaped, becoming longer after flowering. Mid-green.
• NATIVE HABITAT Andes, Ecuador, Peru, Bolivia.
• CULTIVATION Grow as a house or conservatory plant in soil-based mix, in cold areas.
• PROPAGATION By careful division in autumn, or by seed in spring.
• OTHER NAME *S. incarnatum*.

☀ ◊

Z 10–11

HEIGHT
12–24in
(30–60cm)

SPREAD
12in (30cm)

Neck
above

Amaryllidaceae/ Liliaceae	

STENOMESSON MINIATUM

Habit Perennial. **Flowers** Drooping, tubular, borne in sprays of 3–6 during spring and summer. Orange or bright red. **Leaves** Narrowly strap-shaped, appearing after the flowers. Mid-green.
• NATIVE HABITAT Andes, Peru, and Bolivia.
• CULTIVATION Excellent as home or conservatory plant in cold areas, grown in soil-based mix. Elsewhere, ideal for planting in a sunny border.
• PROPAGATION By careful division in autumn, or by seed in spring.
• OTHER NAMES *Urceolina pendula*, *U. peruviana*.

☀ ◊

Z 10–11

HEIGHT
8–12in
(20–30cm)

SPREAD
4–6in
(10–15cm)

Neck
above

Amaryllidaceae/Liliaceae

CLIVIA MINIATA

Habit Robust, clump-forming, rhizomatous, perennial. **Flowers** Open bell- to funnel-shaped, in large clusters of up to 20, borne on leafless, sturdy stems in early spring. Orange, occasionally yellow or red, with yellow petal bases and golden anthers. **Leaves** Evergreen, basal, strap-shaped, and semi-glossy. Dark green.
• NATIVE HABITAT Woodland, S. Africa.
• CULTIVATION Excellent as a conservatory or house plant in cold areas, and good for a shady border in warm climates. Under glass, provide soil-based mix with grit and leaf mold. Water liberally during full growth in spring and summer after flowering, and apply a balanced liquid fertilizer every 2 weeks. Keep bulb almost dry in winter, but resume watering when new growth commences in spring. Specimens grown in containers flower best if kept slightly pot-bound. Outdoors, plant the bulb in fertile, moist but well-drained soil in partial or dappled shade.
• PROPAGATION Separate offsets in early spring after flowering, or sow seed when ripe or in spring.

☼ ◊

Z 10–11

HEIGHT
18in (45cm)

SPREAD
12–24in
(30–60cm)

Neck
above

FRITILLARIAS

Fritillarias are grown for their usually bell-shaped flowers, which are either paired or solitary, borne in sprays or spikes. Many species have very subtle coloring, often with characteristic checkering. Most occur in well-drained habitats, and prefer climates with dry winters and spring rainfall, followed by long, hot summers. Many resent wetness during dormancy. A few species that are found in woodland and damp meadows prefer heavier, moisture-retentive soils.

Fritillarias have varying needs in cultivation, and are classified as follows:
Group 1 Relatively easily to grow in fertile, well-drained soil, in full sun. Suitable for a rock garden or sunny border.
Group 2 Need protection from moisture when dormant. Grow in sharply drained, gritty, moderately fertile soil, in full sun. Suitable for a rock garden, raised bed, or an alpine house or bulb frame.

Group 3 These species are natives of woodland and damp meadows, and are suitable for borders and naturalizing. They need moisture-retentive, fertile soil that does not dry out completely in summer, in sun or light, dappled shade.
Group 4 Intolerant of moisture, and grown in a bulb frame or cold greenhouse to protect them from rain. They need fertile, well-drained soil and full sun.

Propagate by seed sown in autumn in a cold frame. Move to a cold greenhouse upon germination in spring. Leave small species in their pots for two years, and apply a balanced liquid fertilizer as growth begins in spring. Separate offsets or propagate by scaling (see pp. 173–182). Species with large scales, such as *F. pudica*, *F. raddeana*, and *F. acmopetala* suit scaling. An easier method of propagation, but produced in only some species, is to sow rice-grain bulbils in late summer.

F. THUNBERGII
Habit Bulbous, perennial.
Flowers Nodding bells, borne in loose spikes in spring. Creamy-white, with faint, green veins or checkering.
Leaves Linear and glossy. Mid-green.
• CULTIVATION 1.
• OTHER NAME
F. verticillata var. *thunbergii*.
• HEIGHT to 2ft (60cm).
• SPREAD 4–5in (10–12cm).

F. thunbergii

☼ ◊   Z 6–8

F. RADDEANA
Habit Robust, bulbous, perennial.
Flowers Nodding, broadly bell-shaped, borne in sprays of 5–6, occasionally more, in early spring. Creamy-green or pale yellow.
Leaves Lance-shaped. Lustrous, pale green.
• CULTIVATION 1 or 3.
• HEIGHT to 2ft (60cm).
• SPREAD to 8in (20cm).

F. raddeana

☼ ◊   Z 4–9

F. IMPERIALIS
Habit Stout, upright, bulbous, perennial.
Flowers Drooping bells, in sturdy-stemmed sprays of 3–6, crowned with a tuft of leaf-like bracts, borne in early summer. Yellow, orange, or red.
Leaves Lance-shaped. Light green.
• CULTIVATION 1.
• HEIGHT to 5ft (1.5m).
• SPREAD 10–12in (25–30cm).

F. imperialis
Crown imperial

☼ ◊   Z 5–9

F. PUDICA
Habit Slender, bulbous, perennial.
Flowers Drooping, solitary or paired, narrow bells, borne in early spring. Golden-yellow, maturing to red.
Leaves Linear to lance-shaped and slightly glaucous. Mid-green.
• CULTIVATION 4. Forms *rice-grain* bulbils.
• HEIGHT to 6in (15cm).
• SPREAD 2in (5cm).

F. pudica
Yellow fritillary

☼ ◊   Z 2–9

F. RECURVA
Habit Slender, bulbous, perennial.
Flowers Narrowly bell-shaped, drooping, with recurved tips, borne in spike-like sprays in spring. Scarlet, faintly checkered yellow.
Leaves Linear to lance-shaped. Gray-green.
• CULTIVATION 4. Forms *rice-grain* bulbils.
• HEIGHT to 2ft (60cm).
• SPREAD to 4in (10cm).

F. recurva
Scarlet fritillary

☼ ◊   Z 6–9

F. MELEAGRIS
Habit Bulbous, perennial.
Flowers Drooping, bell-shaped, solitary or paired, borne in spring. Purple, pink, strongly checkered pink or purple.
Leaves Linear. Gray-green.
• CULTIVATION 1 or 3. Will naturalize in grass. Prefers heavy soil.
• HEIGHT to 1ft (30cm).
• SPREAD to 3in (8cm).

F. meleagris
Snake's head fritillary

 ◑   Z 3–8

F. PYRENAICA
Habit Slender, bulbous, perennial.
Flowers Broadly bell-shaped, solitary or paired, borne in late spring. Brown-purple checkered, yellow-green inside.
Leaves Lance-shaped, glaucous. Gray-green.
• CULTIVATION 1.
• OTHER NAME
F. nigra of gardens.
• HEIGHT 18in (45cm).
• SPREAD to 3in (8cm).

F. pyrenaica

☼ ◊   Z 6–8

F. PERSICA
Habit Sturdy, upright, bulbous, perennial.
Flowers Drooping, conical, bell-shaped, in dense, terminal spikes of up to 30, borne in spring. Dark purple.
Leaves Lance-shaped and glaucous, appearing along stem. Gray-green.
• CULTIVATION 1. Best in a hot, sunny site.
• HEIGHT to 3ft (1m).
• SPREAD 4in (10cm).

F. persica

☼ ◊   Z 7–8

F. CAMSCHATCENSIS
Habit Variable,
bulbous, perennial.
Flowers Broadly
bell-shaped, drooping,
borne in dense, stout-
stemmed spikes in early
summer. Blackish-purple
or brown.
Leaves Lance-shaped
and glossy. Light green.
• CULTIVATION 3.
Forms rice-grain bulbils.
• HEIGHT 18in (45cm).
• SPREAD to 4in (10cm).

F. camschatcensis
Black sarana

☼ ◗   Z 3–8

F. CIRRHOSA
Habit Bulbous,
perennial.
Flowers Broadly bell-
shaped, drooping, usually
solitary, but occasionally
in pairs or trios, borne in
late spring. Pale green,
often purple-flushed,
with purple checkering.
Leaves Linear.
Gray-green.
• CULTIVATION 3.
• HEIGHT 18in (45cm).
• SPREAD to 3in (8cm).

F. cirrhosa

☼ ◗   Z 6–8

F. ACMOPETALA
Habit Bulbous,
perennial.
Flowers Drooping, bell-
shaped, usually solitary,
occasionally in pairs or
trios, reflexed, borne in
late spring. Pale green,
stained red-brown inside.
Leaves Linear.
Blue-green.
• CULTIVATION 1.
Forms rice-grain bulbils.
• HEIGHT 16in (40cm).
• SPREAD to 3in (8cm).

F. PALLIDIFLORA
Habit Sturdy,
bulbous, perennial.
Flowers Broadly bell-
shaped, foul-smelling,
borne in late spring.
Creamy-yellow,
with green base
and brown-red
checkering inside.
Leaves Lance-shaped,
glaucous. Gray-green.
• CULTIVATION 1 or 3.
• HEIGHT 16in (40cm).
• SPREAD to 3in (8cm).

F. pallidiflora

☼ ◗   Z 5–8

F. PONTICA
Habit Slender,
bulbous, perennial.
Flowers Drooping,
broadly bell-shaped,
solitary, borne in spring.
Pale green, tinted
maroon at the base.
Leaves Lance-shaped,
glaucous. Gray-green.
• CULTIVATION 1 or 2.
Keep bulb dry during
dormancy.
• HEIGHT to 8in (20cm).
• SPREAD 2in (5cm).

F. pontica

☼ ◌   Z 7–8

F. acmopetala

☼ ◌   Z 6–8

Amaryllidaceae/ Liliaceae	POISON BULB

CRINUM ASIATICUM

Habit Clumping, bulbous, perennial. **Flowers** Fragrant, spreading, narrow petals, borne in sprays on sturdy, leafless stems during summer. White. **Leaves** Strap-shaped and basal. Dark green.
• NATIVE HABITAT Tropical southeast Asia.
• CULTIVATION Excellent for growing as a house or conservatory plant in cool climates. Keep barely moist in winter. Needs soil-based mix with added grit and leaf mold.
• PROPAGATION Separate offsets in spring, or sow seed as soon as ripe.

☼ ◊

Z 10–11

HEIGHT
24in (60cm)

SPREAD
24in (60cm)

Nose level

Amaryllidaceae/ Liliaceae	

PANCRATIUM ILLYRICUM

Habit Bulbous, perennial. **Flowers** Fragrant, each with 6 narrow, spreading petals and a small central cup, borne in sprays of up to 20 on a leafless stem, in late spring or early summer. White. **Leaves** Strap-shaped, basal, and semi-erect. Grayish-green.
• NATIVE HABITAT Sandy and rocky areas, Corsica and Sardinia.
• CULTIVATION Suitable for a sheltered border in sun, with moderately fertile, sharply drained soil.
• PROPAGATION Separate offsets in autumn, or sow seeds as soon as ripe.

☼ ◊

Z 8–10

HEIGHT
to 18in
(45cm)

SPREAD
10in (25cm)

8in
(20cm)

Hyacinthaceae/ Liliaceae	

ORNITHOGALUM NARBONENSE

Habit Clump-forming, bulbous, perennial. **Flowers** Star-shaped, borne in pyramidal clusters on bare stems, from late spring to early summer. White. **Leaves** Linear and semi-erect. Gray-green.
• NATIVE HABITAT Wasteland, southern Europe, from the Mediterranean to Caucasus mountains.
• CULTIVATION Suitable for naturalizing in grass or for planting in an herbaceous border. Needs moderately fertile, well-drained soil.
• PROPAGATION By offsets in autumn, or by seed in autumn or spring.

☼ ◊

Z 7–10

HEIGHT
to 36in
(90cm)

SPREAD
4in (10cm)

4in
(10cm)

Alliaceae/Liliaceae	

TRITELEIA HYACINTHA

Habit Upright, cormous, perennial. **Flowers**
Funnel-shaped, in flattened sprays of up to 20,
borne in late spring and early summer. White
or pale blue. **Leaves** Linear and basal, dying
back before the flowers appear. Mid-green.
• NATIVE HABITAT Grassland, chaparral, and
pine woods of western USA.
• CULTIVATION Prefers a warm, sheltered site
with light, sandy, freely draining soil.
• PROPAGATION By seed, when ripe or in spring.
• OTHER NAMES *Brodiaea hyacinthina, B. lactea.*

☼ ◊

Z 6–10

HEIGHT
12–20in
(30–50cm)

SPREAD
3–4in
(8–10cm)

3in
(8cm)

Hyacinthaceae/Liliaceae	CHINCHERINCHEE

ORNITHOGALUM THYRSOIDES

Habit Robust, bulbous, perennial. **Flowers** Star-
shaped cups, borne in dense clusters, in early
summer. White. **Leaves** Basal and narrowly lance-
shaped, withering before flowers. Glossy green.
• NATIVE HABITAT Western Cape, S. Africa.
• CULTIVATION Suitable for planting in a mixed
border with moderately fertile, well-drained soil.
In colder areas, grow as a conservatory or house
plant in soil-based mix. Flowers are excellent
for cutting and last well in water.
• PROPAGATION By offsets in autumn.

☼ ◊

Z 7–10

HEIGHT
12–28in
(30–70cm)

SPREAD
4in (10cm)

4in
(10cm)

Araceae	BLACK JAPANESE JACK-IN-THE-PULPIT

ARISAEMA SIKOKIANUM

Habit Sturdy, tuberous, perennial. **Flowers**
Large, enclosing a club-shaped spike, borne in
late spring or early summer. Deep purple, with
green lining and white spike. **Leaves** Divided
into 3–5 broadly oval segments. Rich green.
• NATIVE HABITAT Woodlands of Japan.
• CULTIVATION Needs an open, leaf-rich, fertile,
moist but well-drained soil that is neutral to acid.
Provide cool shelter in partial or dappled shade.
• PROPAGATION Separate offsets in late summer,
or sow seed as soon as ripe.

☼ ◊

Z 5–9

HEIGHT
12–20in
(30–50cm)

SPREAD
6–12in
(15–30cm)

10in
(25cm)

Melanthiaceae/Liliaceae	

ZIGADENUS FREMONTII

Habit Robust, clumping, bulbous, perennial.
Flowers Star-shaped, borne in broad, pyramidal
spikes in early summer. Pale greenish-yellow.
Leaves Semi-erect, basal, and linear. Gray-green.
• NATIVE HABITAT Scrub, western USA.
• CULTIVATION Needs a dry summer dormancy.
Grows best in a bulb frame or cold greenhouse
where summer rainfall occurs. Elsewhere, suits a
warm, dry, sunny border. All parts are highly toxic.
• PROPAGATION Divide in spring or autumn,
or sow seed as soon as ripe.

☼ ◊

Z 8–9

HEIGHT
12–20in
(30–50cm)

SPREAD
3–4in
(8–10cm)

3–4in
(8–10cm)

| Amaryllidaceae/Liliaceae | PERUVIAN DAFFODIL |

HYMENOCALLIS NARCISSIFLORA

Habit Robust, bulbous, perennial. **Flowers**
Fragrant, small, central cup surrounded by long,
narrow, spreading petals. Borne in stout-stemmed
clusters of 2–5 in summer. White, sometimes with
green-striped inner. **Leaves** Basal, strap-shaped,
and semi-erect, dying down in winter. Dark green.
• NATIVE HABITAT Andes, Peru.
• CULTIVATION In colder areas, grow in a cool
greenhouse or conservatory in soil-based mix with
added leaf-mold and grit. Place in good light, but
shade from hot sun. Outdoors, it suits an

herbaceous or mixed border, but should
be lifted in autumn before frost. Grow in fairly
fertile, moist but well-drained soil that is rich in
organic matter. Pot-grown specimens need an
application of balanced liquid fertilizer every 2–3
weeks when in full growth, and moderate watering.
Reduce water as the leaves wither, keeping the
bulb almost dry when dormant in winter.
• PROPAGATION Separate offsets in spring,
or sow seed as soon as it is ripe.
• OTHER NAMES *H. calathina, Ismene calathina*.

☀ ◊

Z 8–10

HEIGHT
to 24in
(60cm)

SPREAD
12–18in
(30–45cm)

Neck
above

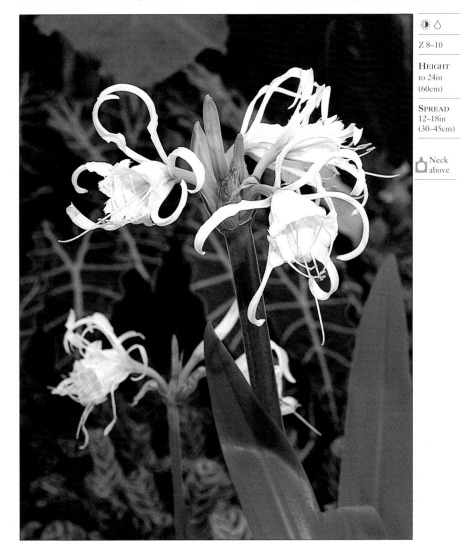

Hyacinthaceae/ Liliaceae	

ORNITHOGALUM ARABICUM

Habit Robust, bulbous, perennial. **Flowers** Fragrant, star-shaped cups, borne in dense, flattened clusters, in early summer. White or creamy-white, with a black base. **Leaves** Strap-shaped, forming basal rosettes. Dark green.
• NATIVE HABITAT Rocky Mediterranean hillsides.
• CULTIVATION Grow in a sheltered site in sun with moderately fertile, well-drained soil. Lift in autumn. In cold areas, grow in a cool greenhouse in soil-based potting mix. Good as cut flowers.
• PROPAGATION By offsets in autumn.

☀ ◌

Z 7–10

HEIGHT
12–18in
(30–45cm)

SPREAD
4–6in
(10–15cm)

4in
(10cm)

Iridaceae	

TRITONIA DISTICHA
subsp. *RUBROLUCENS*

Habit Cormous, perennial. **Flowers** Open funnel-shaped, in one-sided spikes on wiry stems, borne in succession in late summer. Pink. **Leaves** Sword-shaped and erect, forming a basal fan. Mid-green.
• NATIVE HABITAT Grassy hillsides, S. Africa.
• CULTIVATION Prefers light, sandy, well-drained soil. Provide light twiggy support, and protect with a deep, dry, winter mulch.
• PROPAGATION Separate offsets in autumn.
• OTHER NAMES *T. rosea, T. rubrolucens.*

☀ ◌

Z 7–10

HEIGHT
28in
(70cm)

SPREAD
3–4in
(8–10cm)

3–4in
(8–10cm)

Melanthiaceae/ Liliaceae	DEATH CAMAS

ZIGADENUS VENENOSUS

Habit Robust, bulbous, perennial. **Flowers** Small stars, borne in sprays in summer. **Leaves** Linear, basal, and semi-erect. Mid-green.
• NATIVE HABITAT Grassland and open woodland, western USA.
• CULTIVATION Prefers a site in partial or dappled shade, with deep, fertile, moist but well-drained soil that is rich in organic matter. All of the plant is highly toxic and must be handled with care.
• PROPAGATION Divide in spring or autumn, or sow seed as soon as ripe.

☀ ◌

Z 8–9

HEIGHT
12–20in
(30–50cm)

SPREAD
3–4in
(8–10cm)

4in
(10cm)

Alliaceae/Liliaceae	NODDING ONION, WILD ONION

ALLIUM CERNUUM

Habit Vigorous, clump-forming, bulbous, perennial. **Flowers** Small, cup-shaped, borne in loose, drooping clusters of 25–40 in summer. Mid- to deep pink. **Leaves** Basal, narrowly strap-shaped, and semi-erect. Dark green.
• NATIVE HABITAT Rocky mountains, N. America.
• CULTIVATION Prefers moderately fertile, well-drained soil. Excellent for growing in a border that enjoys full sun.
• PROPAGATION By seed when ripe or in spring, or by offsets in autumn.

☀ ◌

Z 4–10

HEIGHT
12–24in
(30–60cm)

SPREAD
3–4in
(8–10cm)

3–4in
(8–10cm)

| Amaryllidaceae/Liliaceae | |

RHODOPHIALA ADVENA

Habit Slender, bulbous, perennial. **Flowers** Open funnel-shaped, held horizontally in sprays of 2–6, borne on leafless stems in late summer and early autumn. Red, yellow, or pink, with yellow-veined center. **Leaves** Basal, semi-upright, and linear, appearing either at the same time as the flowers, or immediately afterwards. Gray-green.
• NATIVE HABITAT Mountainous regions of Chile.
• CULTIVATION Suitable for a raised bed or in a border at the base of a warm, sheltered wall in sun. Needs moderately fertile, sharply drained soil.

Given good drainage and the protection of a dry mulch, it may tolerate occasional low temperatures to 23°F (-5°C). Where cold is prolonged or severe, grow in a cold greenhouse or alpine house. Resents root disturbance, so top-dress annually if pot-grown and repot every third or fourth year.
• PROPAGATION Separate offsets in autumn or spring, or sow seed as soon as ripe.
• OTHER NAME *Hippeastrum advenum.*

☼ ◊

Z 9–10

HEIGHT
to 20in
(50cm)

SPREAD
4–6in
(10–15cm)

Neck
above

Amaryllidaceae/ Liliaceae	RED SPIDER LILY

LYCORIS RADIATA

Habit Slender, bulbous, perennial. *Flowers* Elegant, reflexed, prominent anthers and wavy-margined petals, borne in sprays of 4–6 in late summer. Bright rose-red. *Leaves* Basal, linear, and semi-erect, appearing after flowers. Dark green.
• NATIVE HABITAT Hills and fields, Japan.
• CULTIVATION Suitable for growing in a sunny, sheltered border in fertile, well-drained soil. Needs a warm, dry dormant period in summer.
• PROPAGATION Separate offsets after flowering, or sow seed when ripe.

☼ ◊

Z 8–10

HEIGHT 12–16in (30–40cm)

SPREAD 4in (10cm)

Neck above

Ranunculaceae	PERSIAN BUTTERCUP

RANUNCULUS ASIATICUS [Red form]

Habit Tuberous, perennial. *Flowers* Single- or double-cupped, borne on branching stems in early or mid-summer. Red, pink, yellow, or white, with purple-black center. *Leaves* Long-stalked, deeply lobed, and divided. Pale to deep green.
• NATIVE HABITAT Eastern Mediterranean, northeast Africa, and southwest Asia.
• CULTIVATION Needs fertile, rich, moist but well-drained soil. Must be kept damp during growth. Lift before first frost in colder regions.
• PROPAGATION Divide tuber clusters in autumn.

☼ ◊

Z 8–10

HEIGHT 8–18in (20–45cm)

SPREAD 4–8in (10–20cm)

2in (5cm)

Gesneriaceae	

GLOXINIA PERENNIS

Habit Bushy, rhizomatous, perennial. *Flowers* Solitary bells, borne from early summer through to mid-autumn. Lavender-blue with deep violet base. *Leaves* Heart-shaped, hairy, and glossy. Mid-green, with red-tinted underside.
• NATIVE HABITAT Forests, from Panama to Peru.
• CULTIVATION In cold areas, grow under glass in soilless, potting mix. Water freely when in growth, but keep the rhizome almost dry in winter.
• PROPAGATION By seed or division in spring, or by leaf or stem cuttings in summer.

☽ ◊

Z 10–11

HEIGHT 24in (60cm)

SPREAD 12in (30cm)

1in (2.5cm)

Iridaceae	

PATERSONIA UMBROSA

Habit Sturdy, arching, rather slow-growing, clump-forming, rhizomatous. *Flowers* Iris-like, borne on tough stems in succession from spring through to early summer. Blue-purple. *Leaves* Evergreen, rigid, linear, and basal. Mid-green.
• NATIVE HABITAT Scrubland, western Australia.
• CULTIVATION Needs light, fertile, well-drained soil. In cold areas, grow as a house or conservatory plant in soil-based mix with added grit. Water freely in growth, but sparingly in winter.
• PROPAGATION Divide in autumn.

☼ ◊

Z 9–10

HEIGHT to 3ft (1m)

SPREAD 1–2ft (30–60cm)

1in (2.5cm)

Alliaceae/Liliaceae	STARS OF PERSIA

ALLIUM CRISTOPHII

Habit Robust, bulbous, perennial. *Flowers* Small stars, in large, open, spherical spray of up to 50 flowers, spanning about 8in (20cm), borne on naked, ribbed stems in early summer. Metallic pink-purple. *Leaves* Strap-shaped, basal, and hairy-margined, withering before the flowers appear. Yellowish-green.
• NATIVE HABITAT Rocky slopes in mountain foothills of Turkey and central Asia.
• CULTIVATION Needs moderately fertile, well-drained soil and a warm, sheltered site in full sun. Ideal for planting in an herbaceous or mixed border. This and other large-flowered, brightly colored alliums associate particularly well with low-growing, gray-, silver-, or pale yellow-green-leaved perennials. The cut flowers and seedheads suit drying for winter arrangements.
• PROPAGATION By seed as soon as ripe or in spring, or by offsets in autumn.
• OTHER NAMES *A. christophii*, *A. albopilosum*.

☼ ◊

Z 4–10

HEIGHT
12–24in
(30–60cm)

SPREAD
6–8in
(15–20cm)

3–4in
(8–10cm)

Alliaceae/Liliaceae	

TRITELEIA LAXA

Habit Upright, cormous, perennial. **Flowers**
Funnel-shaped, mostly upright, borne in loose
sprays of up to 25 in early summer. Pale to deep
purple-blue. **Leaves** Linear, basal, dying back at
the same time as or just after flowering. Mid-green.
• NATIVE HABITAT Grassland, chaparral, and pine
woods, western California to south Oregon, USA.
• CULTIVATION Needs light, sandy, freely
draining soil and a warm, sheltered site.
• PROPAGATION By seed when ripe, or in spring.
• OTHER NAME *Brodiaea laxa*.

☼ ◊

Z 6–10

HEIGHT
4–20in
(10–50cm)

SPREAD
3–4in
(8–10cm)

3in
(8cm)

Alliaceae/Liliaceae	

ALLIUM CAERULEUM

Habit Slender, bulbous, perennial. **Flowers** Small
stars, in dense clusters, 1in (2.5cm) span, borne on
stiff stems in early summer. Pale ice-blue. **Leaves**
Linear, withering before the flowers. Mid-green.
• NATIVE HABITAT Northern and central Asia.
• CULTIVATION Easy to grow and flourishes
when planted in full sun. Needs a well-drained,
moderately fertile, but preferably sandy soil.
• PROPAGATION By offsets in autumn, or by
seed when ripe or in spring.
• OTHER NAME *A. azureum*.

☼ ◊

Z 4–10

HEIGHT
24in
(60cm)

SPREAD
2in (5cm)

3–4in
(8–10cm)

Araceae	

ARISAEMA GRIFFITHII

Habit Tuberous, perennial. **Flowers** Hooded,
cobra-like, heavily veined, 10in (25cm) long,
borne in early summer. Green or purple.
Leaves Split into oval leaflets. Olive-green.
• NATIVE HABITAT Forests, eastern Himalaya.
• CULTIVATION Needs an open, moist but well-
drained, soil that is neutral to acid and enriched
with organic matter. Prefers a cool, sheltered site.
Mulch deeply or, in colder areas, lift in autumn.
• PROPAGATION Separate offsets in late summer,
or sow seed as soon as ripe.

☼ ◊

Z 7–9

HEIGHT
to 24in
(60cm)

SPREAD
18in
(45cm)

10in
(25cm)

Araceae	

ARISAEMA JACQUEMONTII

Habit Sturdy, tuberous, perennial. **Flowers**
Narrow, hooded, tapering to a long point, borne
in early summer. Pale green with white stripes.
Leaves Divided into 3–9 narrowly oval, wavy-
edged segments. Rich green.
• NATIVE HABITAT Woodlands of Japan.
• CULTIVATION Needs an open, leaf-rich, moist
but well-drained, neutral to acid soil. Plant in
a cool, sheltered site in partial or dappled shade.
• PROPAGATION Separate offsets in late summer,
or sow seed as soon as ripe.

☼ ◊

Z 7–9

HEIGHT
6–30in
(15–70cm)

SPREAD
12in (30cm)

10in
(25cm)

Araceae	JACK-IN-THE-PULPIT

ARISAEMA TRIPHYLLUM

Habit Tuberous, perennial. *Flowers* Hooded, borne in early summer. Pale green, often purple-lined. *Leaves* Split into 3 thin, oval leaflets. Mid-green. *Fruits* Red berries in autumn.
• NATIVE HABITAT Woodlands. eastern N. America.
• CULTIVATION Needs cool shelter in part shade. Needs leaf-rich, moist, well-drained soil that is neutral to acid with plenty of organic matter.
• PROPAGATION Separate offsets in late summer, or sow seed as soon as ripe.
• OTHER NAME *A. atrorubens*.

Z 4–9

HEIGHT
16–20in
(40–50cm)

SPREAD
12in (30cm)

10in
(25cm)

Hyacinthaceae/Liliaceae	PINEAPPLE LILY

EUCOMIS BICOLOR

Habit Sturdy, bulbous, perennial. *Flowers* Small, star-shaped, in upright, cylindrical spike, borne on maroon-flecked stems, in late summer. Pale green, with purple-edges.•*Leaves* Strap-shaped, semi-erect, with wavy margins. Light green.
• NATIVE HABITAT Damp grasslands in the Drakensberg mountains, S. Africa and Lesotho.
• CULTIVATION Needs fertile, well-drained soil, and a dry, winter mulch in colder regions.
• PROPAGATION Separate offsets in spring, or sow seed as soon as ripe or in spring.

Z 8–10

HEIGHT
12–24in
(30–60cm)

SPREAD
8–12in
(20–30cm)

5in
(12cm)

Amaryllidaceae/ Liliaceae	

CYRTANTHUS MACKENII var. *COOPERI*

Habit Clump-forming, bulbous, perennial. *Flowers* Scented, narrow, tubular, curved, borne in sprays of 4–10 in summer. Yellow or cream. *Leaves* Basal, linear, and semi-erect. Mid-green.
• NATIVE HABITAT S. Africa.
• CULTIVATION Suitable for growing in a cool greenhouse or as a house plant in colder regions. Needs moderately fertile, well-drained soil. Keep barely moist and protect during winter.
• PROPAGATION Separate offsets in spring, or sow seed as soon as ripe.

Z 9–10

HEIGHT
8–12in
(20–30cm)

SPREAD
3–4in
(8–10cm)

Nose
level

Liliaceae/Liliaceae	

CALOCHORTUS BARBATUS

Habit Bulbous, perennial, with branching stems.
Flowers Open, cup-shaped, borne in summer.
Mustard-yellow, often purple-flushed, with purple
inner hairs. **Leaves** Linear and erect. Mid-green.
• NATIVE HABITAT Grasslands, Mexico.
• CULTIVATION Needs sandy, sharply drained soil
and a warm, sheltered site. Dislikes winter
moisture, but suits a bulb frame or cold greenhouse.
• PROPAGATION By seed when ripe, by offsets in
late summer, or by bulbils.
• OTHER NAME *Cyclobothra lutea.*

☀ ◊

Z 6–10

HEIGHT
6–12in
(15–30cm)

SPREAD
2–4in
(5–10cm)

4–6in
(9–15cm)

Ranunculaceae	PERSIAN BUTTERCUP

RANUNCULUS ASIATICUS [Yellow form]

Habit Tuberous, perennial. **Flowers** Single or
double cups, borne on branching stems in early
or mid-summer. Yellow, red, pink, or white, with
purple-black anthers. **Leaves** Long-stalked,
deeply lobed, and divided. Pale to deep green.
• NATIVE HABITAT Eastern Mediterranean,
northeast Africa, and southwest Asia.
• CULTIVATION In colder areas, lift before frost
and keep damp during growth. Needs fertile, moist
but well-drained soil that is rich in organic matter.
• PROPAGATION Divide tuber clusters in autumn.

☀ ◊

Z 8–10

HEIGHT
8–18in
(20–45cm)

SPREAD
4–8in
(10–20cm)

2in
(5cm)

Iridaceae	

CYPELLA HERBERTII

Habit Bulbous, perennial. **Flowers** Borne in
succession in summer. Mustard-yellow, with
purple-marked inner petals. **Leaves** Pleated,
narrowly lance-shaped, in a basal fan. Mid-green.
• NATIVE HABITAT Damp grasslands, S. America.
• CULTIVATION Needs sandy soil that is enriched
with organic matter. Plant in a warm, sheltered
site, either in a rock garden or at the base of a wall.
Also suitable for growing in a cold greenhouse.
• PROPAGATION Separate offsets in late winter
or spring. Sow seed as soon as ripe.

☀ ◊

Z 9–10

HEIGHT
12–20in
(30–50cm)

SPREAD
3–4in
(8–10cm)

3in
(8cm)

Colchicaceae/Liliaceae	CHINESE-LANTERN LILY

SANDERSONIA AURANTIACA

Habit Climbing, tuberous, perennial, with leaf
tendrils. **Flowers** Drooping, urn-shaped, borne in
upper leaf axils during summer. Golden-orange.
Leaves Scattered and lance-shaped. Mid-green.
• NATIVE HABITAT Rocky terrain and lightly
wooded areas in S. Africa.
• CULTIVATION Suitable for growing in borders,
or as conservatory plants. Needs moderately fertile
soil that is rich in organic matter, in a warm, sunny
site. Lift tubers in autumn in colder regions.
• PROPAGATION Divide in autumn or winter.

☀ ◊

Z 9–10

HEIGHT
to 30in
(75cm)

SPREAD
10–12in
(25–30cm)

3–4in
(7–10cm)

Agavaceae	

POLIANTHES GEMINIFLORA

Habit Tuberous, perennial. **Flowers** Drooping, tubular, borne in pairs of tall, upright spikes during summer. Orange-red. **Leaves** Basal, linear, semi-erect, and strap-shaped. Mid-green.
• NATIVE HABITAT Sandy grasslands in Mexico.
• CULTIVATION Grows best as a conservatory or house plant in soil-based mix, in colder areas. Water freely and fertilize regularly during growth. Keep tuber dry during dormancy.
• PROPAGATION By offsets in autumn or spring.
• OTHER NAME *Bravoa geminiflora*.

☼ ◊

Z 9–10

HEIGHT
to 28in
(70cm)

SPREAD
4–6in
(10–15cm)

2in
(5cm)

Iridaceae	PEACOCK FLOWER, TIGER FLOWER

TIGRIDIA PAVONIA

Habit Bulbous, perennial. **Flowers** Iris-like, flattened, borne throughout summer. Orange, red, pink, or yellow, with contrasting center. **Leaves** Pleated, sword-shaped, in basal fans. Mid-green.
• NATIVE HABITAT Sandy grasslands in Mexico.
• CULTIVATION Suitable for growing in a summer border, filling the spaces between other plants. Prefers well-drained soil and a warm, sheltered site. Lift bulb before first frost in autumn.
• PROPAGATION By seed in spring, or by offsets in spring, although these may transmit viruses.

☼ ◊

Z 8–10

HEIGHT
2–5ft
(60cm–1.5m)

SPREAD
5–6in
(12–15cm)

3–4in
(8–10cm)

Iridaceae	

CROCOSMIA 'Jackanapes'

Habit Clump-forming, cormous, perennial. **Flowers** Funnel-shaped, borne on arching, branched spikes during late summer. Bicolored, yellow and orange-red. **Leaves** Basal, sword-shaped, and upright. Bright green.
• NATIVE HABITAT Garden origin.
• CULTIVATION Needs moderately fertile, moist but well-drained soil enriched with organic matter, in partial or dappled shade. Ideal as cut flowers.
• PROPAGATION By division in spring.
• OTHER NAME *C.* 'Fire King'.

☼ ◊

Z 6–9

HEIGHT
16–24in
(40–60cm)

SPREAD
6–8in
(15–20cm)

3in
(8cm)

Amaryllidaceae/ Liliaceae	

NERINE BOWDENII f. *ALBA*

Habit Bulbous, perennial. *Flowers* Funnel-shaped, with recurved, wavy-margined tips and 6 spreading lobes, borne in sprays of 5–10 during autumn. White, often pink-flushed. *Leaves* Strap-shaped, appearing after the flowers. Fresh green.
• NATIVE HABITAT Rocky places, Drakensberg Mountains, S. Africa, and Lesotho.
• CULTIVATION Needs sharp drainage and a sheltered site, such as the base of a warm wall. Provide a deep, dry, winter mulch in cold areas.
• PROPAGATION Divide clumps every 3–5 years.

☼ ◊

Z 8–10

HEIGHT
18–24in
(45–60cm)

SPREAD
5–6in
(12–15cm)

4in
(10cm)

Amaryllidaceae/ Liliaceae	

NERINE 'Orion'

Habit Bulbous, perennial. *Flowers* Funnel-shaped, with spreading, wavy-margined lobes and recurved tips, borne in autumn. Soft, clear pink. *Leaves* Strap-shaped and semi-erect. Mid-green.
• NATIVE HABITAT Garden origin.
• CULTIVATION Ideal as a conservatory plant in soil-based mix, in cold areas. Needs light, sandy, sharply drained soil. Water evenly when in leaf, reduce as leaves wither, and keep dry when dormant. As buds appear, resume watering.
• PROPAGATION Separate offsets in late summer.

☼ ◊

Z 9–10

HEIGHT
12–20in
(30–50cm)

SPREAD
8in (20cm)

Nose
level

Amaryllidaceae/ Liliaceae	

NERINE UNDULATA

Habit Bulbous, perennial. *Flowers* Funnel-shaped, narrow, with crimped lobes and recurved tips, borne in autumn. Pale to rose-pink. *Leaves* Linear, appearing with the flowers. Mid-green.
• NATIVE HABITAT S. Africa.
• CULTIVATION Ideal as a conservatory plant in cold areas. Needs light, sandy, sharply drained soil. Keep just moist in winter, and dry when dormant.
• PROPAGATION Separate offsets during late summer, or sow seed as soon as ripe.
• OTHER NAME *N. crispa.*

☼ ◊

Z9–10

HEIGHT
12–18in
(30–45cm)

SPREAD
4–5in
(10–12cm)

Nose
level

Amaryllidaceae/Liliaceae	RAIN LILY, WINDFLOWER

ZEPHYRANTHES GRANDIFLORA

Habit Slender, bulbous, perennial. *Flowers* Solitary, funnel-shaped, borne on leafless stems in autumn. Deep pink, with a white eye and golden anthers. *Leaves* Basal, linear, semi-erect, and glossy, appearing with the flowers. Fresh green.
• NATIVE HABITAT Grasslands of central America
• CULTIVATION Suitable for a cool greenhouse or conservatory, or as a house plant in colder areas. Grow in soil-based mix with added sharp sand. Alternatively, plant outside and lift in autumn before severe frost. Needs fertile, well-drained soil that is rich in organic matter. Under glass, water freely when in growth and apply a balanced fertilizer every 2 weeks. Reduce water as leaves wither, keeping bulb almost dry during dormancy. Where specimens are grown in containers, they flower best when slightly pot-bound. Excellent for growing in drifts in sunny borders or in rock gardens, in warmer climates.
• PROPAGATION Separate offsets in spring, or sow seed as soon as it is ripe.
• OTHER NAMES *Z. carinata*, *Z. rosea*.

☼ ◊

Z 7–10

HEIGHT
8–12in
(20–30cm)

SPREAD
3–4in
(8–10cm)

4in
(10cm)

Hyacinthaceae/Liliaceae	

SCILLA SCILLOIDES

Habit Slender, perennial. **Flowers** Tiny, star-shaped, borne in dense upright spikes in early autumn. Pale pink. **Leaves** Basal, soft, linear, appearing with the flowers. Mid-green.
• NATIVE HABITAT China and Japan.
• CULTIVATION Needs fertile, well-drained soil enriched with organic matter, in a warm, sheltered site. Excellent for a rock garden or sunny border.
• PROPAGATION Sow seed as soon as ripe, or separate offsets in spring.
• OTHER NAME *S. chinensis*.

☀ ◌

Z 5–10

HEIGHT
6–8in
(15–20cm)

SPREAD
2in (5cm)

3–4in
(8–10cm)

Amaryllidaceae/Liliaceae	

NERINE BOWDENII

Habit Bulbous, perennial. **Flowers** Funnel-shaped, with 6 spreading lobes, recurved, wavy-margined tips, borne in sprays of 5–10 in autumn. Glistening pink. **Leaves** Strap-shaped, appearing after the flowers. Fresh green.
• NATIVE HABITAT Rocky areas, Drakensberg Mountains, S. Africa and Lesotho.
• CULTIVATION Needs sharp drainage and a sheltered site, such as the base of a warm wall. Provide a deep, dry, winter mulch in cold areas.
• PROPAGATION Divide clumps every 3–5 years.

☀ ◌

Z 8–10

HEIGHT
18–24in
(45–60cm)

SPREAD
5–6in
(12–15cm)

4in
(10cm)

Amaryllidaceae/Liliaceae	GUERNSEY LILY

NERINE SARNIENSIS

Habit Bulbous, perennial. **Flowers** Funnel-shaped, with spreading, wavy-margined petals, iridescent, borne in autumn. Deep orange-pink. **Leaves** Strap-shaped and semi-erect, appearing after the flowers. Mid-green.
• NATIVE HABITAT Coastal S. Africa.
• CULTIVATION Ideal for a cool conservatory in colder areas. Needs light, sandy, sharply drained soil. Water moderately when in leaf, but reduce as foliage starts to wither and keep dry in dormancy.
• PROPAGATION Separate offsets in late summer.

☀ ◌

Z 9–10

HEIGHT
18–24in
(45–60cm)

SPREAD
5–6in
(12–15cm)

Nose
level

Amaryllidaceae/Liliaceae	

NERINE 'Brian Doe'

Habit Bulbous, perennial. **Flowers** Funnel-shaped, with reflexed, wavy-margined petals, iridescent, borne in autumn. Deep salmon-pink. **Leaves** Strap-shaped and semi-erect. Mid-green.
• NATIVE HABITAT Garden origin.
• CULTIVATION Ideal as a conservatory plant in soil-based mix, in cold areas. Needs light, sandy, sharply drained soil. Water evenly when in leaf, reduce as leaves wither, and keep dry when dormant. As buds appear, resume watering.
• PROPAGATION Separate offsets in late summer.

☀ ◌

Z 9–10

HEIGHT
12–20in
(30–50cm)

SPREAD
8in (20cm)

Nose
level

| Amaryllidaceae/Liliaceae | AMAZON LILY, EUCHARIST LILY |

EUCHARIS × GRANDIFLORA

Habit Robust, clump-forming, bulbous, perennial. **Flowers** Fragrant, slightly drooping, with 6 spreading petals and 6 protruding stamens fused to form a central cup. Borne on leafless stems, in sprays of up to 6, flowering in early summer and often throughout winter. White. **Leaves** Evergreen, basal, semi-erect, oval, and wavy. Dark green.
• NATIVE HABITAT Moist, open forests, Colombia.
• CULTIVATION Suitable for outdoor cultivation in beds and borders, but in tropical and subtropical

gardens only. In colder areas, grow as a greenhouse or conservatory plant in soil-based potting mix with added leaf-mold and sharp sand. Needs moderately fertile, moist but well-drained soil enriched with organic matter. Water freely and apply a balanced fertilizer monthly during full growth. At other times, water sparingly. Repot every third or fourth year. Popular as a cut flower.
• PROPAGATION Separate offsets after flowering, grow on at 59°F (15°C) until well-established.
• OTHER NAME *E. amazonica* of gardens.

☀ ◊

Z 10–11

HEIGHT
16–24in
(40–60cm)

SPREAD
12in (30cm)

Nose level

Amaryllidaceae/ Liliaceae	

GALANTHUS 'Magnet'

Habit Vigorous, bulbous, perennial. *Flowers* Drooping, pear-shaped, borne in late winter to early spring. White, with inner petals marked green. *Leaves* Narrowly strap-shaped. Gray-green.
• NATIVE HABITAT Garden origin.
• CULTIVATION Perfect for naturalizing in short turf, or in a woodland garden and sufficiently robust for a border. Needs fertile, moist but well-drained soil that does not dry out in summer.
• PROPAGATION Divide clumps after flowering, when leaves begin to wither.

☀ ◐
Z 4–9

HEIGHT
8in (20cm)

SPREAD
3in (8cm)

4in (10cm)

Amaryllidaceae/ Liliaceae	

HIPPEASTRUM 'Apple Blossom'

Habit Robust, bulbous, perennial. *Flowers* Large, open funnel-shaped, in clusters of 2–6, borne on leafless stems in winter. White, with pink-flushed tips. *Leaves* Basal, strap-shaped, and semi-erect, appearing after flowering. Fresh green.
• NATIVE HABITAT Garden origin.
• CULTIVATION Ideal as a conservatory or house plant in colder areas. Prefers general-purpose potting mix. Water well and fertilize every 2 weeks in growth. Needs dry dormancy.
• PROPAGATION Separate offsets in autumn.

☀ ◐
Z 10–11

HEIGHT
12–20in
(30–50cm)

SPREAD
12in (30cm)

Neck above

Amaryllidaceae/ Liliaceae	

HIPPEASTRUM 'Striped'

Habit Robust, bulbous, perennial. *Flowers* Large, open funnel-shaped, in clusters of 2–6, borne on leafless stems in winter. White, with red stripes. *Leaves* Basal, strap-shaped, and semi-erect, appearing after flowering. Fresh green.
• NATIVE HABITAT Garden origin.
• CULTIVATION Ideal as a house or conservatory plant in colder areas. Needs general-pupose potting mix. Water evenly and fertilize every 2 weeks during growth. Keep dry when dormant.
• PROPAGATION Separate offsets in autumn.

☀ ◐
Z 10–11

HEIGHT
20in (50cm)

SPREAD
12in (30cm)

Neck above

Hyacinthaceae/ Liliaceae	

VELTHEIMIA BRACTEATA

Habit Robust, clump-forming, bulbous, perennial. *Flowers* Drooping, tubular, borne in dense, erect spikes in late winter to early spring. Red-pink. *Leaves* Basal and strap-shaped. Mid-green.
• NATIVE HABITAT Grassy or rocky hills, S. Africa.
• CULTIVATION In colder areas, grow as a house or conservatory plant. Needs well-drained potting mix. Water moderately when in growth, but keep the bulb barely moist during dormancy.
• PROPAGATION By offsets, or by seed when ripe.
• OTHER NAMES *V. undulata*, *V. viridifolia*.

☀ ◐
Z 10–11

HEIGHT
12–18in
(30–45cm)

SPREAD
10–15in
(25–38cm)

Neck above

Iridaceae

FREESIA 'Everett'

Habit Slender, cormous, perennial. *Flowers* Fragrant, funnel-shaped, borne in branched, arching spikes from late winter to early spring. Red-pink. *Leaves* Narrowly sword-shaped, upright, forming basal fans. Bright green.
• NATIVE HABITAT Garden origin.
• CULTIVATION Plant corms for winter-flowering during late summer to autumn. Under glass, grow in gritty, soil-based mix with shade from hot sun. Provide good ventilation and a maximum temperature of 55°F (13°C). Water moderately when in growth. Apply a balanced fertilizer on a weekly basis once the flower buds start to appear. Reduce water after flowering, It can be stored dry when dormant. Freesias may be grown outdoors in warm climates, and specially prepared bulbs are available for summer flowering. These may be set out into a warm, sunny border in spring, placed in light, moderately fertile, moist but well-drained soil. Lift in autumn in colder areas. The cut flowers last well in water.
• PROPAGATION Separate offsets in autumn.

☼ ◊

Z 9–10

HEIGHT
to 12in
(30cm)

SPREAD
1in (2.5cm)

3in
(8cm)

Amaryllidaceae/ Liliaceae	

HIPPEASTRUM 'Red Lion'

Habit Robust, bulbous, perennial. **Flowers** Large, open funnels, in clusters of 2–6, borne on leafless stems in winter. Rich red, with yellow anthers. **Leaves** Basal, strap-shaped, semi-erect, appearing with or after the flowers. Fresh green.
• NATIVE HABITAT Garden origin.
• CULTIVATION Grow as a house or conservatory plant in cold areas. Needs moderately fertile, soil-based mix. Water moderately; fertilize every 2 weeks during growth. Keep dry when dormant.
• PROPAGATION Separate offsets in autumn.

☀ ◐

Z 10–11

HEIGHT
12–20in
(30–50cm)

SPREAD
12in (30cm)

Neck above

Amaryllidaceae/ Liliaceae	

HIPPEASTRUM 'Orange Sovereign'

Habit Robust, bulbous, perennial. **Flowers** Large, open funnel-shaped, in clusters of 2–6, borne on leafless stems in winter. Rich orange-red. **Leaves** Basal, strap-shaped, and semi-erect, borne with or just after the flowers. Gray-green.
• NATIVE HABITAT Garden origin.
• CULTIVATION Ideal as a home or conservatory plant in cold areas. Grow in moderately fertile, soil-based mix. Water well and fertilize every 2 weeks during growth. Keep dry when dormant.
• PROPAGATION Separate offsets in autumn.

☀ ◐

Z 10–11

HEIGHT
12–20in
(30–50cm)

SPREAD
12in (30cm)

Neck above

Hyacinthaceae/ Liliaceae	CAPE COWSLIP, LEOPARD LILY

LACHENALIA ORCHIOIDES var. GLAUCINA

Habit Bulbous, perennial. **Flowers** Fragrant, narrowly tubular, borne in dense spikes in late winter. Pale blue, flushed lilac. **Leaves** Strap-shaped and semi-erect. Blue-green, spotted purple.
• NATIVE HABITAT Grasslands, S. Africa.
• CULTIVATION Grow in a cool greenhouse in soil-based mix, in colder areas. Good for rock gardens in warmer climates. Prefers light, well-drained soil. Pot-grown plants need dry dormancy.
• PROPAGATION Separate bulblets in late summer.
• OTHER NAME L. glaucina.

☀ ◐

Z 9–10

HEIGHT
to 12in
(30cm)

SPREAD
2–3in
(5–8cm)

4in
(10cm)

Iridaceae	

FREESIA 'Yellow River'

Habit Slender, cormous, perennial. **Flowers** Fragrant, funnel-shaped, borne in branched, arching spikes in late winter and early spring. Rich yellow. **Leaves** Narrow, basal, and erect. Emerald.
• NATIVE HABITAT Garden origin.
• CULTIVATION Needs gritty, soil-based mix, good ventilation, and a maximum temperature of 55°F (13°C) when grown under glass. Water well and fertilize weekly as flower buds appear. Reduce watering to ensure a dry dormancy.
• PROPAGATION Separate offsets in autumn.

☀ ◐

Z 9–10

HEIGHT
to 12in
(30cm)

SPREAD
1in (2.5cm)

3in
(8cm)

Hyacinthaceae/ Liliaceae	

PUSCHKINIA SCILLOIDES var. *LIBANOTICA* 'Alba'

Habit Bulbous, perennial. *Flowers* Small, star-shaped, open bells, borne in dense, upright clusters in spring. White. *Leaves* Basal, semi-erect, and linear. Rich green.
• NATIVE HABITAT Southeast Europe.
• CULTIVATION Suits a rock garden or naturalizing beneath shrubs. Thrives in any well-drained soil and tolerates partial shade.
• PROPAGATION Separate offsets after the leaves wither in summer.

☼ ◊

Z 3–9

HEIGHT
6in (15cm)

SPREAD
1–2in
(2.5–5cm)

2–3in
(5–8cm)

Hyacinthaceae/ Liliaceae	

ORNITHOGALUM OLIGOPHYLLUM

Habit Slender, bulbous, perennial.
Flowers Widely cup-shaped, borne in broad heads in early spring. Glistening white, with bright-green petal reverse. *Leaves* Basal, almost prostrate, lance-shaped, and glossy. Mid- or grayish-green.
• NATIVE HABITAT Balkan States.
• CULTIVATION Good for growing in a rock garden. Prefers a site with moderately fertile soil.
• PROPAGATION By seed in autumn, or by offsets.
• OTHER NAME *O. balansae.*

☼ ◊

Z 7–10

HEIGHT
to 6in
(15cm)

SPREAD
2–3in
(5–8cm)

4in
(10cm)

Hyacinthaceae/ Liliaceae	

ORNITHOGALUM NUTANS

Habit Sturdy, bulbous, perennial. *Flowers* Star-shaped, nodding, borne in single-sided sprays in spring. Silvery-white, striped green on the petal reverse. *Leaves* Basal, strap-shaped, and semi-erect, appearing before the flowers. Fresh green.
• NATIVE HABITAT Fields and wasteland, Europe and southwest Asia.
• CULTIVATION Tolerates partial shade. Invasive in good conditions, but may be naturalized in grass.
• PROPAGATION By seed in autumn, or by offsets in late summer.

☼ ◊

Z 6–10

HEIGHT
to 24in
(60cm)

SPREAD
2–3in
(5–8cm)

4in
(10cm)

Amaryllidaceae	SPRING SNOWFLAKE

LEUCOJUM VERNUM

Habit Bulbous, perennial. *Flowers* Bell-shaped, borne singly or in pairs on leafless stems, in spring. White, with green tips. *Leaves* Basal, erect, strap-shaped, and glossy. Dark green.
• NATIVE HABITAT Southern and eastern Europe.
• CULTIVATION Suitable for growing in a mixed border, or for naturalizing in turf or in a woodland garden. It can look especially effective when used in waterside plantings.
• PROPAGATION By seed when ripe, or by offsets after the leaves wither.

☀ ◊

Z 4–8

HEIGHT
4–6in
(10–15cm)

SPREAD
3–4in
(8–10cm)

3–4in
(8–10cm)

Amaryllidaceae	

STERNBERGIA CANDIDA

Habit Perennial. *Flowers* Fragrant, funnel-shaped, in late winter and early spring. White. *Leaves* Strap-shaped and basal. Gray-green.
• NATIVE HABITAT Rocky scrub on the edge of cedar forests in southwest Turkey.
• CULTIVATION Dislikes being exposed to winter moisture. Grows best in a bulb frame or alpine house in areas where cold, wet winters are common. Needs moderately fertile, sharply drained soil.
• PROPAGATION By seed when ripe, or by offsets after leaves wither.

☀ ◊

Z 6–9

HEIGHT
4–8in
(10–20cm)

SPREAD
3–4in
(8–10cm)

8in
(20cm)

Hyacinthaceae/ Liliaceae	

ORNITHOGALUM LANCEOLATUM

Habit Dwarf, bulbous, perennial. *Flowers* Star-shaped, borne in compact, almost stemless heads in spring. White, with green-stripes on petal reverse. *Leaves* Prostrate, lance-shaped, and glossy, forming basal rosettes. Mid-green.
• NATIVE HABITAT Dry hillsides, Turkey, Syria, and Lebanon.
• CULTIVATION Suitable for growing in a rock garden, with moderately fertile, well-drained soil.
• PROPAGATION By seed in autumn, or by offsets in late summer.

☀ ◊

Z 5–10

HEIGHT
2–4in
(5–10cm)

SPREAD
4–6in
(10–15cm)

4in
(10cm)

Hyacinthaceae/ Liliaceae	

ORNITHOGALUM MONTANUM

Habit Clump-forming, bulbous, perennial. *Flowers* Star-shaped, in broad clusters, borne on leafless stems in spring. White, with green stripes on petal reverse. *Leaves* Basal, prostrate, and strap-shaped. Pale gray-green.
• NATIVE HABITAT Rocky and grassy hillsides, southern Europe, Turkey, Lebanon, and Israel.
• CULTIVATION Good for growing in a rock garden, or for naturalizing in short turf or beneath shrubs.
• PROPAGATION By seed in autumn, or by offsets in late summer.

☀ ◊

Z 5–10

HEIGHT
4–10in
(10–25cm)

SPREAD
4–6in
(10–15cm)

4in
(10cm)

Liliaceae	FAWN LILY

ERYTHRONIUM CALIFORNICUM

Habit Clumping, bulbous, perennial. **Flowers** Drooping, with reflexed petals, 1–3 borne on sturdy, leafless stems in spring. Creamy-white, with central orange-brown ring and white anthers. **Leaves** Oval. Dark green, mottled brown-green.
• NATIVE HABITAT Scrub, evergreen, and mixed woods in Californian mountains.
• CULTIVATION Excellent for a woodland garden, or as underplantings in a shrub border. Needs a leaf-rich, fertile, moisture-retentive soil.
• PROPAGATION By offsets after flowering.

☼ ◐ ○

Z 3–9

HEIGHT
6–14in
(15–35cm)

SPREAD
4–5in
(10–12cm)

■ 4in
(10cm)

Alliaceae/Liliaceae	

ALLIUM AKAKA

Habit Bulbous, perennial. **Flowers** Small, star-shaped, borne in spherical, almost stemless, sprays in spring. White or pink-flushed, with red center. **Leaves** Basal and broadly oval. Gray-green.
• NATIVE HABITAT Screes and rocky mountain slopes in Caucasus, Turkey, and Iran.
• CULTIVATION Suitable for growing in a sunny rock garden or bulb frame. Needs protection from moisture during winter dormancy.
• PROPAGATION By seed as soon as ripe, or by offsets in autumn.

☼ ○

Z 4–9

HEIGHT
5–6in
(12–15cm)

SPREAD
5–6in
(12–15cm)

■ 3–4in
(8–10cm)

Alliaceae/Liliaceae	

ALLIUM KARATAVIENSE

Habit Sturdy, bulbous, perennial. **Flowers** Small, star-shaped, borne in spherical clusters on leafless stems, in late spring. White to pale pink. **Leaves** Basal, oval, growing horizontally in pairs. Purple-tinted, gray-green with red margins.
• NATIVE HABITAT Mountains, central Asia.
• CULTIVATION Easily grown in a warm, sheltered site in full sun, but must have good drainage. Ideal for planting in a mixed or herbaceous border.
• PROPAGATION By seed as soon as ripe, or by offsets in autumn.

☼ ○

Z 4–9

HEIGHT
4–10in
(10–25cm)

SPREAD
4–10in
(10–25cm)

■ 3–4in
(8–10cm)

Hyacinthaceae/ Liliaceae	

CHIONODOXA FORBESII 'Pink Giant'

Habit Bulbous, perennial. *Flowers* Star-shaped, borne in spikes on leafless stems in early spring. Soft pink, with a white eye. *Leaves* Basal, semi-erect, and broadly linear. Mid-green.
• NATIVE HABITAT Garden origin.
• CULTIVATION Suitable for planting in a rock garden, or for naturalizing beneath deciduous shrubs. Easily grown in any well-drained soil.
• PROPAGATION Separate offsets in summer after leaves wither.
• OTHER NAME *C. siehei* 'Pink Giant'.

☀ ◊

Z 3–9

HEIGHT
4–10in
(10–25cm)

SPREAD
1–2in
(2.5–5cm)

3in
(8cm)

Primulaceae	

CYCLAMEN LIBANOTICUM

Habit Tuberous, perennial. *Flowers* Shuttlecock-shaped with reflexed petals, borne in winter and early spring. Pale to mid-pink, with white base and red mouth. *Leaves* Rounded and heart-shaped. Dull green, with paler patterns and red underside.
• NATIVE HABITAT Among limestone rocks, Lebanese mountains.
• CULTIVATION Grows best in an alpine house, in leaf-rich, gritty soil with added limestone chips.
• PROPAGATION Soak and rinse seed as soon as ripe, then sow in darkness.

☀ ◊

Z 9–10

HEIGHT
4in (10cm)

SPREAD
6in (15cm)

1in
(2.5cm)

Liliaceae	DOG'S-TOOTH VIOLET

ERYTHRONIUM DENS-CANIS

Habit Bulbous, perennial. *Flowers* Drooping, reflexed petals, borne in late spring. Purple, pink, or white, with brown, purple, and yellow basal bands. *Leaves* Oval. Mid-green, with purple-brown marbling.
• NATIVE HABITAT Scrub, meadows, and woodland in Europe and Asia.
• CULTIVATION Excellent for a woodland garden, or for naturalizing in turf. Needs moist but well-drained, leaf-rich, fertile soil in partial shade.
• PROPAGATION Separate offsets after flowering.

☀ ◊

Z 3–9

HEIGHT
6–10in
(15–25cm)

SPREAD
3–4in
(8–10cm)

4in
(10cm)

CROCUS

Crocus are valued for their goblet-shaped flowers and early bloom season. They are grouped by cultivation needs.

Group 1 Gritty, well-drained, poor to moderately fertile soil in full sun.

Group 2 In a bulb frame or alpine house, with a mix of equal parts soil, leaf mold, and grit or sharp sand, in full light. A dry summer dormancy is needed.

Group 3 Fairly moist but well-drained, leaf-rich soil, in sun or partial shade.

Plant spring-flowering corms in autumn, and autumn-flowering ones in late summer. Seed-raised plants take 2 to 4 years before flowering. For propagation, see p. 175. Increase cultivars by separation of cormlets during dormancy. Flowers are produced within 1 to 2 years.

C. TOMMASINIANUS f. ALBUS
Habit Dwarf, cormous, perennial.
Flowers Slender, funnel-shaped, borne in late winter to early spring. Pure white.
Leaves Linear. Dark green, with white stripe.
• CULTIVATION 1. May self-seed. Good for naturalizing in turf.
• HEIGHT to 4in (10cm).
• SPREAD 1in (2.5cm).

C. tommasinianus f. albus

☀ ◊   Z 3–8

C. MALYI
Habit Dwarf, cormous, perennial.
Flowers Long-tubed, funnel-shaped, borne in spring. White, often suffused purple at the base, with yellow throat.
Leaves Linear. Mid-green, with white stripe.
• CULTIVATION 2. Needs to be kept dry in summer dormancy.
• HEIGHT 3in (8cm).
• SPREAD 1½in (4cm).

C. malyi

☀ ◊   Z 3–8

C. VERNUS. subsp. ALBIFLORUS
Habit Dwarf, cormous, perennial.
Flowers Slender, funnel-shaped, with pointed petals, borne in spring. White.
Leaves Linear. Dark green, with white stripe.
• CULTIVATION 1. More difficult to grow than the species.
• HEIGHT 4in (10cm).
• SPREAD 2in (5cm).

C. vernus subsp. *albiflorus*

☀ ◊   Z 3–8

C. SIEBERI 'Albus'
Habit Dwarf, cormous, perennial.
Flowers Goblet-shaped, borne in spring. White, with golden throat.
Leaves Linear. Dark green, with white stripe.
• CULTIVATION 1. Suitable for growing in a rock garden.
• OTHER NAME *C. sieberi* 'Bowles' White'.
• HEIGHT to 3in (8cm).
• SPREAD 1in (2.5cm).

C. sieberi 'Albus'

☀ ◊   Z 3–8

C. BORYI
Habit Dwarf, cormous, perennial.
Flowers Goblet-shaped, borne in autumn. Ivory-white, usually flushed mauve outside.
Leaves Linear. Dark green, with white stripe.
• CULTIVATION 2. Suitable for growing in a bulb frame or alpine house.
• HEIGHT 3in (8cm).
• SPREAD 2in (5cm).

C. boryi

☀ ◊   Z 4–8

C. CHRYSANTHUS 'Snow Bunting'
Habit Dwarf, cormous, perennial. *Flowers* Funnel-shaped, borne in spring. Creamy-white, with pale, blue-gray feathering outside. *Leaves* Linear. Dull mid-green.
• CULTIVATION 1. Suits rock gardens or borders, and naturalizing.
• HEIGHT 3in (7cm).
• SPREAD 2in (5cm).

C. chrysanthus **'Snow Bunting'**

☼ ◊　　　　Z 3–8

C. CHRYSANTHUS 'Eye-catcher'
Habit Dwarf, cormous, perennial. *Flowers* Funnel-shaped, borne in spring. Palest gray, deep purple outer, and yellow throat. *Leaves* Linear. Dull mid-green.
• CULTIVATION 1. Good for growing in a rock garden or border.
• HEIGHT 3in (7cm).
• SPREAD 2in (5cm).

C. chrysanthus **'Eye-catcher'**

☼ ◊　　　　Z 3–8

C. HADRIATICUS
Habit Dwarf, cormous, perennial. *Flowers* Goblet-shaped, borne in autumn. White, with a yellow throat. *Leaves* Linear. Mid-green.
• CULTIVATION 1 or 2. Suits a rock garden.
• OTHER NAME *C. hadriaticus* var. *chrysobelonicus*.
• HEIGHT 3in (8cm).
• SPREAD 1½in (4cm).

C. hadriaticus

☼ ◊　　　　Z 5–8

C. OCHROLEUCUS
Habit Dwarf, cormous, perennial. *Flowers* Funnel-shaped, borne with or before the leaves in late autumn. Creamy-white with pale gold throat. *Leaves* Linear. Bright green.
• CULTIVATION 1 or 2. Suitable for naturalizing in turf.
• HEIGHT 2in (5cm).
• SPREAD 1in (2.5cm).

C. ochroleucus

☼ ◊　　　　Z 6–8

C. CHRYSANTHUS 'Cream Beauty'
Habit Compact, cormous, perennial. *Flowers* Scented, short-tubed, borne in spring. Rich cream, with green-gold base and golden throat. *Leaves* Linear. Dull mid-green.
• CULTIVATION 1. Good for naturalizing in turf.
• HEIGHT 3in (7cm).
• SPREAD 2in (5cm).

C. chrysanthus **'Cream Beauty'**

☼ ◊　　　　Z 3–8

C. CHRYSANTHUS
'Blue Bird'
Habit Dwarf, cormous, perennial.
Flowers Funnel-shaped, borne in spring. Palest blue, with violet outer and golden-yellow throat.
Leaves Linear. Dull mid-green.
• CULTIVATION 1. Good for a border front or rock garden.
• HEIGHT 3in (7cm).
• SPREAD 2in (5cm).

C. chrysanthus 'Blue Bird'

☼ ◊   Z 3–8

C. DALMATICUS
Habit Dwarf, cormous, perennial.
Flowers Goblet-shaped, solitary, borne in late winter and early spring. Pale lilac, with buff or silver overlay outside and faint purple lines.
Leaves Linear. Dark green, with silver stripe.
• CULTIVATION 1. Good for a rock garden.
• HEIGHT 3in (8cm).
• SPREAD 1½in (4cm).

C. dalmaticus

☼ ◊   Z 3–8

C. LAEVIGATUS
Habit Dwarf, cormous, perennial.
Flowers Scented, borne intermittently with the leaves in autumn and winter. Pale lilac-purple, feathered heavy purple.
Leaves Linear. Dark green.
• CULTIVATION 1 or 2. Suitable for naturalizing in grass.
• HEIGHT to 3in (8cm).
• SPREAD 1½in (4cm).

C. laevigatus

☼ ◊   Z 5–8

C. SIEBERI subsp. SUBLIMIS f. TRICOLOR
Habit Slender, cormous, perennial.
Flowers Slender, funnel-shaped, borne in late winter and early spring. Banded lilac, white and deep golden-yellow.
Leaves Linear. Mid-green, with white stripe.
• CULTIVATION 1. Best in a raised bed.
• HEIGHT 1½in (4cm).
• SPREAD 1in (2.5cm).

C. sieberi subsp. *sublimis* f. *tricolor*

☼ ◊   Z 3–8

C. KOTSCHYANUS
Habit Vigorous, dwarf, cormous, perennial.
Flowers Solitary, long-tubed, borne before the leaves in autumn. Pale lilac, with yellow throat.
Leaves Linear. Dark green, with white stripe.
• CULTIVATION 1 or 2.
• OTHER NAME *C. zonatus.*
• HEIGHT to 3in (8cm).
• SPREAD 2in (5cm)

C. kotschyanus

☼ ◊   Z 3–8

C. ETRUSCUS
'Zwanenburg'
Habit Dwarf, cormous, perennial.
Flowers Funnel-shaped, long-tubed, borne in late winter. Lilac-blue, with silver or buff wash outside and purple veins.
Leaves Linear. Dark green, with white stripe.
• CULTIVATION 1. Good for a rock garden.
• HEIGHT 3in (8cm).
• SPREAD 1½in (4cm).

C. etruscus 'Zwanenburg'

☼ ◊   Z 5–8

C. MINIMUS
Habit Dwarf, cormous, perennial.
Flowers Long-tubed, borne in late spring. Mid- to deep lilac-purple, with dark violet feathering or lines outside.
Leaves Linear. Dark green, with white stripe.
• CULTIVATION 1. Good for a rock garden.
• HEIGHT 3in (8cm).
• SPREAD 1in (2.5cm).

C. minimus

☼ ◊   Z 3–8

C. TOMMASINIANUS 'Ruby Giant'
Habit Clump-forming, cormous, perennial.
Flowers Slender, long-tubed, funnel-shaped, borne in late winter and spring. Rich red-purple. A sterile cultivar.
Leaves Linear. Dark green, with white stripe.
• CULTIVATION 1. Will grow in fine turf.
• HEIGHT 4in (10cm).
• SPREAD 1in (2.5cm).

C. tommasinianus **'Ruby Giant'**

☼ ◊   Z 3–8

C. MEDIUS
Habit Dwarf, cormous, perennial.
Flowers Funnel-shaped, long-tubed, borne before the leaves in late autumn Uniform, vivid purple, sometimes paler, with orange-red styles.
Leaves Linear. Mid-green.
• CULTIVATION 1. Good for a rock garden.
• HEIGHT 3in (8cm).
• SPREAD 1in (2.5cm).

C. medius

☼ ◊   Z 3–8

C. TOMMASINIANUS 'Whitewell Purple'
Habit Vigorous, dwarf, cormous, perennial.
Flowers Funnel-shaped, borne in late winter and spring. Red-purple, silver-mauve inside.
Leaves Linear. Dark green, with white stripe.
• CULTIVATION 1. Colonizes rapidly. Good for naturalizing in turf.
• HEIGHT to 4in (10cm).
• SPREAD 1in (2.5cm).

C. tommasinianus **'Whitewell Purple'**

☼ ◊   Z 3–8

C. NUDIFLORUS
Habit Dwarf, cormous, perennial, with stolons.
Flowers Solitary, long-tubed, borne before the leaves in autumn. Rich purple.
Leaves Linear. Dark green.
• CULTIVATION 3. Good for naturalizing, in sun or part-shade, with moist, well-drained soil.
• HEIGHT 10in (25cm).
• SPREAD 2in (5cm).

C. nudiflorus

☼ ◔   Z 3–8

C. BANATICUS
Habit Dwarf, cormous, perennial.
Flowers Solitary, long-tubed, with 3 large outer petals and 3 small, erect, inner ones. Lilac-purple.
Leaves Linear. Dark green, with a paler stripe.
• CULTIVATION 1. Increases slowly.
• OTHER NAME *C. iridiflorus*.
• HEIGHT 4in (10cm).
• SPREAD 2in (5cm).

C. banaticus

☼ ◊   Z 3–8

C. PULCHELLUS
Habit Dwarf, cormous, perennial.
Flowers Goblet-shaped, long-tubed, borne in autumn and winter. Pale lilac-blue, faintly veined violet, with yellow throat.
Leaves Linear. Dark green, with white stripe.
• CULTIVATION 1. Suitable for naturalizing in grass.
• HEIGHT to 5in (12cm).
• SPREAD 1½in (4cm).

C. pulchellus

☼ ◊   Z 3–8

C. IMPERATI 'De Jager'
Habit Dwarf, cormous, perennial.
Flowers Long-tubed, borne in late winter and spring. Violet-purple inside, buff outside.
Leaves Linear and shiny. Dark green.
• CULTIVATION 1. Good for growing in a border or rock garden.
• HEIGHT 4in (10cm).
• SPREAD 1½in (4cm).

C. imperati 'De Jager'

☼ ◊   Z 3–8

C. LONGIFLORUS
Habit Dwarf, cormous, perennial.
Flowers Slender, strongly scented, borne before leaves in autumn. Purple, with darker, outer stripes and yellow center.
Leaves Linear. Dark green, with white stripe.
• CULTIVATION 2. Best grown in an alpine house or bulb frame.
• HEIGHT to 4in (10cm).
• SPREAD 1¼in (3cm).

C. longiflorus

☼ ◊   Z 5–8

C. CORSICUS
Habit Dwarf, cormous, perennial.
Flowers Slender, scented, borne in late spring and early summer. Lilac inside, with paler, violet-striped outside and orange styles.
Leaves Linear. Dark green.
• CULTIVATION 1 or 2. Suits a rock garden.
• HEIGHT to 4in (10cm).
• SPREAD 1½in (4cm).

C. corsicus

☼ ◊   Z 6–9

C. VERNUS 'Remembrance'
Habit Dwarf, cormous, perennial.
Flowers Solitary, goblet-shaped, borne in late spring. Glossy violet.
Leaves Linear. Dark green, with white stripe.
• CULTIVATION 1. Good for naturalizing in grass.
• HEIGHT to 5in (12cm).
• SPREAD 2in (5cm).

C. vernus 'Remembrance'

☼ ◊   Z 3–8

C. VERNUS

Habit Dwarf,
cormous perennial.
Flowers Solitary, goblet-
shaped, borne in spring
or early summer. White,
or shades of lilac-purple.
Leaves Linear. Mid-
green, with white stripe.
• CULTIVATION 1.
Good for naturalizing in
grass, and suitable for
the front of a border.
• HEIGHT to 5in (12cm).
• SPREAD 2in (5cm).

C. vernus

☼ ◊   Z 3–8

C. SPECIOSUS 'Conqueror'

Habit Dwarf,
cormous perennial.
Flowers Solitary,
long-tubed, large,
borne in autumn,
appearing before the
leaves. Deep sky-blue.
Leaves Linear.
Mid-green.
• CULTIVATION 1.
Suitable for borders
and naturalizing.
• HEIGHT to 6in (15cm).
• SPREAD 2in (5cm).

C. speciosus 'Conqueror'

☼ ◊   Z 3–8

C. SPECIOSUS

Habit Dwarf,
cormous, perennial.
Flowers Solitary, long-
tubed, borne in autumn,
appearing before the
leaves. Violet-blue
with darker blue veins
and orange styles.
Leaves Linear.
Mid-green.
• CULTIVATION 1.
Good for naturalizing.
• HEIGHT to 6in (15cm).
• SPREAD 2in (5cm).

C. speciosus

☼ ◊   Z 3–8

C. VERNUS 'Purpureus Grandiflorus'

Habit Free-flowering,
cormous, perennial.
Flowers Single, goblet-
shaped, borne in late
spring. Glossy violet,
with purple base.
Leaves Linear. Dark
green, with white stripe.
• CULTIVATION 1.
Will naturalize in grass.
• HEIGHT to 5in (12cm).
• SPREAD 2in (5cm).

C. vernus 'Purpureus Grandiflorus'

☼ ◊   Z 3–8

C. VERNUS 'Prinses Juliana'

Habit Dwarf,
cormous, perennial.
Flowers Solitary, goblet-
shaped, borne in late
spring. Mid-purple
with darker veins.
Leaves Linear. Dark
green, with white stripe.
• CULTIVATION 1.
Good for naturalizing
in grass.
• HEIGHT to 5in (12cm).
• SPREAD 2in (5cm).

C. vernus 'Prinses Juliana'

☼ ◊   Z 3–8

C. VERNUS 'Queen of the Blues'

Habit Dwarf,
cormous, perennial.
Flowers Solitary, goblet-
shaped, borne in late
spring. Lilac-blue, paler
at the margins and
darker at the base.
Leaves Linear. Dark
green, with white stripes.
• CULTIVATION 1.
Will naturalize in grass.
• HEIGHT to 5in (12cm).
• SPREAD 2in (5cm).

C. vernus 'Queen of the Blues'

☼ ◊   Z 3–8

C. GOULIMYI
Habit Dwarf,
cormous, perennial.
Flowers Funnel-shaped,
long-tubed, fragrant,
borne with the leaves
in autumn. Pale lilac.
Leaves Linear.
Mid-green.
• CULTIVATION 1 or 2.
Best in a warm site in
sun. Suitable for a rock
garden or raised bed.
• HEIGHT 4in (10cm).
• SPREAD 2in (5cm).

C. goulimyi

☼ ◊   Z 3–8

C. CARTWRIGHTIANUS
Habit Dwarf,
cormous, perennial.
Flowers Goblet-shaped,
scented, borne with or
just after the leaves in
autumn and early winter.
White to deep lilac,
with deep purple veins.
Leaves Linear.
Mid-green.
• CULTIVATION 2.
Best in an alpine house.
• HEIGHT 2in (5cm).
• SPREAD 2in (5cm).

C. cartwrightianus

☼ ◊   Z 6–8

C. BIFLORUS
Habit Variable, dwarf,
cormous, perennial.
Flowers Slender, funnel-
shaped, borne in early
spring. Lilac-blue or
white, striped purple or
purple-brown outside.
Leaves Linear. Mid-
green, with white stripe.
• CULTIVATION 1.
Good specimen for
growing in a rock garden.
• HEIGHT 2½in (6cm).
• SPREAD 2in (5cm).

C. biflorus

☼ ◊   Z 3–8

C. ETRUSCUS
Habit Dwarf,
cormous, perennial.
Flowers Funnel-shaped,
long-tubed, borne in late
winter and spring. Pale
purple-blue, violet veins
and silver wash outside.
Leaves Linear. Dark
green, with white stripe.
• CULTIVATION 1.
Good specimen for
growing in a rock garden.
• HEIGHT 3in (8cm).
• SPREAD 1½in (4cm).

C. etruscus

☼ ◊   Z 5–8

C. SPECIOSUS
'Oxonian'
Habit Dwarf,
cormous, perennial.
Flowers Solitary, long-
tubed, borne in autumn.
Violet-mauve, with
darker veins outside.
Leaves Linear, after
flowering. Mid-green.
• CULTIVATION 1.
Good for naturalizing
in turf.
• HEIGHT to 6in (15cm).
• SPREAD 2in (5cm).

C. speciosus 'Oxonian'

☼ ◊   Z 3–8

C. SIEBERI
'Hubert Edelsten'
Habit Dwarf,
cormous, perennial.
Flowers Goblet-shaped,
borne in late winter and
early spring. Pale lilac,
with yellow throat. Deep
purple and white outside.
Leaves Linear. Dark
green, with white stripe.
• CULTIVATION 1.
Good for a rock garden.
• HEIGHT to 3in (8cm).
• SPREAD 1in (2.5cm).

C. sieberi
'Hubert Edelsten'

☼ ◊   Z 3–8

C. BAYTOPIORUM
Habit Dwarf,
cormous, perennial.
Flowers Slender,
goblet-shaped, borne
during early spring.
Pale turquoise-blue,
with darker veins.
Leaves Linear and
smooth. Dark green.
• CULTIVATION 2.
Grow in an alpine
house or bulb frame.
• HEIGHT 2in (5cm).
• SPREAD 1in (2.5cm).

C. baytopiorum

☼ ◊   Z 4–8

C. CHRYSANTHUS
'Blue Pearl'
Habit Dwarf,
cormous, perennial.
Flowers Fragrant,
funnel-shaped, borne
in spring. White, with
yellow throat and lilac-
blue outer petals.
Leaves Linear. Green,
with white stripe.
• CULTIVATION 1.
Suitable for naturalizing.
• HEIGHT 3in (7cm).
• SPREAD 2in (5cm).

C. chrysanthus
'Blue Pearl'

☼ ◊   Z 3–8

C. VERNUS
'Pickwick'
Habit Dwarf,
cormous, perennial.
Flowers Goblet-shaped,
borne in late spring.
White, with deep and
pale lilac stripes and
deep purple base.
Leaves Linear. Green,
with white stripe.
• CULTIVATION 1.
Good for naturalizing.
• HEIGHT to 5in (12cm).
• SPREAD 2in (5cm).

C. vernus 'Pickwick'

☼ ◊   Z 3–8

C. CHRYSANTHUS
'Ladykiller'
Habit Dwarf,
cormous, perennial.
Flowers Funnel-shaped,
borne in late winter or
mid-spring. White,
marked deep violet-
purple outside.
Leaves Linear. Mid-
green, striped white.
• CULTIVATION 1.
Suitable for naturalizing.
• HEIGHT 3in (7cm).
• SPREAD 2in (5cm).

C. chrysanthus
'Ladykiller'

☼ ◊   Z 3–8

C. CHRYSANTHUS
'E.A. Bowles'
Habit Dwarf,
cormous, perennial.
Flowers Goblet-shaped,
borne in spring. Rich
lemon-yellow, purple
feathering and bronze
base on outer petals.
Leaves Linear. Dark
green, with white stripe.
• CULTIVATION 1.
Suitable for naturalizing.
• HEIGHT 3in (7cm).
• SPREAD 2in (5cm).

C. chrysanthus
'E.A. Bowles'

☼ ◊   Z 3–8

C. 'Golden Bunch'
Habit Dwarf,
cormous, perennial.
Flowers Scented,
well-rounded, borne in
clusters of 5 in late
winter and early spring.
Bright yellow or orange.
Leaves Linear.
Grayish-green.
• CULTIVATION 1.
Ideal for a rock garden.
• OTHER NAME
C. ancyrensis
'Golden Bunch'.
• HEIGHT 2in (5cm).
• SPREAD 1½in (4cm).

C. 'Golden Bunch'

☼ ◊   Z 3–8

C. CVIJICII
Habit Slender,
cormous, perennial.
Flowers Solitary, funnel-
shaped, borne just before
the leaves in spring.
Golden-yellow, or cream.
Leaves Linear. Mid-
green, striped silver.
• CULTIVATION 2.
Suits an alpine house
or bulb frame that does
not dry out.
• HEIGHT 4in (10cm).
• SPREAD 1½in (4cm).

C. cvijicii

☼ ◊   Z 3–8

C. GARGARICUS
Habit Dwarf, perennial,
with tiny corms.
Flowers Slender,
solitary, borne in spring.
Bright orange-yellow.
Leaves Linear. Dark
green, with white stripe.
• CULTIVATION 3.
Needs to be grown in
a sunny or part-shaded
site, with moist, but
well-drained soil.
• HEIGHT 1½in (4cm).
• SPREAD 1in (2.5cm).

C. gargaricus

☼ ◊   Z 5–8

Alliaceae/Liliaceae	

ALLIUM ACUMINATUM

Habit Bulbous, perennial. *Flowers* Small, open
bell-shaped, borne in a loose, hemispherical spray
in early summer. Purplish-pink. *Leaves* Linear,
channeled, basal, and stem-clasping. Mid-green.
• NATIVE HABITAT Western N. America.
• CULTIVATION Prefers moderately fertile,
well-drained soil. Suitable for planting in a
warm, sunny herbaceous border or rock garden.
• PROPAGATION By seed as soon as ripe,
or by offsets in autumn.
• OTHER NAME *A. murrayanum.*

☀ ◊

Z 4–9

HEIGHT
4–12in
(10–30cm)

SPREAD
2–3in
(5–8cm)

3–4in
(8–10cm)

Alliaceae/Liliaceae	

ALLIUM OREOPHILUM

Habit Dwarf, bulbous, perennial. *Flowers* Small,
bell-shaped, borne in loose, domed clusters in early
summer. Bright purplish-pink. *Leaves* Linear,
sheathing the stem at the base. Mid-green.
• NATIVE HABITAT Stony mountain slopes of
Caucasus and central Asia.
• CULTIVATION Grow in moderately fertile, well-
drained soil, in a herbaceous border or rock garden.
• PROPAGATION By seed as soon as ripe, or by
offsets in autumn.
• OTHER NAME *A. ostrowskianum.*

☀ ◊

Z 4–9

HEIGHT
2–8in
(5–20cm)

SPREAD
3–4in
(8–10cm)

3–4in
(8–10cm)

Ranunculaceae	

ANEMONE BLANDA 'Radar'

Habit Spreading, tuberous, perennial.
Flowers Solitary, upright, flattened saucers, borne
in early spring. Deep magenta, with a white center.
Leaves Deeply lobed and toothed. Dark green.
• NATIVE HABITAT Garden origin.
• CULTIVATION Needs moderately fertile soil
that is rich in organic matter, and prefers a site
in dappled shade or sun. Useful for underplanting,
especially beneath deciduous trees and shrubs.
• PROPAGATION Separate offset tubers when
dormant in summer.

☀ ◊

Z 4–8

HEIGHT
2–4in
(5–10cm)

SPREAD
4–6in
(10–15cm)

2–3in
(5–8cm)

Ranunculaceae	

ANEMONE × *FULGENS*

Habit Tuberous, perennial. *Flowers* Single,
erect cup, borne on sturdy stems in spring or early
summer. Rich red, with dark center. *Leaves* Basal,
divided, deeply lobed, and toothed. Mid-green.
• NATIVE HABITAT Garden origin.
• CULTIVATION Easily grown in light, sandy soil
that is well-drained. Prefers a warm, sunny site.
Excellent for planting at the front of a sunny
border or in a rock garden.
• PROPAGATION Separate offset tubers when
dormant in summer.

☀ ◊

Z 8–10

HEIGHT
4–12in
(10–30cm)

SPREAD
6in (15cm)

2–3in
(5–8cm)

Iridaceae	HARLEQUIN FLOWER

SPARAXIS TRICOLOR

Habit Cormous, perennial. **Flowers** Open-tubed, borne in spring. Orange, purple, red, pink, or white, with black or red center. **Leaves** Upright and lance-shaped, forming basal fans. Mid-green.
• NATIVE HABITAT Damp, rocky areas, S. Africa.
• CULTIVATION Good for the base of a warm sunny wall in mild areas. Where frost occurs, grow in a cool greenhouse. Needs light, fertile, well-drained soil. Provide a deep, dry, winter mulch.
• PROPAGATION Separate offsets when dormant, or sow seed as soon as ripe.

☼ ◊

Z 9–10

Height
4–16in
(10–40cm)

Spread
3in (8cm)

4in
(10cm)

Araceae	MOUSETAIL PLANT

ARISARUM PROBOSCIDEUM

Habit Spreading, often mat-forming, rhizomatous, perennial. **Flowers** Small, hooded, with a long, slender tip resembling a mouse's tail, borne in spring. Deep brown-purple, fading to whitish-blue. **Leaves** Glossy and arrow-shaped. Dark green.
• NATIVE HABITAT Woodland in Italy and Spain.
• CULTIVATION Suits a woodland, rock garden, or shady border. Needs moist but well-drained soil, rich in organic matter, in partial or dappled shade.
• PROPAGATION Sow seed in spring, or divide rhizome in autumn.

◐ ◊

Z 7–9

Height
6in (15cm)

Spread
From 4in
(10cm)

2in
(5cm)

Colchicaceae/Liliaceae	

BULBOCODIUM VERNUM

Habit Cormous, perennial. **Flowers** Stemless, widely funnel-shaped, borne in spring. Pinkish-purple. **Leaves** Linear, glossy, growing longer after flowering. Dark green.
• NATIVE HABITAT Meadows in the Pyrenees, and in the southwest and central Alps.
• CULTIVATION Suits a rock garden or raised bed, or naturalizing in turf. Needs well-drained soil enriched with organic matter, in open, sunny site.
• PROPAGATION Sow seed in autumn or spring, or separate offsets in summer.

☼ ◊

Z 3–9

Height
1¼–1½ in
(3–4cm)

Spread
1¼–2in
(3–5cm)

3in
(8cm)

Iridaceae	

ROMULEA BULBOCODIUM

Habit Slender, cormous, perennial. **Flowers** Solitary, upright funnels, borne in spring. Pale to deep lilac, with white or yellow center. **Leaves** Basal, linear, recurved, and channeled. Mid-green.
• NATIVE HABITAT Sandy, rocky, coastal sites and scrubland in Portugal and southern Spain.
• CULTIVATION Suitable for a trough, raised bed or bulb frame. Keep dry during summer dormancy.
• PROPAGATION By seed when ripe, or by offsets when dormant.
• OTHER NAME *R. grandiflorum.*

☼ ◊

Z 9–10

HEIGHT
2–4in
(5–10cm)

SPREAD
1–2in
(2.5–5cm)

3in
(8cm)

Iridaceae	WINECUPS

BABIANA RUBROCYANEA

Habit Cormous, perennial. **Flowers** Funnel-shaped, borne in spikes of 5–10 in spring. Blue-purple, with scarlet base. **Leaves** Erect, folded, lance-shaped, and hairy. Fresh green.
• NATIVE HABITAT Grassland and hills, S. Africa.
• CULTIVATION Suitable for planting at the front of a sunny border. Grow as a house or conservatory plant in colder areas. Needs light, fertile, well-drained soil enriched with organic matter.
• PROPAGATION By seed as soon as ripe, or by offsets when dormant.

☼ ◊

Z 9–10

HEIGHT
6–8in
(15–20cm)

SPREAD
2in (5cm)

8in
(20cm)

Alliaceae/Liliaceae	

IPHEION UNIFLORUM 'Froyle Mill'

Habit Clump-forming, bulbous, perennial. **Flowers** Fragrant, solitary, facing upwards, star-shaped, borne on strong, slender stems in spring. Dusky violet. **Leaves** Semi-erect and narrowly strap-shaped. Bluish-green.
• NATIVE HABITAT Garden origin.
• CULTIVATION Suitable for growing in a rock garden or for underplanting in an herbaceous border. Needs moderately fertile, moist but well-drained soil that is rich in organic matter.
• PROPAGATION Divide when dormant in summer.

◑ ◊

Z 6–9

HEIGHT
4–6in
(10–15cm)

SPREAD
2–3in
(5–8cm)

3in
(8cm)

Iridaceae	

GYNANDRIRIS SISYRINCHIUM

Habit Cormous, perennial. **Flowers** Small, iris-like, borne on wiry stems in spring, opening in the afternoon. Pale lavender to violet-blue, marked white, yellow, or orange. **Leaves** Basal, narrow, channeled, semi-erect, or prostrate. Mid-green.
• NATIVE HABITAT In open scrubland, from the Mediterranean to southwest Asia.
• CULTIVATION Needs moisture in winter and early spring, followed by a dry, summer dormancy.
• PROPAGATION By seed as soon as ripe, or by offsets in summer.

☼ ◊

Z 9–10

HEIGHT
4–12in
(10–30cm)

SPREAD
3–4in
(8–10cm)

3in
(8cm)

Hyacinthaceae/ Liliaceae	FEATHER GRAPE HYACINTH

MUSCARI COMOSUM 'Plumosum'

Habit Bulbous, perennial. **Flowers** Branching, feathery, sterile spikes of threads, borne in spring. Purple. **Leaves** Basal and linear. Mid-green.
• NATIVE HABITAT Garden origin.
• CULTIVATION Suitable for planting at the front of a mixed or herbaceous border, or in a rock garden. Needs moist but well-drained, moderately fertile soil, and a warm, sunny site.
• PROPAGATION By offsets in summer.
• OTHER NAMES *M. c.* 'Monstrosum', *Leopoldia comosa* var. *plumosum*.

☼ ◊

Z 2–9

HEIGHT
10in (25cm)

SPREAD
4–5in
(10–12cm)

4in
(10cm)

Hyacinthaceae/ Liliaceae	STRIPED SQUILL

PUSCHKINIA SCILLOIDES

Habit Bulbous, perennial. **Flowers** Small, bell-shaped, borne in dense, upright spikes in spring. Pale blue, with darker median stripe on petal. **Leaves** Basal, semi-erect, and linear. Green.
• NATIVE HABITAT Snow-flushed meadows, from Caucasus to Lebanon.
• CULTIVATION Good for a rock garden or for planting beneath shrubs. Tolerates partial shade.
• PROPAGATION Separate offsets after the leaves wither in summer.
• OTHER NAMES *P. libanotica, P. hyacinthoides.*

☼ ◊ ◑

Z 3–9

HEIGHT
6in (15cm)

SPREAD
1–2in
(2.5–5cm)

2–3in
(5–8cm)

Hyacinthaceae/ Liliaceae	

HYACINTHELLA LEUCOPHAEA

Habit Bulbous, perennial. **Flowers** Small, bell-shaped, borne in short spikes on leafless stems in spring. Palest milky-blue. **Leaves** Basal, strap-shaped, and semi-erect. Mid-green.
• NATIVE HABITAT Dry grassland and rocky slopes, throughout eastern Europe.
• CULTIVATION Grow in gritty, moderately fertile soil and provide a sheltered, sunny site. Protect from summer rainfall, preferably with a bulb frame.
• PROPAGATION By seed as soon as ripe, or by offsets in summer when dormant.

☼ ◊

Z 6–9

HEIGHT
8in
(20cm)

SPREAD
1–2in
(2.5–5cm)

2–3in
(5–8cm)

HYACINTHS

Cultivars of *Hyacinthus orientalis* (known as hyacinths) are valued for their flowers and sweet, pervasive scent. Hyacinths are ideal for planting in spring borders and bedding, and are also suitable for indoor containers.

Outside, plant bulbs 4in (10cm) deep and spaced 3in (8cm) apart, during autumn. Hyacinths thrive in sunny or partially shaded sites, with any moderately fertile, well-drained soil. Container-grown bulbs need a soil-based potting mix, and those raised in bowls without drainage holes need bulb fiber. Hyacinths are ideal for forcing to use in indoor displays (see p. 167).

Propagate by scooping and scoring, (see p. 182), by separation of offsets when dormant, or by twin scaling (see p. 179).

H. ORIENTALIS
'White Pearl'
Habit Bulbous, perennial.
Flowers Fragrant, waxy, single, tubular, bell-shaped, borne in erect spikes in mid-spring. Pure white.
Leaves Narrowly lance-shaped and channeled. Bright green.
• HEIGHT 8–12in (20–30cm).
• SPREAD 3in (8cm).

H. orientalis
'White Pearl'

☼ ◊   Z 6–9

H. ORIENTALIS
'Lady Derby'
Habit Bulbous, perennial.
Flowers Fragrant, waxy, single, tubular, bell-shaped, borne in early spring. Soft rose-pink.
Leaves Narrowly lance-shaped and channeled. Bright green.
• HEIGHT 8–12in (20–30cm).
• SPREAD 3in (8cm).

H. orientalis
'Lady Derby'

☼ ◊   Z 6–9

H. ORIENTALIS
'Queen of the Pinks'
Habit Bulbous, perennial.
Flowers Fragrant, waxy, single, tubular bells, in erect, crowded spikes, borne in late spring. Clear, deep pink.
Leaves Narrowly lance-shaped and channeled. Bright green.
• HEIGHT 8–12in (20–30cm).
• SPREAD 3in (8cm).

H. orientalis 'Queen of the Pinks'

☼ ◊   Z 6–9

H. ORIENTALIS
'Distinction'
Habit Bulbous, perennial.
Flowers Fragrant, waxy, single, tubular bells, in slender, open spikes, borne in early spring. Deep red-purple.
Leaves Narrowly lance-shaped and channeled. Bright green.
• HEIGHT 8–12in (20–30cm).
• SPREAD 3in (8cm).

H. orientalis 'Distinction'

☼ ◊   Z 6–9

H. ORIENTALIS
'Jan Bos'
Habit Bulbous,
perennial.
Flowers Fragrant,
waxy, single, tubular
bells, in upright spikes,
borne in early spring.
Cerise-crimson.
Leaves Narrowly lance-
shaped and channeled.
Bright green.
• HEIGHT 8–12in
(20–30cm).
• SPREAD 3in (8cm).

H. orientalis
'Jan Bos'

☼ ◊   Z 6–9

H. ORIENTALIS
'Violet Pearl'
Habit Bulbous,
perennial.
Flowers Fragrant,
waxy, single, tubular
bells, in upright spikes,
borne in early spring.
Pinkish-violet.
Leaves Narrowly lance-
shaped and channeled.
Bright green.
• HEIGHT 8–12in
(20–30cm).
• SPREAD 3in (8cm).

H. orientalis
'Violet Pearl'

☼ ◊   Z 6–9

H. ORIENTALIS
'Delft Blue'
Habit Bulbous,
perennial.
Flowers Fragrant, waxy,
single, tubular bells,
borne in erect spikes in
early spring. Soft, violet-
flushed blue.
Leaves Narrowly lance-
shaped and channeled.
Bright green.
• HEIGHT 8–12in
(20–30cm).
• SPREAD 3in (8cm).

H. orientalis
'Delft Blue'

☼ ◊   Z 6–9

H. ORIENTALIS
'Ostara'
Habit Bulbous,
perennial.
Flowers Fragrant, single,
tubular bells, in large,
dense spikes, borne in
early spring. Violet-blue,
with a darker stripe.
Leaves Narrowly lance-
shaped and channeled.
Bright green.
• HEIGHT 8–12in
(20–30cm).
• SPREAD 3in (8cm).

H. orientalis 'Ostara'

☼ ◊   Z 6–9

H. ORIENTALIS
'Blue Jacket'
Habit Bulbous,
perennial.
Flowers Fragrant, waxy,
single, tubular bells,
borne in erect spikes in
early spring. Navy-blue,
with purple veins.
Leaves Narrowly lance-
shaped and channeled.
Bright green.
• HEIGHT 8–12in
(20–30cm).
• SPREAD 3in (8cm).

H. orientalis
'Blue Jacket'

☼ ◊   Z 6–9

H. ORIENTALIS
'City of Haarlem'
Habit Bulbous,
perennial.
Flowers Fragrant, waxy,
single, tubular bells, in
dense, upright spikes,
borne in late spring.
Soft primrose-yellow.
Leaves Narrowly lance-
shaped and channeled.
Bright green.
• HEIGHT 8–12in
(20–30cm).
• SPREAD 3in (8cm).

H. orientalis
'City of Haarlem'

☼ ◊   Z 6–9

H. ORIENTALIS
**'Princess Maria
Christina'**
Habit Bulbous,
perennial.
Flowers Scented, waxy,
single, tubular bells, in
spikes, borne in early
spring. Apricot-pink.
Leaves Narrowly lance-
shaped and channeled.
Bright green.
• HEIGHT 8–12in
(20–30cm).
• SPREAD 3in (8cm).

H. orientalis **'Princess
Maria Christina'**

☼ ◊   Z 6–9

Iridaceae	

IRIS 'Katharine Hodgkin'

Habit Very vigorous, dwarf, bulbous, perennial.
Flowers Delicately marked, spotted and lined,
borne in late winter or very early spring. Pale
yellow, heavily suffused with pale blue. Dark blue
markings, with darker golden-yellow stains on the
falls. **Leaves** Erect, square-sectioned, emerging
with the flowers, then elongating after flowering
to 12in (30cm). Pale to mid-green.
• NATIVE HABITAT Garden origin.
• CULTIVATION Excellent for pocket plantings
in a rock garden or at the front of a border. Grow
in shallow pots in an alpine house, or in a bulb
frame to protect the full beauty of the flowers from
the severest winter weather. Needs well-drained,
neutral to slightly alkaline soil, in an open site in
full sun. Will spread slowly to form colonies where
conditions suit. In an alpine house, use a soil-based
potting mix with additional grit. Water moderately
when bulb is in growth, and keep almost dry, but
not arid, when dormant in summer.
• PROPAGATION Separate offsets as the leaves
wither and replant immediately.

☼ ◌

Z 6–9

HEIGHT
2½–5in
(6–12cm)

SPREAD
2–3in
(5–7cm)

2–3in
(5–8cm)

Hyacinthaceae/ Liliaceae	

BELLEVALIA HYACINTHOIDES

Habit Bulbous, perennial. *Flowers* Small, dark-veined bells, borne in loose sprays in spring. Pale blue. *Leaves* Fleshy and strap-shaped. Mid-green.
• NATIVE HABITAT Rocky hillsides, Greece.
• CULTIVATION Best in a bulb frame in areas with cold, wet winters. Needs a dry, summer dormancy. Grow in well-drained soil and a warm, sunny site.
• PROPAGATION Sow seed when ripe, or separate offsets when dormant in summer.
• OTHER NAMES *Strangweja spicata, Hyacinthus spicatus.*

☼ ◊

Z 7–9

HEIGHT
2–6in
(5–15cm)

SPREAD
2in (5cm)

💧 4in (10cm)

Hyacinthaceae/ Liliaceae	

SCILLA MISCHTSCHENKOANA

Habit Dwarf, bulbous, perennial. *Flowers* Small stars, in lengthening spikes, borne in late winter or early spring. Pale silvery-blue, with darker stripes. *Leaves* Semi-erect and linear. Mid-green.
• NATIVE HABITAT Rocks and alpine meadows, from Transcaucasia to northwest Iran.
• CULTIVATION Grow in well-drained soil in a sunny site, or in deep pots in an alpine house.
• PROPAGATION Sow seed as soon as ripe, or separate offsets when dormant in summer.
• OTHER NAME *S. tubergeniana.*

☼ ◊

Z 1–8

HEIGHT
4–6in
(10–15cm)

SPREAD
2in (5cm)

💧 3–4in (8–10cm)

Hyacinthaceae/ Liliaceae	

BRIMEURA AMETHYSTINA

Habit Bulbous, perennial. *Flowers* Small bells, borne in slender spikes in spring. Pale to deep blue. *Leaves* Linear and channeled. Bright green.
• NATIVE HABITAT Mountain meadows, Pyrenees.
• CULTIVATION Suitable for planting in pockets in a rock garden or in a raised bed. Needs well-drained soil that is rich in organic matter. Prefers partial shade, but will tolerate full sun.
• PROPAGATION Sow seed when ripe or divide established clumps when dormant in summer.
• OTHER NAME *Hyacinthus amethystinus.*

☼ ◊

Z 5–9

HEIGHT
4–10in
(10–25cm)

SPREAD
1–2in
(2.5–5cm)

💧 2in (5cm)

Tecophilaeaceae/ Liliaceae	

TECOPHILAEA CYANOCROCUS 'Leichtlinii'

Habit Cormous, perennial. *Flowers* Open funnels, borne in spring. Blue, with white center. *Leaves* Basal, semi-erect, and lance-shaped. Mid-green.
• NATIVE HABITAT Rocky, alpine grassland, Chile.
• CULTIVATION Suitable for a rock garden in mild areas. Elsewhere, can be grown more safely in an alpine house. Needs well-drained, sandy soil, and a warm, sheltered site that is never completely dry.
• PROPAGATION Sow seeds as soon as ripe, or separate offsets in late summer.

☼ ◊

Z 7–9

HEIGHT
3–4in
(8–10cm)

SPREAD
2–3in
(5–8cm)

💧 2in (5cm)

Hyacinthaceae/ Liliaceae	

SCILLA SIBERICA 'Spring Beauty'

Habit Bulbous, perennial. **Flowers** Small, bell-shaped, borne in loose spikes in spring. Deep rich blue, faintly flushed violet-blue. **Leaves** Basal and broadly linear. Rich green.
• NATIVE HABITAT Garden origin.
• CULTIVATION Needs moderately fertile, preferably sandy soil, enriched with organic matter, sited in dappled shade or sun. Excellent for a rock garden or for planting beneath shrubs.
• PROPAGATION By offsets in summer dormancy.
• OTHER NAME *S. siberica* 'Atrocaerulea'.

☼ ◊

Z 1–8

HEIGHT
4–6in
(10–15cm)

SPREAD
6in (5cm)

3–4in
(8–10cm)

Hyacinthaceae/ Liliaceae	

MUSCARI AUCHERI

Habit Bulbous, perennial. **Flowers** Small, almost spherical, becoming paler in the upper spray, borne in spring. Bright blue, with white-rimmed mouth. **Leaves** Basal and strap-shaped. Grayish-green.
• NATIVE HABITAT Sunny hillsides, Turkey.
• CULTIVATION Good for planting in a rock garden, or at the front of a border. Grow in moderately fertile, well-drained soil in a sunny site.
• PROPAGATION Sow seed as soon as ripe, or separate offsets in summer.
• OTHER NAME *M. lingulatum*.

☼ ◊

Z 2–9

HEIGHT
2–6in
(5–15cm)

SPREAD
2–3in
(5–8cm)

4in
(10cm)

Hyacinthaceae/ Liliaceae	

CHIONODOXA LUCILIAE

Habit Bulbous, perennial. **Flowers** Star-shaped, upward-facing, borne in early spring. Clear blue, with a white eye. **Leaves** Basal, broadly linear, and often recurved. Mid-green.
• NATIVE HABITAT Stony hillsides, Turkey.
• CULTIVATION Suitable specimen for pocket or drift plantings, either in a rock garden or in an alpine house. Grow in any well-drained soil.
• PROPAGATION Sow seed as soon as ripe, or separate offsets in summer.
• OTHER NAME *C. gigantea*.

☼ ◊

Z 3–9

HEIGHT
2–4in
(5–10cm)

SPREAD
1–2in
(2.5–5cm)

3in
(8cm)

Hyacinthaceae/ Liliaceae	

CHIONODOXA FORBESII

Habit Bulbous, perennial. **Flowers** Star-shaped, outward-facing, borne in spikes in early spring. Blue, with a white eye. **Leaves** Basal, semi-erect, and broadly linear. Mid-green.
• NATIVE HABITAT Hillsides, western Turkey.
• CULTIVATION Suitable for a rock garden, or for naturalizing beneath deciduous shrubs. Easily grown in any well-drained soil.
• PROPAGATION Separate offsets in summer after leaves wither, or sow seed as soon as ripe.
• OTHER NAMES *C. siehei, C. tmolusi.*

☼ ◊

Z 3–9

HEIGHT
4–8in
(10–20cm)

SPREAD
2in (5cm)

3in
(8cm)

Tecophiliaeaceae/ Liliaceae	CHILEAN BLUE CROCUS

TECOPHILAEA CYANOCROCUS

Habit Cormous, perennial. **Flowers** Open funnel-shaped, upward-facing, borne in spring. Rich gentian-blue. **Leaves** Basal, semi-erect, and narrowly lance-shaped. Mid-green.
• NATIVE HABITAT Rocky alpine grassland, Chile.
• CULTIVATION Ideal for a rock garden in mild areas, but best grown in an alpine house elsewhere. Provide well-drained, sandy soil and a sheltered site that never dries out completely.
• PROPAGATION Sow seeds as soon as ripe, or separate offsets in late summer.

☼ ◊

Z 7–9

HEIGHT
3–4in
(8–10cm)

SPREAD
2–3in
(5–8cm)

2in
(5cm)

Hyacinthaceae/ Liliaceae	

MUSCARI ARMENIACUM

Habit Vigorous, bulbous, perennial. **Flowers** Small, tubular, borne in dense spikes in spring. Blue, with constricted, white mouth. **Leaves** Basal, linear, appearing in autumn. Mid-green.
• NATIVE HABITAT Grassy hills, southeast Europe.
• CULTIVATION Ideal for a rock garden or at the front of a border. Grow in any moderately fertile, well-drained soil in sun. Can be invasive.
• PROPAGATION Separate offsets or divide clumps in summer, or sow seed when ripe.
• OTHER NAMES *M. woronowii, M. polyanthum.*

☼ ◊

Z 2–9

HEIGHT
6–8in
(15–20cm)

SPREAD
3–4in
(8–10cm)

4in
(10cm)

Hyacinthaceae/ Liliaceae	

MUSCARI NEGLECTUM

Habit Bulbous, perennial. **Flowers** Small, egg-shaped, borne in dense spikes in spring. Blue-black, with white-rimmed mouth. **Leaves** Basal, linear to cylindrical, and channeled. Mid-green.
• NATIVE HABITAT Europe and northern Africa
• CULTIVATION Good for interplanting in a mixed or herbaceous border. Tolerant of any well-drained soil. Increases rapidly and can be invasive.
• PROPAGATION Sow seed as soon as ripe, or separate offsets in summer. Self-seeds freely.
• OTHER NAME *M. racemosum.*

☼ ◊

Z 2–9

HEIGHT
4–8in
(10–20cm)

SPREAD
3–4in
(8–10cm)

4in
(10cm)

Ranunculaceae	

ANEMONE BLANDA 'Ingramii'

Habit Spreading, perennial, with knobby tubers.
Flowers Solitary, erect, flattened, saucer-shaped,
borne in early spring. Intense, deep-blue. *Leaves*
Deeply lobed and semi-erect. Dark green.
• NATIVE HABITAT Garden origin.
• CULTIVATION Needs moderately fertile soil in
dappled shade or sun. Ideal for rock gardens or for
naturalizing beneath deciduous trees and shrubs.
• PROPAGATION Separate offset tubers when
dormant in summer.
• OTHER NAME *A. blanda* 'Atrocaerulea'.

☼ ◐

Z 6–9

HEIGHT
2–4in
(5–10cm)

SPREAD
4–6in
(10–15cm)

💧 2–3in
(5–8cm)

Hyacinthaceae/ Liliaceae	

× *CHIONOSCILLA ALLENII*

Habit Sturdy, bulbous, perennial. *Flowers*
Small, star-shaped, borne in short spikes in spring.
Mid- to deep blue. *Leaves* Basal, semi-erect,
and lance-shaped. Rich green.
• NATIVE HABITAT Natural hybrid, between
Chionodoxa forbesii and *Scilla bifolia*, occurring
where both parents grow in proximity.
• CULTIVATION Good for planting in a rock garden
or beneath trees and shrubs. Grow in any well-
drained soil in sun or light, dappled shade.
• PROPAGATION Separate offsets in summer.

☼ ◐

Z 3–9

HEIGHT
4–6in
(10–15cm)

SPREAD
1–2in
(2.5–5cm)

💧 3in
(7cm)

Iridaceae	

IRIS 'Joyce'

Habit Bulbous, perennial. *Flowers* Borne in late
winter or very early spring. Deep sky-blue, with
yellow-stained, darker blue falls. *Leaves* Upright
and square-sectioned. Pale to mid-green.
• NATIVE HABITAT Garden origin.
• CULTIVATION Good for an alpine house or for
pocket plantings in a rock garden. Needs well-
drained, neutral to slightly alkaline soil. Prefers
an open site in full sun.
• PROPAGATION Separate offsets when the
leaves wither and replant immediately.

☼ ◐

Z 5–9

HEIGHT
5in (12cm)

SPREAD
2–3in
(5–7cm)

💧 2–3in
(5–8cm)

Iridaceae	

IRIS HISTRIOIDES 'Major'

Habit Robust, bulbous, perennial. *Flowers*
Borne in early spring. Deep blue-violet, with
yellow-stained, darker-spotted falls. *Leaves*
Erect and square-sectioned. Pale to mid-green.
• NATIVE HABITAT Sunny hillsides, Turkey.
• CULTIVATION Excellent for growing in a rock
garden, alpine house, or bulb frame. Needs well-
drained, neutral to slightly alkaline soil, and
must be kept dry during summer dormancy.
• PROPAGATION Separate offsets as the leaves
wither and replant immediately.

☼ ◐

Z 6–9

HEIGHT
4–6in
(10–15cm)

SPREAD
2–3in
(5–7cm)

💧 2–3in
(5–8cm)

Hyacinthaceae/ Liliaceae	

LEDEBOURIA SOCIALIS

Habit Bulbous, perennial. **Flowers** Small, bell-shaped, borne in spikes in late spring. Purple-green. **Leaves** Evergreen, lance-shaped, and fleshy. Silver-green, with dark-green spots.
• NATIVE HABITAT S. Africa.
• CULTIVATION Suits a greenhouse or conservatory in colder regions. Needs sandy soil, plenty of water during growth, and dry dormancy in winter.
• PROPAGATION Sow seed in spring or autumn, or separate offsets in spring.
• OTHER NAMES *Scilla socialis, S. violacea.*

☼ ◊

Z 9–10

HEIGHT
2–4in
(5–10cm)

SPREAD
3–4in
(8–10cm)

Neck above

Hyacinthaceae/ Liliaceae	

MUSCARI MACROCARPUM

Habit Bulbous, perennial, persistent fleshy roots. **Flowers** Scented, small, tubular, borne in spikes in spring. Dull violet, opening to yellow with brown rim. **Leaves** Basal and linear. Gray-green.
• NATIVE HABITAT Greece and western Turkey.
• CULTIVATION Suitable for planting in a rock garden, bulb frame, or alpine house. Grow in well-drained soil, choosing a sunny site to ensure a warm and dry summer dormancy.
• PROPAGATION By ripe seed or by summer offsets.
• OTHER NAME *M. moschatum* var. *flavum.*

☼ ◊

Z 2–9

HEIGHT
4–8in
(10–20cm)

SPREAD
4–6in
(10–15cm)

4in
(10cm)

Araceae	

ARUM ITALICUM subsp. *ITALICUM* 'Marmoratum'

Habit Tuberous, perennial. **Flowers** Borne in early summer. Pale green, with yellow spike. **Leaves** Arrow-shaped, glossy. Dark green, cream-veined. **Fruits** Orange-red berries in autumn.
• NATIVE HABITAT Europe and northern Africa.
• CULTIVATION Flowers best in sun in fertile soil, rich in organic matter. Leaves are larger in shade.
• PROPAGATION Sow seed as soon as ripe, or divide tubers after flowering.
• OTHER NAME *A. italicum* 'Pictum'.

☼ ◊

Z 6–9

HEIGHT
10–12in
(25–30cm)

SPREAD
8–12in
(20–30cm)

to 6in
(15cm)

Iridaceae	

IRIS WINOGRADOWII

Habit Vigorous, dwarf, bulbous, perennial.
Flowers Single, borne in early spring. Pale primrose-yellow with broad, green-spotted falls, usually marked deeper, rich yellow at the center.
Leaves Erect, narrow, and square-sectioned. Very short when emerging with the flowers, but will reach 12in (30cm). Pale to mid-green.
• NATIVE HABITAT Open grassland and damp meadows, Caucasus mountains.
• CULTIVATION Excellent for pocket plantings in a rock garden, trough, or raised bed. Needs

moisture-retentive but well-drained, fertile soil that is neutral to slightly alkaline. Grows best in an open site in full sun. Bulbs should not be allowed to dry out completely during summer dormancy. New root growth begins in summer when the leaves start to wither.
• PROPAGATION Sow seed when ripe or in spring.

☼ ◊

Z 7–9

HEIGHT
3–4in
(7–10cm)

SPREAD
2½–3in
(6–7cm)

2–3in
(5–8cm)

Liliaceae	GOLDEN FAIRY LANTERN

CALOCHORTUS AMABILIS

Habit Slender, bulbous, perennial. **Flowers** Nodding, open, fringed bells, borne on branching stems in spring and early summer. Deep yellow. **Leaves** Erect and lance-shaped. Grayish-green.
• NATIVE HABITAT Scrubland and forests in Californian mountains.
• CULTIVATION Provide a warm, sheltered site in full sun, preferably in sandy soil. Grows well in a bulb frame. Protect the bulb from excess rain.
• PROPAGATION By seed as soon as ripe, or by offsets in late summer.

☼ ◊

Z 7–9

HEIGHT
4–12in
(10–30cm)

SPREAD
2–4in
(5–10cm)

4–6in
(9–15cm)

Iridaceae	

IRIS DANFORDIAE

Habit Bulbous, perennial. **Flowers** Single, with tiny standards, borne in late winter and early spring. Yellow, with green-spotted falls. **Leaves** Erect, slim, and squared. Pale to mid-green.
• NATIVE HABITAT Sunny hillsides, Turkey.
• CULTIVATION Suitable for growing in a rock garden, trough, alpine house, or bulb frame. Needs well-drained, neutral to slightly alkaline soil and a dry, summer dormancy.
• PROPAGATION Separate offsets as leaves wither and replant immediately. Sow seed when ripe.

☼ ◊

Z 6–9

HEIGHT
2–4in
(5–10cm)

SPREAD
2in (5cm)

2–3in
(5–8cm)

Colchicaceae/Liliaceae	

COLCHICUM LUTEUM

Habit Cormous, perennial. **Flowers** Goblet-shaped, up to 4 per corm, borne in early spring. Golden- to straw-yellow. **Leaves** Semi-erect and narrowly linear. Mid-green.
• NATIVE HABITAT Bare slopes in Himalaya, Tibet, northern India, and Afghanistan.
• CULTIVATION Best grown in a bulb frame to give protection from excessive rainfall. Needs gritty, sharply drained soil and a dry summer dormancy.
• PROPAGATION Sow seed when ripe, or separate cormlets in summer.

☼ ◊

Z 7–9

HEIGHT
2–4in
(5–10cm)

SPREAD
2–3in
(5–8cm)

4in
(10cm)

Hyacinthaceae/ Liliaceae	

DIPCADI SEROTINUM

Habit Bulbous, perennial. **Flowers** Nodding, small, tubular, in loose spikes, borne on a leafless stem in spring. Bronze or dull orange-red, flushed green. **Leaves** Basal and linear. Gray-green.
• NATIVE HABITAT Dry, rocky areas in southwest Europe and northern Africa.
• CULTIVATION Suitable for growing in a rock garden, bulb frame, or alpine house. Protect from winter moisture. Needs light, well-drained soil.
• PROPAGATION Sow seed when ripe, or separate offsets when dormant in summer.

☼ ◊

Z 8–10

HEIGHT
4–12in
(10–30cm)

SPREAD
2–3in
(5–8cm)

2in
(5cm)

Araceae	

ARISAEMA CANDIDISSIMUM

Habit Tuberous, perennial. **Flowers** Fragrant, elegant, cowl-like, borne in early summer. White, striped pink and green. **Leaves** Solitary, divided into 3 oval leaflets. Mid-green.
• NATIVE HABITAT Shady slopes and forests, western China.
• CULTIVATION Needs leaf-rich, moist but well-drained soil, enriched with organic matter. Provide a cool, sheltered site in partial or dappled shade.
• PROPAGATION Separate offsets in late summer, or sow seed as soon as ripe.

☼ ◐

Z 7–9

HEIGHT
16in (40cm)

SPREAD
4–6in
(10–15cm)

🌡 10in
(25cm)

Amaryllidaceae/ Liliaceae	

HIPPEASTRUM STRIATUM

Habit Bulbous, perennial. **Flowers** Funnels, borne in sprays of up to 4, on stout stems in spring or summer. Coral-red, with a green, central stripe. **Leaves** Basal and strap-shaped. Bright green.
• NATIVE HABITAT Brazil.
• CULTIVATION Grow as a house or conservatory plant. Water freely during growth but reduce as leaves wither, keeping bulb dry when dormant.
• PROPAGATION Separate offsets in autumn, or sow seed when ripe.
• OTHER NAME *H. rutilum.*

☼ ◊

Z 10–11

HEIGHT
12in (30cm)

SPREAD
8–10in
(20–25cm)

🌡 Neck
above

Hyacinthaceae/Liliaceae	

ALBUCA HUMILIS

Habit Dwarf, perennial. **Flowers** Small, narrowly bell-shaped, borne in loose spikes of 1–3 from late spring to early summer. White, with green stripe, later flushed pink on the outside. **Leaves** Basal and linear. Dark green.
• NATIVE HABITAT Grasslands, southern Africa.
• CULTIVATION Needs light, well-drained soil. Grow in a cool greenhouse or conservatory in cool areas. Elsewhere, plant in a mixed border.
• PROPAGATION Sow seed when ripe, or separate offsets in autumn.

☼ ◊

Z 9–10

HEIGHT
2–4in
(5–10cm)

SPREAD
2–3in
(5–8cm)

🌡 2in
(5cm)

Primulaceae	

CYCLAMEN PURPURASCENS

Habit Tuberous, perennial. **Flowers** Scented, conical, borne in mid- and late summer. Pale to deep carmine-red. **Leaves** Evergreen, rounded, and heart-shaped. Dark green, often with faint, silver mottling and purple-red underside.
• NATIVE HABITAT Alpine woods, central Europe.
• CULTIVATION Grow in leaf-rich, gritty, moist but well-drained, alkaline soil. Do not allow to dry out.
• PROPAGATION Soak and rinse seed as soon as ripe, and sow in darkness.
• OTHER NAMES *C. europeum, C. fatrense.*

☼ ◊

Z 5–9

HEIGHT
4in
(10cm)

SPREAD
4–6in
(10–15cm)

🌡 1in
(2.5cm)

Hypoxidaceae	

RHODOHYPOXIS BAURII 'Douglas'

Habit Clump-forming, bulbous, perennial, with corm-like rootstock. **Flowers** Erect, flattened, with 6 petals overlapping in 2 ranks, borne in succession in early summer. Rich, deep red. **Leaves** Basal, hairy, and narrowly lance-shaped. Dark green.
• NATIVE HABITAT Garden origin.
• CULTIVATION Suits a rock garden, raised bed, or trough. Needs gritty, well-drained soil, enriched with organic matter. Dislikes excessive winter moisture.
• PROPAGATION Separate offsets in late autumn.
• OTHER NAME *R.* 'Douglas'.

☼ ◊

Z 9–10

HEIGHT
2–4in
(5–10cm)

SPREAD
1–2in
(2.5–5cm)

▣ 1in
(2.5cm)

Hypoxidaceae	

RHODOHYPOXIS BAURII 'Albrighton'

Habit Clump-forming, bulbous, perennial, with corm-like rootstock. **Flowers** Erect, flattened, with 6 petals overlapping in 2 ranks, borne in succession in early summer. Deep red-pink. **Leaves** Basal, hairy, and narrowly lance-shaped. Dark green.
• NATIVE HABITAT Garden origin.
• CULTIVATION Good for a rock garden, raised bed or trough, with gritty, well-drained soil rich in organic matter. Dislikes excessive winter moisture.
• PROPAGATION Separate offsets in late autumn.
• OTHER NAME *R.* 'Albrighton'.

☼ ◊

Z 9–10

HEIGHT
2–4in
(5–10cm)

SPREAD
1–2in
(2.5–5cm)

▣ 1in
(2.5cm)

Amaryllidaceae/ Liliaceae	BLOOD LILY, CAPE TULIP

HAEMANTHUS COCCINEUS

Habit Bulbous, perennial. **Flowers** Clusters of tiny flowers, up to 4in (10cm) span, borne on leafless stems in summer. Red, with yellow anthers. **Leaves** Strap-shaped, borne after the flowers. Mid-green, often purple-marked.
• NATIVE HABITAT Hillsides, southern Africa.
• CULTIVATION Needs fertile, gritty, well-drained soil. Grow as a house or conservatory plant in cooler areas. Under glass, water moderately when in growth, keeping bulb dry after leaves wither.
• PROPAGATION By ripe seed, or by spring offsets.

☼ ◊

Z 10–11

HEIGHT
to 12in
(30cm)

SPREAD
8–12in
(20–30cm)

▣ Neck
above

Amaryllidaceae/ Liliaceae	FIRE LILY

CYRTANTHUS BRACHYSCYPHUS

Habit Clumping, bulbous, perennial. **Flowers** Tubular, slightly curved, in sprays, borne on bare stems in spring and summer. Flame-red. **Leaves** Semi-erect and lance-shaped. Bright green.
• NATIVE HABITAT S. Africa.
• CULTIVATION In colder regions, grow as a house plant in moderately fertile soil. Water freely during growth, keeping just moist when dormant.
• PROPAGATION Sow seed as soon as it is ripe, or separate offsets in spring.
• OTHER NAME *C. parviflorus.*

☼ ◊

Z 9–10

HEIGHT
8–12in
(20–30cm)

SPREAD
4in (10cm)

Nose level

Alliaceae/Liliaceae	CHIVES

ALLIUM SCHOENOPRASUM

Habit Clump-forming, bulbous, perennial. **Flowers** Tiny, bell-shaped, in dense sprays, borne on leafless stems in summer. Pink-purple. **Leaves** Upright and narrowly cylindrical. Dark green.
• NATIVE HABITAT Europe, Asia, and N. America.
• CULTIVATION Grow in a herb garden or as border edging. Needs moist but well-drained, fertile soil. Leaves and flowers are edible. For culinary use, cut leaves frequently to ensure continuous supply.
• PROPAGATION Divide clumps in spring, or sow ripe seed. Bulbs cannot usually be purchased.

☼ ◊

Z 3–9

HEIGHT
5–10in
(12–25cm)

SPREAD
2–4in
(5–10cm)

2in
(5cm)

Alliaceae/Liliaceae	

ALLIUM NARCISSIFLORUM

Habit Clump-forming, perennial, rhizomatous. **Flowers** Bell-shaped, in loose, drooping sprays, borne in summer. Pink-purple. **Leaves** Narrow, strap-shaped, and stem-sheathing. Gray-green.
• NATIVE HABITAT Portugal, France, northern Italy.
• CULTIVATION Suitable for a rock garden or at the front of a mixed or herbaceous border that is sunny and dry. Needs fertile, well-drained soil.
• PROPAGATION Sow seed as soon as ripe or in spring. Divide in spring.
• OTHER NAME *A. pedemontanum* of gardens.

☼ ◊

Z 4–9

HEIGHT
6–14in
(15–35cm)

SPREAD
3–4in
(8–10cm)

3–4in
(8–10cm)

Alliaceae/Liliaceae	

ALLIUM CYATHOPHORUM var. FARRERI

Habit Vigorous, bulbous, perennial. **Flowers** Small, drooping, bell-shaped, borne in loose sprays in summer. Deep violet-purple. **Leaves** Basal, erect, and narrowly strap-shaped. Mid-green.
• NATIVE HABITAT Grassy mountain slopes, China.
• CULTIVATION Good for a rock garden as border edging or in gravel plantings. Needs moist but well-drained soil that is rich in organic matter.
• PROPAGATION Sow seed when ripe or in spring, or separate offsets in autumn. May self-seed.
• OTHER NAME *A. farreri.*

☼ ◊

Z 4–9

HEIGHT
6–12in
(15–30cm)

SPREAD
2in (5cm)

3–4in
(8–10cm)

Zingiberaceae

ROSCOEA HUMEANA

Habit Robust, tuberous, perennial. *Flowers* Hooded upper petal, 1½in (4cm) across, surrounded by overlapping bracts. Borne in succession on leafy stems in the upper leaf axils, during early summer. Rich purple. *Leaves* Oblong to oval, 1–2 or occasionally 3, and stem-sheathing. Leaves are usually only partially developed at flowering time, and do not reach their full length until after the flowers. Dark, rich green.

• NATIVE HABITAT Grassy mountain slopes in the Yunnan and Sichuan provinces of southwest China.

• CULTIVATION Excellent for growing in a peat bed, woodland garden or damp, shaded border. Prefers climates with cool summers, and may prove to be almost fully hardy if planted deeply and protected with a generous, winter mulch of leaf-mold or similar. Needs moist but well-drained, leaf-rich, acid soil in a cool, sheltered position with partial or dappled shade.

• PROPAGATION By seed, or by division in spring.

☀ ◐

Z 7–9

HEIGHT
6–10in
(15–25cm)

SPREAD
6in
(15cm)

6in
(15cm)

Hyacinthaceae/ Liliaceae	

SCILLA PERUVIANA

Habit Clumping, bulbous, perennial. **Flowers**
Small star-shaped, borne in conical spikes in early
summer. Purple-blue or white. **Leaves** Almost
evergreen, basal, semi-erect, and lance-shaped,
appearing as old leaves fade in autumn. Mid-green.
• NATIVE HABITAT Mediterranean, northern Africa.
• CULTIVATION Grow in a sunny rock garden or at
the front of an herbaceous border, with fertile soil
enriched with organic matter.
• PROPAGATION By seed as soon as ripe, or by
offsets in autumn.

☼ ◊

Z 8–10

HEIGHT
6–12in
(15–30cm)

SPREAD
4–6in
(10–15cm)

1–2in
(2–5cm)

Iridaceae	

IRIS 'Cantab'

Habit Bulbous, perennial. **Flowers** Fragrant,
solitary, borne in late winter and early spring.
Pale blue, with darker, yellow-crested falls. **Leaves**
Erect, narrow, and squared. Pale to mid-green.
• NATIVE HABITAT Garden origin.
• CULTIVATION Excellent for a rock garden, raised
bed, or trough. Needs well-drained, fertile soil that
is neutral to slightly alkaline in a sunny, open site.
• PROPAGATION Separate offsets from established
clumps as the leaves wither. Bulbs may split
naturally, taking several years to bloom.

☼ ◊

Z 6–9

HEIGHT
4–6in
(10–15cm)

SPREAD
1–2in
(2.5–5cm)

2–3in
(5–7cm)

Iridaceae	

IRIS 'Harmony'

Habit Bulbous, perennial. **Flowers** Solitary,
fragrant, borne in late winter. Royal-blue, with
yellow crest and white stains. **Leaves** Upright,
narrow, and square-sectioned. Pale to mid-green.
• NATIVE HABITAT Garden origin.
• CULTIVATION Good for a rock garden, alpine
house, trough, or raised bed. Needs fertile, neutral
to slightly alkaline soil in a warm, sheltered site.
• PROPAGATION Separate offsets from established
clumps as the leaves wither. Bulbs may split
naturally, taking several years to bloom.

☼ ◊

Z 6–9

HEIGHT
4–6in
(10–15cm)

SPREAD
1–2in
(2.5–5cm)

2–3in
(5–7cm)

Zingiberaceaee	

ROSCOEA CAUTLEYOIDES

Habit Robust, tuberous, perennial. *Flowers* Hooded, borne in succession during mid-summer. Pale yellow, white, or purple. *Leaves* Linear to lance-shaped. Mid- to dark green.
• NATIVE HABITAT Grassy mountain slopes in the Yunnan and Sichuan provinces of northwest China.
• CULTIVATION Excellent in a peat bed, damp border, or woodland. Needs a leaf-rich, moist but well-drained, acid soil, in a cool, sheltered site.
• PROPAGATION Sow seed as soon as ripe, or divide in early spring.

☼ ◊

Z 7–9

HEIGHT
to 22in
(55cm)

SPREAD
4–6in
(10–15cm)

6in
(15cm)

Amaryllidaceae/ Liliaceae	

CHLIDANTHUS FRAGRANS

Habit Bulbous, perennial. *Flowers* Fragrant funnels, borne in sprays of 3–5 in summer. Yellow. *Leaves* Basal, semi-erect, and linear. Gray-green.
• NATIVE HABITAT Andes, Peru.
• CULTIVATION Grow as a house or conservatory plant in cold regions. Needs sandy, well-drained soil or potting mix, that is rich in organic matter. Water freely when in growth, but withhold water as leaves start to wither so that bulb is stored dry during winter dormancy.
• PROPAGATION In spring, by seed or by offsets.

☼ ◊

Z 8–10

HEIGHT
12in (30cm)

SPREAD
3in (8cm)

Nose
level

Alliaceae/Liliaceae	GOLDEN GARLIC

ALLIUM MOLY

Habit Sturdy, clump-forming, bulbous, perennial. *Flowers* Star-shaped, borne in dense clusters of up to 30 in summer. Bright golden-yellow. *Leaves* Basal and lance-shaped. Gray-green.
• NATIVE HABITAT Shady rocks and screes in the mountains of southwest and southern Europe.
• CULTIVATION Excellent as underplantings beneath shrubs or for naturalizing in a woodland garden. Tolerant of light, dappled shade.
• PROPAGATION By seed as soon as ripe, or by offsets in autumn. Self-seeds and spreads rapidly.

☼ ◊

Z 3–9

HEIGHT
6–10in
(15–25cm)

SPREAD
2in (5cm)

3–4in
(8–10cm)

Hypoxidaceae/Liliaceae	STARFLOWER, STARGRASS

HYPOXIS ANGUSTIFOLIA

Habit Slender, cormous, perennial. *Flowers* Small, star-shaped, upward-facing, borne in spikes in summer. Yellow. *Leaves* Grass-like, hairy, semi-upright, and linear. Mid-green.
• NATIVE HABITAT S. Africa.
• CULTIVATION Suitable as a conservatory or house plant in colder areas. Needs moist but well-drained, fertile soil, and shade from hot sun. Protect from excess wet in summer and winter.
• PROPAGATION By seed in spring, or by offsets in autumn.

☼ ◊

Z 5–9

HEIGHT
4–8in
(10–20cm)

SPREAD
2in (5cm)

1in
(3cm)

Colchicaceae/Liliaceae	

COLCHICUM SPECIOSUM 'Album'

Habit Vigorous, cormous, perennial. **Flowers** Sturdy, weather-resistant, goblet-shaped, borne in autumn. White. **Leaves** Semi-erect and oval, produced from late winter to spring. Mid-green.
• NATIVE HABITAT Stony slopes and subalpine meadows in the Caucasus region.
• CULTIVATION Good for a mixed or herbaceous border, or at the foot of a rockery. Suitable for naturalizing in grass. Needs deep, fertile soil that is well-drained but not too dry, in a warm, sunny site.
• PROPAGATION Separate offsets in summer.

☼ ◊

Z 4–9

HEIGHT
4–8in
(10–20cm)

SPREAD
up to 1ft
(30cm)

4in
(10cm)

Amaryllidaceae/ Liliaceae	AUTUMN SNOWFLAKE

LEUCOJUM AUTUMNALE

Habit Slender, bulbous, perennial. **Flowers** Drooping bells, borne in open sprays of 2–4 in late summer and early autumn. White, tinted red at the base. **Leaves** Basal, thread-like, and upright, appearing with or just after the flowers. Mid-green.
• NATIVE HABITAT Woodland, scrub, and grassland, in southwest Europe and northern Africa.
• CULTIVATION Grow in moist but well-drained soil. Prefers a warm, sunny site.
• PROPAGATION By seed as soon as ripe, or by offsets as leaves start to wither.

☼ ◊

Z 5–9

HEIGHT
4–6in
(10–15cm)

SPREAD
2in (5cm)

1–2in
(4–5cm)

Primulaceae	

CYCLAMEN HEDERIFOLIUM f. ALBUM

Habit Tuberous, perennial. **Flowers** Shuttlecock-shaped, with reflexed petals, borne in autumn, with or before the leaves. Pure white. **Leaves** Ivy-like. Green-marbled, with silvery-green mottling.
• NATIVE HABITAT In woods and among rocks, in the Mediterranean.
• CULTIVATION Prefers gritty, well-drained soil enriched with leaf mold, in sun or dappled shade.
• PROPAGATION Soak and rinse seed as soon as ripe, then sow in darkness.
• OTHER NAME C. neapolitanum var. album.

☼ ◊

Z 5–9

HEIGHT
to 4in
(10cm)

SPREAD
4–6in
(10–15cm)

1–2in
(3–5cm)

Amaryllidaceae/ Liliaceae	RAINFLOWER, WINDFLOWER

ZEPHYRANTHES CANDIDA

Habit Slender, clump-forming, bulbous, perennial. **Flowers** Solitary, star-shaped, borne in succession from late summer to autumn. White, often with red-tinted exterior. **Leaves** Evergreen, basal, upright, and linear. Mid-green.
• NATIVE HABITAT Marshland in Argentina.
• CULTIVATION Ideal for a rock garden or at the front of an herbaceous border. Needs fertile, moist but well-drained soil enriched with organic matter.
• PROPAGATION By seed when ripe, or by division in spring.

☼ ◊

Z 7–10

HEIGHT
4–8in
(10–20cm)

SPREAD
3in (8cm)

4in
(10cm)

Primulaceae	

CYCLAMEN AFRICANUM

Habit Tuberous, perennial. *Flowers* Cone-shaped, with reflexed petals, borne in autumn, appearing just before the leaves. Shades of pink, with maroon-rimmed mouth. *Leaves* Heart-shaped. Bright green, with paler green marks.
• NATIVE HABITAT Algeria.
• CULTIVATION Best grown in a cool greenhouse or alpine house. Needs fertile, sharply drained potting mix, and dry dormancy as leaves fade.
• PROPAGATION Soak and rinse seed as soon as ripe, then sow in darkness.

☼: ◐ ◊

Z 8–9

HEIGHT
5–6in
(12–15cm)

SPREAD
9in (23cm)

¾in
(2cm)

Primulaceae	

CYCLAMEN MIRABILE

Habit Tuberous, perennial. *Flowers* Slender, reflexed, fringed, borne in autumn. Pale pink, with maroon-stained mouth. *Leaves* Heart-shaped, with scalloped margins, appearing with the flowers. Mid-green, with red-purple underside.
• NATIVE HABITAT Scrubland, southwest Turkey.
• CULTIVATION Needs leaf-rich, gritty, sharply drained soil. Best grown in an alpine house to ensure dry conditions when dormant.
• PROPAGATION Soak and rinse seed as soon as ripe, then sow in darkness.

☼: ◐ ◊

Z 8–9

HEIGHT
4in (10cm)

SPREAD
12–15in
(30–40cm)

¾in
(2cm)

Colchicaceae/Liliaceae	AUTUMN CROCUS, MEADOW SAFFRON

COLCHICUM AUTUMNALE

Habit Vigorous, cormous, perennial. *Flowers* Long-tubed, goblet-shaped, up to 8, borne in autumn. Lavender-pink. *Leaves* Erect, glossy, and lance-shaped, appearing in spring. Mid-green.
• NATIVE HABITAT Meadows in Europe.
• CULTIVATION Suitable for naturalizing in grass. Good in a mixed or herbaceous border or at the foot of a bank. Needs deep, fertile, well-drained soil that is not too dry, in a warm, open, sunny site.
• PROPAGATION Sow seed when ripe, or separate offsets in summer.

☼ ◊

Z 4–9

HEIGHT
4–6in
(10–15cm)

SPREAD
4–6in
(10–15cm)

4in
(10cm)

Colchicaceae/Liliaceae	

COLCHICUM BYZANTINUM

Habit Vigorous, free-flowering, cormous, perennial. *Flowers* Open funnel-shaped, up to 20, borne in autumn. Lilac. *Leaves* Erect, ribbed, and oval, appearing in spring. Mid-green.
• NATIVE HABITAT Origin unknown.
• CULTIVATION Suitable for naturalizing in grass, or for planting at the foot of a bank in a rock garden. Needs deep, fertile, well-drained soil that is not too dry. Prefers a warm, open, sunny site.
• PROPAGATION Separate offsets in summer.
• OTHER NAME *C. autumnale* 'Major'.

☼ ◊

Z 4–9

HEIGHT
5in (12cm)

SPREAD
4in (10cm)

4in
(10cm)

Primulaceae	

CYCLAMEN GRAECUM

Habit Tuberous, perennial, fleshy roots. **Flowers**
Cone-shaped, reflexed petals and dark-rimmed
mouth, borne in autumn. Pink to carmine-red.
Leaves Heart-shaped, appearing after the flowers.
Dark green, with silver and paler green markings.
• NATIVE HABITAT Greece.
• CULTIVATION Grow in deep containers in an
alpine house with soil-rich, fertile, sharply drained
potting mix. Needs a dry, summer dormancy.
• PROPAGATION Soak and rinse seed as soon as
ripe, then sow in darkness.

☀ ◇

Z 8–9

HEIGHT
4in (10cm)

SPREAD
6in (15cm)

¾in
(2cm)

Primulaceae	

CYCLAMEN ROHLFSIANUM

Habit Tuberous, perennial. **Flowers** Scented,
shuttlecock-shaped, with prominent anthers, in
autumn. Pale pink with deep red mouth. **Leaves**
Heart-shaped, shiny, scalloped, appearing with the
flowers. Rich green, with silver-green markings.
• NATIVE HABITAT Libya.
• CULTIVATION Grow in a cool greenhouse with
a soil-based, sharp-drained potting mix. Water in
growth, but keep dry during summer dormancy.
• PROPAGATION Soak and rinse seed as soon as
ripe, then sow in darkness.

☀ ◇

Z 8–9

HEIGHT
4–5in
(10–13cm)

SPREAD
6in (15cm)

¾in
(2cm)

Amaryllidaceae/ Liliaceae	

HABRANTHUS ROBUSTUS

Habit Robust, bulbous, perennial. **Flowers**
Solitary, open funnel-shaped, borne in late summer
to early autumn, with or just after the leaves. Pale
pink. **Leaves** Basal and strap-shaped. Mid-green.
• NATIVE HABITAT Dry uplands in Brazil.
• CULTIVATION Needs soil-based, gritty potting
mix, and a cool greenhouse. Water lightly, but
increase as leaves emerge. Keep moist in dormancy.
• PROPAGATION By seed as soon as ripe, or by
offsets in winter.
• OTHER NAME *Zephyranthes robusta*.

☀ ◇

Z 9–10

HEIGHT
8–12in
(20–30cm)

SPREAD
3–4in
(8–10cm)

3–4in
(7–10cm)

Primulaceae	

CYCLAMEN CILICIUM

Habit Tuberous, perennial. **Flowers** Slender,
shuttlecock-shaped, borne in autumn with the
leaves. White or pink, with carmine-rimmed
mouth. **Leaves** Rounded to heart-shaped.
Mid-green, with extensive paler-green markings.
• NATIVE HABITAT In woods and among rocks,
in southern Turkey.
• CULTIVATION Grow in leafy, gritty, moist but
well-drained soil. Prefers sun or dappled shade.
• PROPAGATION Soak and rinse seed as soon
as ripe, then sow in darkness.

☀ ◇

Z 5–9

HEIGHT
2in (5cm)

SPREAD
3in (8cm)

1in
(2–3cm)

Primulaceae	

CYCLAMEN HEDERIFOLIUM

Habit Tuberous, perennial. *Flowers* Shuttlecock-shaped, with reflexed petals, borne during mid- and late autumn, appearing with or before the leaves. Pale to deep pink, with a darker flush towards the mouth. *Leaves* Variable, but usually ivy-like. Dark-green marbling, mottled with pale green and silvery-green.

• NATIVE HABITAT In woods and among rocks, in the Mediterranean.

• CULTIVATION Needs leafy, gritty, well-drained soil, enriched with organic matter. Suitable for growing in a rock garden in sun or dappled shade. Excellent for naturalizing beneath shrubs, at a hedge base, or below conifers, especially as dormant tubers need to be well-protected from excessive summer rainfall. Mulch annually with leaf mold or similar as soon as leaves start to wither. May self-seed, forming extensive colonies where suitable conditions are found.

• PROPAGATION Soak and rinse ripe seed, then sow in darkness, and germinate at 45–54°F (6–12°C).

• OTHER NAME *C. neapolitanum.*

☀ ◌

Z 5–9

HEIGHT
4–5in
(10–13cm)

SPREAD
6in (15cm)

1–2in
(3–5cm)

Colchicaceae/Liliaceae

COLCHICUM CILICIUM

Habit Cormous, perennial. *Flowers* Widely funnel-shaped, up to 25, borne in autumn. Purplish-pink. *Leaves* Semi-erect, oval to lance-shaped, appearing in spring. Mid-green.
• NATIVE HABITAT Rocks and screes, or scrubland, in foothills of Turkey, Syria, and Lebanon.
• CULTIVATION Grow in a raised bed or at the foot of rock garden. Needs deep, well-drained soil that is not too dry, in an open, sunny site.
• PROPAGATION Sow seed when ripe, or separate offsets in summer.

☼ ◊

Z 5–9

HEIGHT
4in (10cm)

SPREAD
3in (8cm)

4in
(10cm)

Colchicaceae/Liliaceae

COLCHICUM AGRIPPINUM

Habit Cormous, perennial. *Flowers* Narrowly funnel-shaped with heavy, checkered markings, 1 or 2, borne in early autumn. Deep purplish-pink. *Leaves* Semi-erect, narrow, and slightly wavy, appearing in early spring. Mid-green.
• NATIVE HABITAT Origin uncertain.
• CULTIVATION Suitable for a grassy bank or rock garden, placed either at the foot of a rockery or on rock ledges. Needs deep, well-drained soil that is not too dry, and prefers an open, sunny site.
• PROPAGATION Separate offsets in summer.

☼ ◊

Z 4–9

HEIGHT
3–4in
(8–10cm)

SPREAD
3in (8cm)

4in
(10cm)

Colchicaceae/Liliaceae

COLCHICUM BIVONAE

Habit Robust, cormous, perennial. *Flowers* Fragrant, goblet-shaped, strongly checkered, borne in autumn. Purplish-pink, with white base. *Leaves* Semi-erect, oval to strap-shaped, appearing in spring. Mid-green.
• NATIVE HABITAT Italy and western Turkey.
• CULTIVATION Needs deep, well-drained soil that is not too dry. Grows best in an open, sunny site.
• PROPAGATION Sow seed when ripe, or separate offsets in summer.
• OTHER NAMES *C. bowlesianum, C. sibthorpii.*

☼ ◊

Z 4–9

HEIGHT
4–6in
(10–15cm)

SPREAD
4in (10cm)

4in
(10cm)

Colchicaceae/Liliaceae

COLCHICUM 'Waterlily'

Habit Vigorous, cormous, perennial. *Flowers* Fully double, up to 5, borne in autumn. Pinkish-lilac. *Leaves* Semi-erect, narrowly oval, appearing in winter or spring. Mid-green.
• NATIVE HABITAT Garden origin.
• CULTIVATION Suitable for planting at the front of a border or at the foot of a bank in a rock garden. Emerging leaves can crowd smaller plants. Needs deep, fertile, well-drained soil that is not too dry. Grows best in a warm, open, sunny site.
• PROPAGATION Separate offsets in summer.

☼ ◊

Z 5–9

HEIGHT
5in (12cm)

SPREAD
4in (10cm)

4in
(10cm)

Colchicaceae/Liliaceae	

MERENDERA MONTANA

Habit Cormous, perennial. **Flowers** Upright, funnel-shaped, borne in autumn. Purple to red-purple. **Leaves** Linear and channeled, appearing with or just after the flowers. Mid-green.
• NATIVE HABITAT Stony ground and dry turf, in the Pyrenees and Iberian Peninsula.
• CULTIVATION Grow in a sunny rock garden, or raised bed in well-drained, moderately fertile soil.
• PROPAGATION By seed in spring, or by offsets in summer.
• OTHER NAMES *M. bulbocodium, M. pyrenaica.*

☼ ◊

Z 6–9

HEIGHT
2in (5cm)

SPREAD
2in (5cm)

2–3in
(5–7cm)

Araceae	

ARUM PICTUM

Habit Tuberous, perennial. **Flowers** Hooded, with short spikes, borne in autumn. Black-purple. **Leaves** Arrow-shaped, leathery, and glossy. Dark green, with fine, cream veins.
• NATIVE HABITAT Shady places, Mediterranean.
• CULTIVATION Grow in an alpine house in fertile soil enriched with organic matter, or plant outdoors in sunny shelter. Water freely in growth, but reduce as leaves wither to allow dry dormancy.
• PROPAGATION Sow seed as soon as ripe, or divide clumps of tubers after flowering.

☼ ◊

Z 7–9

HEIGHT
6–10in
(15–25cm)

SPREAD
6in (15cm)

4–6in
(9–15cm)

Araceae	

BIARUM TENUIFOLIUM

Habit Tuberous, perennial. **Flowers** Ill-scented, slender, often twisted, cowl-like, borne in autumn. Green, flushed dark purple, surrounding black-purple spike. **Leaves** Basal, upright, and lance-shaped, appearing after the flowers. Green.
• NATIVE HABITAT Rocky hillsides, Mediterranean.
• CULTIVATION Needs light, gritty, sharply drained soil. Grow in a warm, sheltered site at the base of a sunny wall. May spread where conditions suit.
• PROPAGATION Sow seed in spring, or separate offset tubers in summer.

☼ ◊

Z 7–9

HEIGHT
4–8in
(10–20cm)

SPREAD
2–3in
(5–8cm)

2in
(5cm)

Amaryllidaceae	AUTUMN DAFFODIL

STERNBERGIA LUTEA

Habit ·Free-flowering, bulbous, perennial. **Flowers** Goblet-shaped, borne in autumn. Deep yellow. **Leaves** Narrowly lance-shaped, appearing with the flowers. Dark green.
• NATIVE HABITAT Stony hillsides, from the Mediterranean to Iran and central Asia.
• CULTIVATION Suitable for growing in a rock garden or raised bed. Needs a warm, sunny site, with sharply drained, moderately fertile soil.
• PROPAGATION Sow seed as soon as ripe, or separate offsets when dormant.

☼ ◊

Z 6–9

HEIGHT
6in (15cm)

SPREAD
3in (8cm)

6in
(15cm)

Amaryllidaceae/ Liliaceae	DOUBLE COMMON SNOWDROP

GALANTHUS NIVALIS 'Flore Pleno'

Habit Robust, bulbous, perennial. *Flowers* Pear-shaped, honey-scented, drooping, irregularly doubled, borne in winter to early spring. White, with green marks inside. *Leaves* Basal, semi-erect, and narrowly lance-shaped. Gray-green.
• NATIVE HABITAT Woodlands, from the Pyrenees to Ukraine; elsewhere, naturalized.
• CULTIVATION Grow in moist but well-drained, fertile soil in partial or dappled shade.
• PROPAGATION Divide clumps before the leaves wither after flowering, and replant immediately.

☼ ◑

Z 3–9

HEIGHT
4–6in
(10–15cm)

SPREAD
2in (5cm)

2–3in
(5–7cm)

Amaryllidaceae/ Liliaceae	

GALANTHUS NIVALIS 'Pusey Green Tip'

Habit Robust, bulbous, perennial. *Flowers* Pear-shaped, drooping, irregularly doubled, borne in winter to early spring. White, with pale-green markings on outer tips. *Leaves* Basal, semi-erect, and narrowly lance-shaped. Gray-green.
• NATIVE HABITAT Garden origin.
• CULTIVATION Grow in moist but well-drained, fertile soil. Prefers partial or dappled shade.
• PROPAGATION Divide clumps before the leaves wither after flowering (known as "in the green"), and replant immediately.

☼ ◑

Z 3–9

HEIGHT
4–6in
(10–15cm)

SPREAD
2in (5cm)

2–3in
(5–7cm)

Amaryllidaceae/ Liliaceae	

GALANTHUS GRACILIS

Habit Slender, bulbous, perennial. *Flowers* Pear-shaped, scented, drooping, borne in late winter and early spring. White, with green inner tips and base. *Leaves* Linear and twisted. Gray-green.
• NATIVE HABITAT Woodlands in Bulgaria, Greece, and Turkey.
• CULTIVATION Grow in moist but well-drained, fertile soil in partial or dappled shade.
• PROPAGATION Divide clumps after flowering, or sow seed when ripe. Species hybridize freely.
• OTHER NAMES *G. elwesii* var. *minor, G. graecus*.

☼ ◑

Z 3–9

HEIGHT
4in (10cm)

SPREAD
2in (5cm)

2–3in
(5–7cm)

Amaryllidaceae/ Liliaceae	

GALANTHUS RIZEHENSIS

Habit Slender, bulbous, perennial. *Flowers* Small, pear-shaped, drooping, borne in late winter to early spring. White, with green-marked tips. *Leaves* Linear and recurved. Dark green.
• NATIVE HABITAT Woodlands in mountain foothills of northeastern Turkey.
• CULTIVATION Grow in moist but well-drained, fertile soil, in a partial- or dapple-shaded site.
• PROPAGATION Divide clumps after flowering, or sow seed when ripe. Species hybridize freely and may not come true from seed.

☼ ◑

Z 3–9

HEIGHT
5in (12cm)

SPREAD
2in (5cm)

2–3in
(5–7cm)

Amaryllidaceae/ Liliaceae	

GALANTHUS ELWESII

Habit Robust, bulbous, perennial. *Flowers* Honey-scented, slender, pear-shaped, drooping, borne in late winter. White, with green, often merging, marks on tips and base. *Leaves* Strap-shaped and sometimes twisted. Gray-green.
• NATIVE HABITAT Balkans and western Turkey.
• CULTIVATION Grow in moist but well-drained, fertile soil in partial or dappled shade.
• PROPAGATION Divide clumps after flowering, or sow seed when ripe. Species hybridize freely and may not come true from seed.

☼ ◐

Z 3–9

HEIGHT
5–9in
(12–22cm)

SPREAD
3in (8cm)

2–3in
(5–7cm)

Amaryllidaceae/ Liliaceae	

GALANTHUS 'Atkinsii'

Habit Vigorous, bulbous, perennial. *Flowers* Slender, stretched pear-shaped, drooping, with short stalks, borne in late winter. White, with green heart on inner petals. *Leaves* Linear. Gray-green.
• NATIVE HABITAT Garden origin.
• CULTIVATION Grow in moist but well-drained, fertile soil, preferably in partial or dappled shade. As with other robust variants, *G.* 'Atkinsii' is ideal for naturalizing.
• PROPAGATION Divide clumps before leaves wither after flowering, and replant immediately.

☼ ◐

Z 3–9

HEIGHT
8in (20cm)

SPREAD
3in (8cm)

2–3in
(5–7cm)

Amaryllidaceae/ Liliaceae	

GALANTHUS IKARIAE subsp. *IKARIAE*

Habit Bulbous, perennial. *Flowers* Pear-shaped, drooping, borne in late winter or early spring. White, with large, green mark on inner tip. *Leaves* Strap-shaped and glossy. Bright green.
• NATIVE HABITAT Aegean Islands and Turkey.
• CULTIVATION Grow in moist but well-drained, fertile soil. Prefers partial or dappled shade.
• PROPAGATION Divide clumps after flowering, or sow seed when ripe. Species hybridize freely.
• OTHER NAMES *G. latifolius* of gardens, *G. platyphyllus.*

☼ ◐

Z 3–9

HEIGHT
4–6in
(10–15cm)

SPREAD
2in (5cm)

2–3in
(5–7cm)

Amaryllidaceae/ Liliaceae	

GALANTHUS NIVALIS 'Scharlockii'

Habit Robust, bulbous, perennial. *Flowers* Pear-shaped, drooping, with conspicuous hoods divided in two, borne in late winter to spring. White, with pale-green, outer marks. *Leaves* Basal, semi-erect, and narrowly lance-shaped. Gray-green.
• NATIVE HABITAT Rhineland woods in Germany.
• CULTIVATION Grow in moist but well-drained, humus-rich soil, in partial or dappled shade.
• PROPAGATION Divide after flowering, or sow seed when ripe.
• OTHER NAME *G.* 'Scharlockii'.

☼ ◐

Z 3–9

HEIGHT
4–6in
(10–15cm)

SPREAD
2in (5cm)

2–3in
(5–7cm)

Amaryllidaceae/ Liliaceae	

GALANTHUS PLICATUS subsp. BYZANTINUS

Habit Bulbous, perennial. **Flowers** Pear-shaped, drooping, borne in late winter to early spring. White, with green marks on inner tips and base. **Leaves** Broadly linear, with recurved margins. Dull, dark green, with gray-green central bands.
• NATIVE HABITAT Fields and scrub in Turkey.
• CULTIVATION Grow in moist but well-drained, fertile soil. Prefers partial or dappled shade.
• PROPAGATION Divide after flowering, or sow seed when ripe. May not come true from seed.

☀ ◐

Z 3–9

HEIGHT
to 8in
(20cm)

SPREAD
3in (8cm)

2–3in
(5–7cm)

Amaryllidaceae/ Liliaceae	

GALANTHUS 'S. Arnott'

Habit Vigorous, bulbous, perennial. **Flowers** Strongly scented, rounded, pear-shaped, borne in winter to early spring. White, with green, inverted "V"-shape on inner tips. **Leaves** Basal, semi-erect, and narrowly lance-shaped. Gray-green.
• NATIVE HABITAT Garden origin.
• CULTIVATION Grow in moist but well-drained, fertile soil, in partial or dappled shade.
• PROPAGATION Divide after flowering.
• OTHER NAMES G. 'Arnott's Seedling', G. 'Sam Arnott'.

☀ ◐

Z 3–9

HEIGHT
8in (20cm)

SPREAD
3in (8cm)

2–3in
(5–7cm)

Primulaceae	

CYCLAMEN COUM subsp. ALBUM

Habit Tuberous, perennial. **Flowers** Cone-shaped, borne in winter or early spring. White, stained carmine-red at mouth. **Leaves** Rounded, appearing with the flowers. Dark green, sometimes with silver marks.
• NATIVE HABITAT In woods, scrub, and among rocks, from Bulgaria to Lebanon.
• CULTIVATION Grow in leaf-rich, fertile, gritty, well-drained soil. Prefers sun or dappled shade.
• PROPAGATION Soak and rinse seed as soon as ripe, then sow in darkness.

☀ ○

Z 5–9

HEIGHT
to 4in
(10cm)

SPREAD
2–4in
(5–10cm)

1–2in
(3–5cm)

Primulaceae	

CYCLAMEN PERSICUM

Habit Tuberous, perennial. **Flowers** Scented, shuttlecock-shaped, with reflexed petals, in winter and early spring. White or pink. **Leaves** Heart-shaped. Dark green, often with silver-marbled outside, and pale- or purple-green underside.
• NATIVE HABITAT Southeast Mediterranean.
• CULTIVATION Grow in moderately fertile, potting mix. Water evenly in growth, reduce as leaves wither, keeping tuber dry when dormant.
• PROPAGATION Soak and rinse seed, then sow in darkness at 54–59°F (12–15°C), in late summer.

☀ ○

Z 9–10

HEIGHT
4–8in
(10–20cm)

SPREAD
4–6in
(10–15cm)

Nose
level

Amaryllidaceae/Liliaceae

GALANTHUS NIVALIS 'Sandersii'

Habit Delicate, bulbous, slender, perennial.
Flowers Scented, drooping, pear-shaped, borne
in winter to early spring. White, with yellow, inner
marks and yellow base. *Leaves* Basal, semi-erect,
and narrowly lance-shaped. Gray-green.
• NATIVE HABITAT Garden origin.
• CULTIVATION Grow in moist but well-drained,
fertile soil. Prefers to be sited in partial or dappled
shade. This species is less vigorous than many
other variants and is more delicate in all of its
parts. Suitable for naturalizing beneath shrubs

or in light woodland, but needs a little more care
to maintain colonies. Be careful not to plant among
strong-growing grass or other, more robust plants.
Application of a general, balanced fertilizer after
flowering is beneficial.
• PROPAGATION Divide clumps before leaves
start to wither after flowering (known as "in the
green"). Replant immediately, at the same depth,
taking care to avoid damage to the bulb and roots.
• OTHER NAMES *G.* 'Howick Yellow',
G. 'Lutescens', *G. nivalis flavescens.*

☼ ◊

Z 3–9

HEIGHT
4in (10cm)

SPREAD
1–2in
(2.5–5cm)

2in
(5cm)

Primulaceae	

CYCLAMEN PERSICUM 'Pearl Wave'

Habit Tuberous, perennial. *Flowers* Slender, scented, shuttlecock-shaped, frilly-edged, borne in winter to early spring. Deep pink. *Leaves* Heart-shaped. Dark green, marked silver and pale green.
• NATIVE HABITAT Garden origin.
• CULTIVATION Grow as a house or conservatory plant. Water evenly during growth, avoiding the crown. Apply low-nitrogen fertilizer every 2 weeks, reduce as leaves fade, keeping dry when dormant.
• PROPAGATION Soak and rinse seed, then sow in darkness at 54–59°F (12–15°C), in late summer.

☼ ◊

Z 9–10

HEIGHT
4–8in
(10–20cm)

SPREAD
4–6in
(10–15cm)

Nose
level

Primulaceae	

CYCLAMEN COUM subsp. COUM

Habit Tuberous, perennial. *Flowers* Compact, shuttlecock-shaped, with dark-stained mouth, borne in winter or early spring. Bright carmine-pink. *Leaves* Rounded, appearing with the flowers. Plain, dark green, or silver-marked.
• NATIVE HABITAT In woods and scrubland, in Bulgaria, Caucasus, Turkey, and Lebanon.
• CULTIVATION Grow in leaf-rich, fertile, gritty, well-drained soil in sun or dappled shade.
• PROPAGATION Soak and rinse seed as soon as ripe, then sow in darkness.

◐ ◊

Z 5–9

HEIGHT
to 4in
(10cm)

SPREAD
2–4in
(5–10cm)

1–2in
(3–5cm)

Primulaceae	

CYCLAMEN PERSICUM 'Esmeralda'

Habit Tuberous, perennial. *Flowers* Shuttlecock-shaped, with broad petals, borne in winter. Carmine-red. *Leaves* Heart-shaped. Dark green, with silver marks.
• NATIVE HABITAT Garden origin.
• CULTIVATION Grow as a house or conservatory plant. Water evenly during growth, avoiding the crown. Apply low-nitrogen fertilizer every 2 weeks, reduce as leaves fade, keeping dry when dormant.
• PROPAGATION Soak and rinse seed, then sow in darkness at 54–59°F (12–15°C), in late summer.

☼ ◊

Z 9–10

HEIGHT
4–8in
(10–20cm)

SPREAD
4–6in
(10–15cm)

Nose
level

Primulaceae	

CYCLAMEN PERSICUM Kaori Series

Habit Tuberous, perennial. *Flowers* Shuttlecock-shaped, fragrant, borne in winter. Various colors. *Leaves* Heart-shaped. Dark green, silver veined.
• NATIVE HABITAT Garden origin.
• CULTIVATION In cooler areas, grow as a house or conservatory plant in moderately fertile, potting mix. Water during growth, avoiding the crown. Apply low-nitrogen fertilizer every 2 weeks, reduce as leaves fade, keeping dry when dormant.
• PROPAGATION Soak and rinse seed, then sow in darkness, at 54–59°F (12–15°C), in late summer.

☼ ◊

Z 9–10

HEIGHT
4–8in
(10–20cm)

SPREAD
4–6in
(10–15cm)

Nose
level

Primulaceae	

CYCLAMEN PERSICUM 'Renown'

Habit Tuberous, perennial. **Flowers** Shuttlecock-shaped, slender, fragrant, borne in winter and early spring. Scarlet. **Leaves** Heart-shaped. Bright silver-green, with dark-green center.
• NATIVE HABITAT Garden origin.
• CULTIVATION Grow as a house or conservatory plant in cool areas.. Water during growth, avoiding the crown. Apply low-nitrogen fertilizer every 2 weeks, reduce as leaves fade. Needs dry dormancy.
• PROPAGATION Soak and rinse seed, then sow in darkness at 54–59°F (12–15°C), in late summer.

☀ ◊

Z 9–10

HEIGHT
4–8in
(10–20cm)

SPREAD
4–6in
(10–15cm)

Nose level

Hyacinthaceae/ Liliaceae	

LACHENALIA ALOIDES var. QUADRICOLOR

Habit Bulbous, perennial. **Flowers** Drooping, tubular, borne in winter. Flame bud, opening to green and yellow spike. **Leaves** Strap-shaped. Bluish-green.
• NATIVE HABITAT Western Cape, southern Africa.
• CULTIVATION Needs light, well-drained soil and dry dormancy in summer.
• PROPAGATION Sow seed when ripe, or separate bulblets in late summer or autumn.
• OTHER NAMES Lachenalia tricolor.

☀ ◊

Z 9–10

HEIGHT
6–10in
(15–25cm)

SPREAD
2–3in
(5–8cm)

4in
(10cm)

Ranunculaceae	WINTER ACONITE

ERANTHIS HYEMALIS

Habit Clump-forming, tuberous, perennial. **Flowers** Stemless, cup-shaped, borne in late winter to early spring. Bright yellow. **Leaves** Dissected, forming a ruff immediately beneath the flower. Bright green.
• NATIVE HABITAT Southern France to Bulgaria.
• CULTIVATION Grow in fertile, moist but well-drained, fertile soil. Prefers dappled or partial shade. Spreads rapidly to form colonies.
• PROPAGATION By seed in late spring, or by division of colonies immediately after flowering.

☀ ◊

Z 4–9

HEIGHT
2–4in
(5–10cm)

SPREAD
3–4in
(8–10cm)

2in
(5cm)

Hyacinthaceae/ Liliaceae	

LACHENALIA ALOIDES 'Nelsonii'

Habit Bulbous, perennial. **Flowers** Drooping, tubular, borne in dense spikes in winter and early spring. Bright yellow, tinted green. **Leaves** Semi-erect and strap-shaped. Mid-green, spotted purple.
• NATIVE HABITAT Garden origin.
• CULTIVATION Needs light, well-drained soil. Water moderately in growth, keeping dry in summer dormancy. Resume watering once growth starts in autumn. Good for a cool conservatory.
• PROPAGATION Separate bulblets in late summer or autumn during dormancy.

☀ ◊

Z 9–10

HEIGHT
6–10in
(15–25cm)

SPREAD
2–3in
(5–8cm)

4in
(10cm)

CARING FOR BULBS

Most bulbous and cormous plants have a period of dormancy underground after flowering, and so need relatively little attention for most of the year. Their long-term success, however, depends on the initial selection of healthy stock and correct planting. Most importantly, the needs of the individual species must be matched to the prevailing conditions of soil, moisture, light, and warmth in the planting site.

Conserving bulbs in their habitat is of utmost importance, and strict legislation governs their importation. It is good practice to check that bulbs are from cultivated rather than wild-collected sources, and to reject stock of dubious origin. Responsible producers propagate from cultivated plants and usually label their stock accordingly.

The size and quality of bulbs offered by commercial producers tends to vary considerably, so it is best to examine them thoroughly before making a purchase. Check that they are plump, firm, and healthy, with strong growing points and no obvious signs of damage,

disease, or soft tissue. It is worth bearing in mind that bulb offsets are unlikely to flower in their first season; the same is also true of bulbs that are smaller than average for their type.

Different types of bulb are sold at different times of year, and it is always best to buy upon availability. This ensures that they have not sprouted into growth, or suffered overheating or desiccation in storage. In particular, shade-loving bulbs and those native to damp woodland (such as *Erythronium)*, will deteriorate if kept dry for too long. These are usually sold in moist bark or sawdust and any whose packaging material is dust-dry should be rejected. A few plants, notably *Cyclamen*, establish best when the fibrous roots that emerge from the tubers have been allowed to grow unchecked by dry conditions.

The more expensive pot-grown specimens often prove better value, as they establish more readily. Similarly, snowdrops often fail to establish well from dry bulbs, and specialist growers usually supply them "in the green."

HOW TO SELECT BULBS

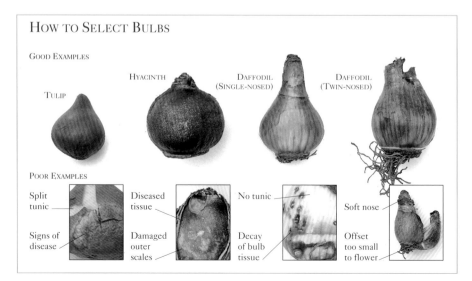

GOOD EXAMPLES

TULIP

HYACINTH

DAFFODIL
(SINGLE-NOSED)

DAFFODIL
(TWIN-NOSED)

POOR EXAMPLES

Split tunic

Signs of disease

Diseased tissue

Damaged outer scales

No tunic

Decay of bulb tissue

Soft nose

Offset too small to flower

CHOOSING CORMS, TUBERS, AND BULBOUS PLANTS

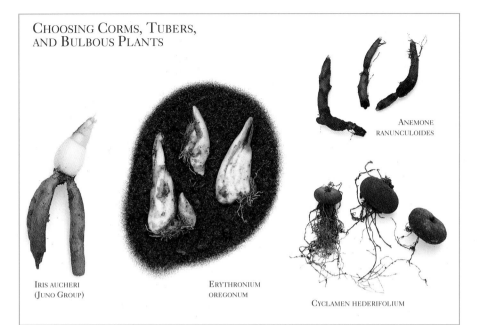

ANEMONE
RANUNCULOIDES

IRIS AUCHERI
(JUNO GROUP)

ERYTHRONIUM
OREGONUM

CYCLAMEN HEDERIFOLIUM

SOIL PREPARATION AND PLANTING

The conditions of a bulb's native habitat provide valuable clues to its needs in cultivation. Most hardy bulbs originate from Mediterranean-type climates, where they experience cool, damp winters, with adequate moisture in spring, followed by a hot, dry summer during which they are dormant. Bulbs will thrive in a warm, sunny site, in well-drained soils that warm quickly in spring and become dry during summer.

Soil should be moderately fertile, enriched with organic matter and, for most bulbs, neutral to slightly alkaline. A few species, for example *Crocus tommasinianus, C. vernus* and their cultivars, tolerate heavier soils that remain moist during the growing period, provided that the soil dries out during dormancy. Bulbs that are native to swamp or waterside habitats need moist soils that do not dry out in summer. For most other bulbs, good drainage is vital since they will rot during dormancy in wet or poorly aerated soils.

Sandy soils suit many bulbs because they are free-draining and warm up rapidly in spring. To improve the soil's deficiency in nutrients and organic matter, dig in well-rotted compost or manure to below the level of the bulbs, at least three months before planting. Fertilize annually at the recommended rate, in spring. Sandy loams (and well-cultivated sandy soils) will benefit from organic matter, but they do not need additional fertilizer in the first year.

For smaller bulbs in rock gardens or raised beds, provide essential good drainage by incorporating sufficient coarse sand into the top 12in (30cm), making up about one-third by volume.

Although they are usually very fertile, heavy clay soils need to be improved considerably if bulbs are to thrive. Install a drainage system if subsoil drainage is poor. Then add coarse sand at a rate of 2 bucketfuls per sq. yd (sq. m), and plenty of well-rotted organic matter, to improve structure and drainage.

When to plant

Dry bulbs usually become available towards the natural end of their dormant period. They should be planted as soon as possible after purchase, before root growth begins. In spring-flowering bulbs, dormancy starts between late summer (as with most *Narcissus*) and early autumn. All autumn-flowering bulbs should be planted by late summer although some, such as the autumn crocuses and colchicums, need a longer growing season and should be in place by mid-summer. Summer-flowering genera, such as *Galtonia* and *Gladiolus*, and bulbs grown "in the green," are planted in early to mid-spring.

How to plant

As a general rule, the planting depth of dry bulbs is determined by their size. In open ground, most need to be covered with soil to about 3–5 times the bulb's height (deeper in light than in heavy soil), and should be spaced at 2–3 times their own width apart. Fork some bonemeal into the bottom of the planting hole, and lay a bed of coarse sand into which the bulbs are gently firmed. This avoids air pockets, deters slugs and, in wetter areas, aids drainage. Cover with soil, breaking down any clods into fine crumbs. Firm gently for good soil contact. Plant several bulbs to a large hole dug out with a spade, or singly to a trowel-made hole. Random rather than symmetrical spacing of the bulbs achieves the most natural effects.

When planting "in the green," set the bulbs at the same depth as they were planted before and water in thoroughly. If setting out pot-grown bulbs, allow them to die back naturally and then plant as for dry bulbs. Dig a hole that is large and deep enough for the entire potful without disturbance. If planted at about the right depth, many bulbs adjust themselves to their preferred depth by means of contractile roots. In the wild, this adaptation protects them from the predations of animals and the extremes of weather.

PLANTING BULBS IN THE OPEN

1 *Dig out a large hole in well-prepared ground and plant the bulbs in a sand bed, growing points uppermost and at least twice their depth and width apart.*

2 *For the most natural effects, position the bulbs randomly on the base of the hole. Once they are in position, gently draw the soil over them by hand to avoid displacing them.*

3 *Tamp down the soil over the planted area gently but firmly with the back of a rake. Do not step heavily on the soil surface, since this may damage the bulbs' growing points.*

PLANTING LARGE BULBS IN GRASS

1 *Scatter bulbs randomly over the planting area, and then adjust to make sure that they are at least their own width apart.*

2 *Make an individual hole for each bulb, about 4–6in (10–15cm) deep, with a bulb planter.*

3 *Trickle in a pinch of bonemeal mixed with some core soil from the bulb planter. Position the bulb in place, growing point up.*

4 *Break up the lower two-thirds of the soil core, and cover the bulb with the loose soil. Set the remaining circle of turf back in place.*

5 *Firm the turf gently to ensure good soil contact, while avoiding damage to the growing point. Fill any gaps with loose soil.*

PLANTING SMALL BULBS IN GRASS

1 *Use a spade or half-moon edger to cut an "H" shape in the turf. Make the cut deep enough to penetrate the soil beneath.*

2 *Undercut the turf and fold back the flaps. Loosen the soil beneath with a handfork to a depth of 3in (7cm).*

3 *Press bulbs gently and randomly into the soil, at least 1in (2.5cm) apart. Score the turf beneath with a fork. Roll back and firm.*

Planting corms and tubers

For most corms and tubers, the planting technique and the calculation of depth is the same as for bulbs. However, they usually need slightly wider spacings to accommodate their roots. Several bulbs, mainly woodland natives, will establish themselves more rapidly and are more likely to flower in their first season if planted during root growth. Dry corms or tubers, however, are far less reliable. Woodland natives prefer a leaf-rich, moist but well-drained soil, so it is best to incorporate plenty of well-rotted organic matter such as leaf-mold into the soil. On planting, spread the roots gently and evenly in the hole prepared, then cover with soil and firm gently to exclude air spaces.

Cyclamen differ from other tuberous plants in that they grow near the soil surface in their natural habitat. For this reason, they will fail to thrive or flower if planted too deeply. Plant the tubers so that the growing tips are just at soil level, and allow a space between each of at least their own width. If preferred, the tips can be just covered with a loose mulch of leaf mold or coarse sand.

Bulbs in containers

Usually, bulbs are grown in pots for purely ornamental purposes, as decoration for balconies or patios outdoors, or to force prepared bulbs for display inside homes. In some cases, pot cultivation is needed to give greater control over growing conditions. This might be because a species is frost-tender and requires the protection of a heated greenhouse or home. Sometimes, the bulb needs a dry dormancy with protection from summer or winter wet even though it is frost-hardy. Some simply prefer soils that differ from those in the garden. Hardy bulbs that need special seasonal care can be grown in a cold greenhouse, in a pot or border, or in an alpine house or bulb frame outdoors.

Clay pots are better for species that dislike excessive moisture since they dry out more rapidly than plastic ones. However, plastic pots are especially useful for woodlanders which prefer even, moist conditions. All pots must have adequate drainage, and it is best to use "pot feet" outdoors to allow free drainage from the bottom of the pot and to give clay pots added frost protection.

How to Plant Bulbs in Pots

1 *Put a layer of soil mix at the bottom of the pot. Plant bulbs at twice their own depth and one bulb's width apart.*

2 *Cover the bulbs with soil mix to within ½in (1cm) of the pot rim. Top-dress with coarse sand, and label the pot (see insert).*

Preparing clay pots
Before planting bulbs in clay pots, place a layer of crocks or pebbles over the drainage hole and then add soil mix.

Soil mixes for bulbs under cover

All soil mixes for bulbs, corms, and tubers must be free-draining and well-aerated. The following mixes suit pots, greenhouse borders, and bulb frames. A mix of 2 parts peat (or substitute), 3 parts coarse sand, and 4 parts loam, with additional base fertilizer at a rate of 1oz/gallon (25g/5 liters) and garden lime at 1oz/4 gallons (25g/18 liters); this mix suits most mature bulbs. For species that hate lime, use acid loam as a replacement. A mix for woodland bulbs consists of 3 parts leaf mold, 2 parts loam, and 1 part grit or coarse sand. Commercial soil mix can be mixed with at least one-third by volume of coarse sand or grit to ensure good drainage. If planting bulbs directly into a bulb frame or greenhouse border, mix sufficient soil mix to make a bed 12in (30cm) deep over a 2in (5cm) deep layer of well-rotted compost or garden manure.

Planting bulbs in pots

In containers, bulbs can be planted at the same depth as those grown outdoors. For some large bulbs, like *Hippeastrum*, the nose needs to be at surface level. All large bulbs need at least 1in (2.5cm) of moist soil mix below them. Fill pots to within ½in (1cm) of the rim, top-dress with grit, and then label with name and date. Do not water until the soil mix is dry and root growth starts. After planting, keep pots in a cold greenhouse or frame, preferably plunged in a sand bed to prevent pots freezing in winter, or drying out or overheating in summer.

BULBS IN A PLUNGE BED

Plunging in sand
Plunge pots to their rims in a bed of coarse sand or into the soil at the base of the cold frame. Check regularly to ensure that the soil mix does not dry out.

FORCING HYACINTHS FOR INDOOR DISPLAY

1 *Set the bulbs on a layer of moist bulb fiber with the bulb crown just above the surface. Put in a cool, dark place. Keep the medium just moist, watering carefully between the bulbs if it dries out.*

2 *After 8 weeks, or when the shoots reach 2in (5cm) high and the flower spike is just visible, bring into bright, indirect light in a cool room. On exposure to light, the leaves will soon turn green.*

ROUTINE CARE

Once bulbs are planted in suitable conditions, they need little attention. The most common reason for poor flowering is overcrowding, but this is easily remedied by lifting, dividing, and replanting in a fresh site.

Bulbs in grass
When naturalized in grass, bulbs need even less attention than those planted elsewhere. To promote flower formation, feed occasionally with a high-potash fertilizer, rather than a high-nitrogen feed which encourages grass growth at the expense of bulbs. The timing of mowing is crucial. Whether bulbs are spring-, summer-, or autumn-flowering, they must be allowed to complete their foliage growth and to die back naturally before cutting. Leaves provide the food source that fuels the growth and flowers for the next season.

For early-flowering bulbs, such as narcissus, make the first cut about 6 weeks after flowering, when the foliage begins to yellow. Where bulbs that colonize by self-seeding, such as *Galanthus*, are grown delay the first cut for a further 3 weeks. Seed capsules generally ripen after the leaves have faded. It is easier to cut the bulb foliage first with shears before trying to mow.

Autumn-flowering species, like *Colchicum*, begin leaf growth before the end of the mowing season. In this case, either stop mowing as the growing tips emerge, or raise the mower blades to avoid them. Do not mow when shoots are too tall to escape the blades.

Deadheading
Regular deadheading of flowered bulbs, whether in grass or in beds and borders, improves the vigor of the bulbs. It prevents them from wasting energy in the production of unwanted seed, and helps the formation of the next season's flowerbuds within the bulb. In borders, cut down dead, dry flower stems at the base with pruners. If seed is needed for self-sowing or propagation, leave a few pods to ripen and harvest before cutting back the faded leaves.

CUTTING AFTER FLOWERING

Keep clumps of leaves in place until they begin to fade and turn yellow naturally. Bulbs (here, Narcissus*) growing in grass are best cut back to the ground with shears before using a lawnmower.*

DEADHEADING

Dead, dry flower stems (here, Allium*) should be cut down at the base, using pruners. If seed is needed, leave several seedheads in place. Collect the seed as soon as the capsule begins to split.*

Bulbs in borders and woodland

The level of care needed for bulbs in borders and woodland depends on whether they are grown as permanent plantings or used as temporary fillers. Permanent plantings, for example *Narcissus*, require little maintenance unless or until flowering is reduced by overcrowding. This is resolved by lifting and dividing bulbs.

In well-prepared ground, provide one or two applications of a high-potash, low-nitrogen fertilizer during growth after the first year. Care of temporary plantings, such as tulips, is the same as first-year care for permanent ones; the essential difference being that bulbs are lifted at the end of the growing season, as the foliage fades.

Staking

Tall bulbs with slender stems, for example *Gladiolus*, usually need staking. This is best done as soon as they are tall enough for a tie to be put around them. Insert the stake carefully, to avoid bruising or damaging the bulb, then tie in the stem using soft twine or raffia. Tie in again when the stem approaches its

STAKING BULBS IN GROUPS

For clump-forming bulbs, like Lilium, *insert stakes at the center of the clump, taking care not to pierce the bulbs. Tie stems to the stakes with soft twine or raffia using a figure-eight loop.*

STAKING

1 *Support single-stemmed plants such as* Gladiolus *with a stake. Insert the cane carefully when the stem reaches about 6in (15cm) tall. Tie in the stem to the stake with soft twine or raffia.*

2 *As the stem approaches its full height and flowerbuds begin to show, tie in the stem again, just below the lowest flowerbud, to prevent the stem from breaking when the flowers open.*

HOW TO DIVIDE AN OVERCROWDED CLUMP

1 *Carefully lift overcrowded clumps of bulbs as the leaves fade after flowering. Use a garden fork, taking care not to spear the bulbs with the tines.*

2 *Divide the clump of bulbs by hand, teasing it apart, first into smaller clumps, then into individual bulbs. Discard any dead or damaged material.*

3 *Discard any bulbs that are unhealthy. Clean healthy bulbs carefully by rubbing off loose tunics, before planting them back individually in soil that has been prepared well.*

full height, and is about to flower. Where bulbs are planted in groups as, for example, with lilies, set the stakes at the center of the clump so that they are disguised as the foliage grows. In this case, tie the twine in a figure-eight loop so that the stems do not chafe against the stakes.

Removing dead leaves

When bulbs in the border have finished flowering, allow the leaves to die back completely before removing them. Do not cut them down or tie them in knots when they are still green, since this depletes the bulbs' vigor and reduces its flowering potential for the following year.

Dividing overcrowded bulbs

If the flowering performance of mature bulbs begins to deteriorate, the most likely cause is overcrowding. Lift the crowded clumps only when bulbs are completely dormant, before root growth begins. Check that they are firm, with no signs of soft tissue or rot, and discard any that appear suspect. If bulbs are healthy, separate the clump into individual bulbs, and replant in irregular drifts at the appropriate depths and spacings. For natural effects, set young offsets between full-size bulbs. Alternatively, grow the offsets on in a nursery bed or in pots, and feed them regularly with a high-potash, low-nitrogen fertilizer during the growing season. Transfer to their final site, during dormancy, when they reach flowering size, which may take several years.

Flowering problems

Bulbs occasionally fail to flower for reasons other than overcrowding, namely infestation, fungus, rot, or bulb blindness (see p. 183). A few species, such as *Fritillaria recurva* and *Iris danfordiae*, do not flower regularly even in their native habitat, often because they form many tiny bulblets. If the foliage is healthy, leave the bulbs undisturbed and they will bloom eventually.

Lifting, drying, and storing

Bulbs used as temporary fillers should be left in place until the foliage begins to turn yellow. Then lift and clean them, and lay them on a wire mesh tray to dry. If they show signs of fungal disease, dust with fungicide. Store them in a clearly labeled paper bag in cool, dry conditions until it is time for replanting. Bulbs may be lifted when they are still in growth, particularly where they have been used for bedding (for example, tulips), in order to free space for other plantings. Lift the plants immediately after flowering, when the leaves are still green, and transfer them to a nursery bed until the leaves fade naturally.

Bulbs in containers outdoors

It is important that bulbs in containers are not allowed to dry out during their growing period. Feed them at alternate waterings with a high-potash fertilizer. The foliage of spring-flowering bulbs should be left to die back naturally, then lift, dry, and store as for outdoor bulbs. Replant in fresh soil mix in autumn. If containers are needed for summer plantings, transfer bulbs "in the green" to another part of the garden where they can be allowed to die back naturally before storing. Alternatively, bulbs like crocus and daffodils can be transferred to the open garden for naturalizing. A few bulbs, notably lilies, do not thrive if allowed to dry out completely during their dormant period. These are best plunged in their pots in a shaded cold frame during dormancy, and repotted in fresh soil mix in spring.

Routine care of bulbs under cover

Bulbs grown in frames need similar care to those grown outdoors in borders, but special care must be given for feeding and watering. Remove covers at the beginning of the growing season, but replace them during periods of cold weather or prolonged heavy rain, and again at the start of the dormant season. When in growth, water the bulbs in dry weather and apply a liquid fertilizer

HOW TO LIFT, DRY, AND STORE BULBS

1 *When leaves turn yellow, about 4–6 weeks after flowering, gently lift the bulbs (here,* Tulipa) *with a fork. Store them temporarily in labeled containers.*

2 *Clean the soil off the bulbs and rub off any loose tunics. Cut or carefully pull off the dying foliage. Discard damaged or diseased bulbs.*

3 *Place the bulbs on a wire tray and allow them to dry overnight. Dust with fungicide, then store in a cool dry place in clearly labeled paper bags.*

every 2–3 weeks. Change to a high-potash fertilizer in the latter part of the season to ensure good flowering in the following year. Container-grown bulbs under cover may be left in their pots for several years. Replace the top layer of soil mix annually, at the start of the growing season; this will usually be sufficient to replenish nutrients, at least until they become overcrowded. If the soil mix is not replenished, feed by applying a high-potash, low-nitrogen fertilizer at alternate waterings during the growing season. Reduce the water gradually as the leaves being to fade

after flowering, and store the dry bulbs in their pots during dormancy. Repot, when they become overcrowed, at the end of the natural dormant period. Several bulbs, in particular woodland natives and those like *Muscari*, whose roots do not die back during summer dormancy, should be kept just moist when dormant with sufficient water to prevent desiccation. Summer-flowering bulbs, like *Galtonia*, usually originate from climates with wet summers and become dormant in winter. Where these bulbs are grown under cover, they must be watered throughout summer.

REPOTTING OVERCROWDED BULBS

1 At the end of dormancy, remove some soil mix from the pot and inspect the bulbs (here, Narcissus). Repot if overcrowded.

2 Tip out the contents of the pot, and separate the bulbs from the soil mix. Discard any dead material as well as bulbs that show signs of damage or disease.

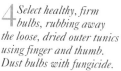

3 Separate pairs of bulbs, or clumps bearing large offsets into individual bulbs, by gently pulling them apart.

4 Select healthy, firm bulbs, rubbing away the loose, dried outer tunics using finger and thumb. Dust bulbs with fungicide.

5 Replant into pots of fresh, moist soil mix, at twice their own depth and at least one bulb's width apart.

PROPAGATION

In the wild, bulbs increase by seed and by forming offsets or bulblets, usually at the base of the bulb. A few of them, including some lilies, produce bulblets on the underground stems or grow stem bulbils from the leaf axils. All of these natural forms of multiplication can be exploited in cultivation to increase stocks. Although raising bulbs from seed demands considerable patience for many species, it can be one of the most economical and rewarding ways of gaining large numbers of new plants. A range of more specialized techniques, including sectioning, scooping, and scoring, are used for the propagation of bulbs that are naturally slow to form offsets or bulblets. These techniques can also be used for bulbs that cannot be raised from seed because they are hybrids of complex parentage.

Dividing bulbs
During the growing season, offsets are often formed from the main parent bulb, usually within the bulb tunic. This is one of the simplest ways of increasing bulbs. The offsets can be separated every second or third year or so, and planted out separately, or potted up and grown on until they reach flowering size. When left in place, the clumps become overcrowded so that offsets develop flowers more slowly, and flowering of the parent bulb may also be impaired.

Propagation from offsets
Some bulbs, such as *Crinum*, may be increased by dividing an established clump just before growth begins in spring. Lift the clump and clean off any soil and loose material. Gently pull the offset away from the parent bulb or cut through the basal plate where the offset is attached to the parent. Dust any cut surfaces with fungicide before re-planting the larger offsets and the parent bulb in the garden. Pot up smaller offsets, either singly or several to a large pot, and grow on for one or two seasons in a cold greenhouse.

Propagating from bulblets or bulbils
Bulbs raised from bulblets generally flower a year or two earlier than those raised from seed. Separate the bulblets from the parent bulb when dormant. Towards the end of the dormancy, insert them in rows, spaced at their own width apart, in trays of soil-based potting

HOW TO PROPAGATE BULBS FROM OFFSETS

1 *In spring, before active growth begins, lift the clump of bulbs (here.* Crinum) *with a garden fork. Shake off excess soil.*

2 *Select a large bulb with several well-developed offsets. Gently tease offsets away, taking care to preserve any roots.*

3 *Replant individual offsets, 1in (2.5cm) deep, in 6in (15cm) pots of moist soil mix. Water in and label.*

HOW TO PROPAGATE GLADIOLUS BY CORMELS

1 *Lift the corm with a handfork, as the foliage fades after flowering. Cormels will have developed around the base of the corm. Overwinter in a cool, dry place.*

2 *In late winter or early spring, separate the cormels from the parent corm – they should come away easily. The cormels will vary in size but all can be used for propagation.*

3 *Half-fill a tray with moist, gritty soil mix. Insert cormels, growing points up, in rows spaced 1in (2.5cm) apart. Fill the tray with soil mix, level, firm, and label with name and date.*

mix, and label with name and date. Transfer the containers to a shaded part of the garden or cold frame so the bulblets can grow on, keeping the soil mix moist. If growing on in clay pots, plunge them in a sandbed or the soil base of the cold frame to prevent from drying out. Feed the bulbs regularly with a half-strength, high-potash fertilizer during their first growing season. When the foliage has died back completely at the end of the growing season, tip the young bulbs out of their pot, separate, and clean them. If they are large enough to plant out at the end of the first season, set them into the final flowering site. If not, pot up into potting mix recommended for mature bulbs and grow on for a further year.

Bulbils, such as those formed on the stems of some lilies, for example *Lilium longiflorum and L. pardalinum*, are treated in a similar way but do not need such a deep covering of soil mix. Collect ripe stem bulbils from the parent and loosen during late summer. Set them on the surface of a shallow pot of soil-based seed mix, pressing them gently into the surface. Simply cover with a layer of grit, name and date them, and grow on in a cold frame. In the next autumn, pot them up separately or plant all of the young bulbs in their final flowering site.

Gladiolus cormels

Small cormels form at the base of the gladiolus corm. Store the parent corm and cormels in a dry, frost-free place overwinter. Remove them from the parent corm just before the start of a new growing season in late winter or early spring. Then, set them in trays of soil mix and treat them as for bulblets or plant them in rows, 1in (2.5cm) apart, in light, well-drained, fertile soil in a nursery bed. Alternatively, plant the young cormels in a frost-free frame in cold areas. Grow them on in a nursery bed (in mild areas) or frame for a further two to three years, until they reach flowering size; then lift and plant in their final flowering site, as for mature corms.

Growing bulbs from seed

One attraction of raising bulbs from seed is that it costs relatively little. Moreover, the offspring raised from seed are virus-free, initially, since most viruses cannot be transmitted by seed (see p. 183). With most propagation other than by seed, any diseases present in the parent are passed on to the offspring.

Most seed-raised bulbs take between three and five years to reach flowering size. A few plants, like *Cardiocrinum*, die after flowering, but by sowing seed annually, healthy stock will mature and flower in each growing season.

With most species, seed capsules are easily visible, since they are produced at the tips of the flowered stems. Some genera, like *Crocus*, produce seed capsules at or just above ground level. Observe the ripening seed capsules carefully, removing them as they begin to turn brown and split. Seed is often shed rapidly at this stage and can easily be lost. Extract seed promptly and store in labeled paper bags in cool, dry conditions until sown.

ONE-YEAR-OLD BULB SEEDLINGS

At the end of the first growing season, seedlings (here Fritillaria meleagris*) are often not vigorous enough to pot on. Let the foliage die back and keep the soil mix barely moist.*

HOW TO PROPAGATE BULBS FROM SEED

1 *Fill a pot to within ½in (1cm) of the rim with commercial seed mix and a quarter-part coarse sand, and firm. Sow seed evenly on the surface.*

2 *Just cover the seed with a thin, even layer of sieved soil mix. It should be just deep enough to conceal the seed. Top-dress with a ½in (1cm) layer of grit, and label with name and date.*

3 *Plunge the seed pot in damp sand or gravel in an open frame in a shaded site in the garden. Water as often as required to keep the soil mix evenly moist.*

Autumn is the best time to sow the seed of most hardy bulbs, but if it is available earlier in the season, then sow it at once; it will usually germinate in the following spring. The seed of hardy cyclamen ripens by mid-summer and is best sown as soon as ripe. Dry seed should be soaked for 24 hours and rinsed well before sowing.

The seeds of most lilies also ripens between late summer and early autumn, but they exhibit one of two types of germination, depending on the species. With epigeal germination, shoot and root growth occur almost concurrently and seeds usually, but not always, germinate within 2–6 weeks of sowing. In hypogeal germination, root growth occurs first and shoot growth is initiated by a cold period. It may be several months before obvious signs of hypogeal germination are seen.

Seed mix for bulbs

Combine a commercial soil-based seed mix with a quarter-part by volume of coarse sand to ensure essential good drainage. Alternatively, mix 2 parts sterile soil, 1 part peat, and 1½ parts seed-grade perlite or coarse sand. To this mix, add superphosphate and lime at 1oz/4 gallons (25g/18 liters) each, but omit the lime for acid-loving species such as *Lilium superbum*. Most woodland species prefer a mix that contains leaf mold. For this, mix equal parts sterilized leaf mold, peat, and soil, with an additional 1½ parts of seed-grade perlite or coarse sand.

Sowing seed

Fill a half-pot to within ½in (1cm) of the rim and firm gently. Sow seed thinly and evenly on the surface about ¼in (5mm) apart for small seed, and space large seeds at least one seed's width apart. Just cover seeds with sieved soil mix, top with a layer of grit, and label with name and date. Place in a shaded site, in an open frame or plunge bed, and keep moist. Keep the seed of marginally hardy and tender bulbs in frost-free conditions over winter. The seed of many tender species germinates more rapidly at 70°F (21°C). However, if germination has not occurred within 6–8 weeks in warmth, transfer the seeds to a cooler place.

POTTING UP SEEDLINGS

1 *Empty out the entire contents of the pot. Some of the tiny bulbs, (here,* Fritillaria raddeana*) will be visible in the soil mix. Separate and remove the bulbs from the soil mix carefully.*

2 *Prepare a pot with fresh, gritty bulb soil mix, and replant the young bulbs. Ensure that they are set at twice their own depth, and at least a bulb's width apart.*

Care of seedlings

On germination, bring pots of seedlings into full light in a cold frame or cold greenhouse. Keep soil mix moist during growth, and stop watering when leaves show signs of fading naturally. Woodland natives, such as *Erythronium* and some *Crocus* species from mountainous areas, which do not experience a dry dormancy in nature, should be kept barely moist. Resume watering in early autumn or as soon as signs of growth are seen. Unless seedlings are growing very vigorously, most bulb seedlings are best left undisturbed in their pots for two growing seasons. Apply a half-strength, high-potash fertilizer every 2–3 weeks during the second season.

When foliage dies back toward the end of the dormant period, empty the pot contents. Separate and clean the young bulbs, and pot up in the soil mix recommended for mature bulbs. A technique that suits slow-growing bulbs and many woodland species, since it avoids repeated root disturbance, is to transfer the contents of the pot intact to a larger pot of bulb soil mix and grow on. Most bulbs are best grown on in pots until they are suitable for planting out, usually at 2–3 years old. Continue feeding during the growing season until the bulbs are large enough to be established successfully outdoors. Then plant out the entire potful of bulbs at the end of the dormant period, just as they are coming into growth. Feed when planting to avoid any delay in flowering.

EXTRACTING CYCLAMEN SEED

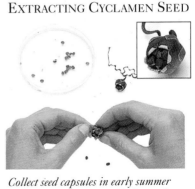

Collect seed capsules in early summer when they begin to split. Shake out the seeds and soak for 24 hours, rinsing well before sowing.

PLANTING OUT "WOODLAND" BULBS

1 *Plant out woodland species without separating the young bulbs. Invert a pot of two year-old bulbs, (here,* Erythronium*) and slide out the mass of bulbs and soil mix.*

2 *Plant the entire potful of soil mix and bulbs, so that the top of the bulb mass is at least 1in (2.5cm) below the surface. Firm the site gently, label, and water lightly.*

Scaling

An important technique used in the propagation of lilies, scaling can also be used for other bulbs with distinct scales, such as some species of *Fritillaria*. Most lily bulbs consist of concentric rings of scales arising from a basal plate. If these are separated from the parent by a small piece of basal plate, the basal tissue is capable of generating new bulblets.

Good hygiene is essential for all variations of this technique, and the cutting surface, tools, and hands must be scrupulously clean. Lift the dormant parent bulbs in late summer or early autumn before root growth begins. Gently remove about six of the outermost scales from the parent bulb and then replant the parent as usual, to flower the following season. The whole bulb may be scaled if larger numbers of offspring are needed. Select only plump, disease-free, unblemished scales. Place them in a plastic bag with fungicide powder, and shake gently to coat them thoroughly. Transfer the scales to a clean plastic bag with damp vermiculite or perlite. Seal and place in a warm dark place at 21°C (70°F),

HOW TO SCALE LILIES

1 Clean the bulb. Remove and discard withered or damaged outer scales. Snap off 6 plump scales close to the base of the bulb.

2 Place some fungicide powder in a plastic bag. Put the scales in the bag and shake gently. Transfer to a clean plastic bag.

3 Add a mix of equal parts peat and perlite, then inflate and seal the bag. Store at 70°F (21°C) in the dark.

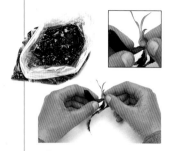

4 When small bulblets develop on the scales, remove them if they are soft. If firm, leave them attached to the bulblets.

5 Plant clusters of bulblets singly in small pots. Top-dress with grit, label, and leave in a warm, light place. Grow on in a cold frame.

6 In autumn, when bulbs have grown on, remove from the pots, separate, and pot up individually or plant out in their flowering site.

for about three months. Place the
bag at the bottom of a refrigerator
(not a freezer) for a further 6–8 weeks.
At the end of this period, bulblets
should have formed at the base of each
scale. Insert one or more scales,
each with small bulblets attached, into
pots of free-draining propagating soil
mix with the tip of the parent scale
just below the surface. Keep the pots
in a shaded greenhouse or cold frame
and transfer them in summer to a
plunge bed to keep cool and evenly
moist. At the end of the first growing
season, separate the bulblets and pot
them up singly into the soil mix
recommended for mature bulbs.
Grow them on in a cool greenhouse
or cold frame until the following spring,
and then either pot up or plant out in
their flowering site.

Alternatively, dust the scales
with fungicide and set them in trays
filled with a mix of 2 parts vermiculite
or damp perlite and 1 part coarse sand.
Keep them moist and shaded in a warm
area at 70°F (21°C) for two months.
To promote leaf growth, the scales
should be moved to a shaded, cool
but frost-free frame in spring. Pot
them up individually at the end of
the growing season, and grow on for
a further year before planting out.

Twin-scaling

This modified form of chipping can
produce numerous offspring and
is used for bulbs with tightly packed
scales, like daffodils, hyacinths,
and snowdrops. The parent bulb is
sectioned into pairs of scales, each
with a piece of basal plate. After
steeping in fungicide, twin scales are
treated as for single scales. Cut tissue
is very susceptible to disease, hence
the success of twin-scaling depends
on good hygiene. Use a liquid fungicide
to ensure good penetration between
the scales. Sterilize the knife blade
and work surface (a sheet of glass is
ideal) with denatured alcohol, before
and between each operation.

TWIN-SCALING

1 *Remove the bulb's outer tunic (here,
Narcissus), and using a sharp knife,
trim off the bulb nose and roots, taking
care not to damage the basal plate.*

2 *Place the bulb upside down on its
nose end. Cut downard through the
basal plate, dividing it into sections,
each with a piece of basal plate.*

3 *Divide the sections into pairs
of scales by peeling back the layers.
Use a sharp scalpel to cut each
pair away with a piece of basal
plate attached (see inset).*

Cutting bulbs into sections

Sectioning bulbs is a technique that is seldom used by amateur gardeners, although it can produce a rapid increase in numbers. It is especially useful for bulbs that do not produce offsets freely or, like cultivars, do not come true from seed (as in tulips and *Gladiolus*). As with twin-scaling, perfect hygiene is necessary to ensure success.

Chipping

The technique of chipping suits bulbs that are formed from tightly packed scales surrounding a central growing point, such as *Hippeastrum*, *Narcissus*, and *Galanthus*. Select clean, healthy parent bulbs at the end of the dormant period, between mid-summer and autumn. Work on a clean, sterile surface and sterilize the knife blade with denatured alcohol, both before and between cutting up different bulbs. Use a sharp, thin-bladed knife to trim off the nose and roots. Divide the bulb, by cutting through the center of the basal plate. Subdivide each half, so that each section or "chip" has a piece of basal plate. Small bulbs, like *Galanthus* or *Narcissus*, are usually cut into 4–8 pieces, while large bulbs, like *Hippeastrum*, will yield up to 16 chips from one bulb. Treat the chips with liquid fungicide and drain for 5–10 minutes. Place them in a plastic bag containing damp vermiculite or perlite, and seal plenty of air inside. Put in a dark place at 70°F (21°C). Check regularly for any signs of rotting. After about 12 weeks, separate the small bulblets that will have formed at the base of the chips and transfer into a shallow pot of well-drained soil mix. For hardy species, harden off and transfer to a cold frame to grow on, but maintain tender species at their minimum recommended temperature. Bulbs grown from chips generally reach flowering size within 2–4 years.

Sectioning corms and tubers

Some corms, such as *Crocosmia* or *Gladiolus*, and the tubers of cyclamen, for example *Cyclamen hederifolium*, form multiple growing points on their surface. Provided that the corms and tubers are large and healthy, they can be sectioned at the end of their dormancy to produce new plants relatively quickly.

SECTIONING TUBERS FOR PROPAGATION

1 *Take a large, healthy tuber (here, Cyclamen* hederifolium*), and with a clean, sharp knife, cut verticially into 2–3 pieces, each piece with at least one growing point. Dust cut surfaces with fungicide.*

2 *Leave pieces on a wire tray in a warm, dry place for 48 hours, to callus over (see inset). Pot sections individually into pots of sharply drained soil mix, with the growing point at the surface. Top-dress with grit.*

Select large tubers or corms that are free from all signs of pests or disease. Cut them into sections, each with at least one growing point, and dust the cut surfaces with fungicide. Put the sections in a warm, dry place for at least 48 hours, to allow the cut surfaces to form calluses. Prepare 5–6cm (2–3in) deep pots, by placing a few crocks at the bottom and then filling them almost full with well-drained, propagating soil mix. Set the corm or tuber with the growing point uppermost, just at the soil mix surface, and then top-dress with grit. Label with name and date and leave them in a cold greenhouse until growth begins. Keep the sections sufficiently moist so as to prevent desiccation, until they start to grow.

Transfer the sections to a cold frame and grow on. Plenty of light and good ventilation are essential, but make sure that sufficient shade from hot sun is also provided. Water the young plants, taking care that they do not dry out during growth. Full-size corms or tubers will usually be produced by the end of the first growing season, and are ready to plant for flowering in the following year.

HOW TO PROPAGATE BULBS BY CHIPPING

1 *When foliage dies down, lift dormant bulb. Select a large, healthy specimen (here,* Hippeastrum*). Trim off the nose and roots.*

2 *Place the bulb on a clean surface, basal plate uppermost. Divide in half by cutting downards through the basal plate.*

3 *Cut each half of the bulb again in the same way, making sure that the basal plate is divided equally between the sections.*

4 *Repeat until the bulb has been cut into 16 chips. Soak in fungicide for 10–15 minutes. Stir occasionally. Drain on a wire tray.*

5 *Half-fill a plastic bag with moist vermiculite. Put several chips in the bag, seal, and store in a warm dark place.*

6 *When bulblets appear on the basal plate of the chips, plant them singly into small pots of well-drained soil mix.*

Scooping and scoring

Commonly used to increase hyacinths commercially, scooping and scoring are techniques that induce bulblet production by cutting into the basal plate tissue. Rhizomes respond to cutting in a similar way by producing small rhizomes on the cut surfaces.

To score hyacinths, take a mature bulb in late summer at the end of the normal dormant period. Make two "V"-shaped cuts at right angles to each other, ¼in (5mm) deep, through the bulb's basal plate. Dust the cut surfaces with fungicide, place in a bag of damp perlite or vermiculite, and keep in a warm, dark place. Check regularly, and when bulblets have formed on the cut surfaces, set the bulb upside down in a tray of sharp-draining soil mix made up of equal parts peat (or substitute) and grit. The tips of the bulblets should be just below the surface of the soil mix. After one year, carefully separate the bulblets that have formed on the cut surfaces and plant them in trays in a cold greenhouse to grow on, as described for bulblets (see p. 173).

Scooping hyacinths is a more fruitful modification of this technique. The basal plate of the parent bulb is scooped out with a special knife or sharpened spoon, to a depth no greater than one-quarter of the overall height of the bulb, leaving the rim of the basal plate intact. The scooping action removes the central growing shoot of the bulb, stimulating bulblets to form around the cut surfaces of the basal plate. Dust the exposed surfaces with fungicide and place the bulb upside down in a warm, dry, dark place for about a week, while the cut surface calluses over. For convenience, support the bulbs in a tray of dry sand, with the cut surfaces exposed above the surface of the sand. After 7 days, water the sand to increase humidity and to prevent the bulb drying out. Numerous small bulblets will form after 12–14 weeks. These can be separated from the parent bulb and grown on as for bulblets.

(see p. 173)

HOW TO PROPAGATE HYACINTHS BY SCOOPING

1 *Use a clean, sharpened teaspoon to scoop out the inner part of the bulb's basal plate. Leave the outer rim intact, and discard the basal plate.*

2 *Dip the cut surfaces in fungicide then lay the bulbs, with their scored side uppermost, on trays of dry sand. Put the tray in a warm, airy place.*

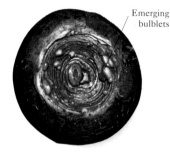

Emerging bulblets

3 *Water the sand just sufficiently to keep it moist. When bulblets form on the scooped base, separate from the parent bulb and pot up.*

PESTS, DISEASES, AND DISORDERS

Some of the most common bulb problems are identified below.

BULB BLINDNESS Bulbs that fail to flower are referred to as "blind". This can be caused by overcrowding and is often accompanied by stunted leaves. It is easily remedied by lifting and dividing overcrowded bulbs, then replanting them in fresh soil. Where bulbs fail to flower as a result of drought, usually they will recover by the next season. Regular watering of pot-grown plants during growth helps to avoid this problem, but outdoors this is more difficult, especially if watering limits are enforced. Bulbs that were immature when planted can also be blind, but they will recover in later seasons. Avoid this problem by planting good-sized stock.

BULB FLIES If bulbs are blind or bear spindly leaves, check a sectioned bulb for larvae and their detritus. The large narcissus fly, *Merodon equestris*, attacks sound bulbs and has brownish-white larvae, ¾in (2cm) long. The small narcissus fly, *Eumerus* species, attacks damaged bulbs and its larvae grow to ⅜in (8mm) long. There is no chemical treatment, so affected bulbs must be destroyed. Avoid planting in warm, dry, shady sites, and firm at the bulb neck as foliage dies down to deter egg-laying.

BULB SCALE MITE This microscopic white mite, *Steneotarsonemus laticeps*, causes stunted growth and curved leaves, and makes saw-toothed scars on leaf margins and flower stems. Bulbs must be discarded since no chemical control is available for use.

INK SPOT FUNGUS This causes black blotches on leaves, inky stains on bulbs, and yellow dots or black craters on bulb scales. Destroy affected bulbs and dust healthy stock with fungicide.

STORAGE ROTS These affect bulbs, corms, and tubers, especially if damaged. Discolored, sunken patches develop on the bulb's surface, and the rot spreads throughout the tissue. Dust undamaged bulbs with fungicide before storing.

VIRUSES The presence of a virus in a plant can be identified from mottling and streaking of the leaves and flowers. Sometimes, growth deformities can also be detected. Virus infection is usually spread by sap-sucking insects such as aphids. The only remedy is to destroy the affected stocks, and use an insecticide to control the aphid vectors.

COMMON NARCISSUS PROBLEMS

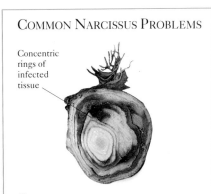

Concentric rings of infected tissue

EELWORM
Nematodes distort, stunt and eventually rot bulbs. Destroy affected bulbs and those within a 3ft (1m) radius. To kill nematodes without harming the bulb, immerse dormant bulbs in a water bath at a constant 112°F (44°C) for 3 hours.

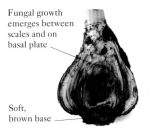

Fungal growth emerges between scales and on basal plate

Soft, brown base

BASAL ROT
This soil-borne fungus spreads rapidly in warm, moist soil. It produces a soft, brown base, followed by pink fungal growth. Destroy affected bulbs. Clean soil from bulbs, treat with fungicide, then store in a cool, dry, and airy place.

GLOSSARY OF TERMS

Italicized words have their
own entry.

ACID (of soil) With a *pH* value
of less than 7; see also *alkaline*
and *neutral.*

ALKALINE (of soil) With a
pH value of more than 7; some
plants will not tolerate alkaline
soils and must be grown in soil
that is *neutral* or *acid.*

ALPINE HOUSE An unheated
greenhouse that is used for the
cultivation of mainly alpine and
bulbous plants. An alpine house
provides greater ventilation and
usually more light than a
conventional greenhouse.

ALTERNATE (of leaves)
Borne singly at each *node*,
successively on either side
of a *stem.*

ANTHER The part of
a *stamen* that produces pollen;
it is usually borne on a *filament.*

APEX The tip or growing
point of any organ such as
a leaf or *shoot.*

AXIL The angle between a
leaf and *stem* where an axillary
bud develops.

BEDDING PLANT A plant
that is mass planted to provide
a temporary display.

BLOOM 1. A flower or blossom.
2. A fine, waxy, whitish or
bluish-white coating found
on *stems*, leaves, or fruits.

BRACT A modified leaf at
the base of a *flower* or flower
cluster. Bracts may resemble
normal leaves or can be reduced
and scale-like in appearance;
they are often large and
brightly colored.

BUD A rudimentary or
condensed *shoot* that
contains embryonic leaves
or *flowers.*

BULB A storage organ that
consists of mainly fleshy *scales*
and swollen modified leafbases
on a much reduced *stem.*
Bulbs usually, but not always,
grow underground.

BULBIL A small bulb-like
organism that is often borne
in a leaf *axil* or in a *flower head.*
It may be used for propagation.

BULBLET A small *bulb* that
is produced at the base of
a mature one.

CALYX (pl. calyces) The outer
part of a *flower*, that encloses
the *petals* in *bud* and is formed
from the *sepals.*

CAPSULE A dry fruit that
splits open when ripe to release
its *seeds.*

CARPEL The female portion
of a *flower*, or part of it, made up
of an *ovary*, a *stigma*, and a *style.*

CORM A *bulb*-like underground
storage organ consisting mainly
of a swollen stem base, and
often surrounded by a *tunic.*

CORMEL A small *corm* that
develops around a mature one,
usually outside the main corm
tunic, as in gladiolus.

CORMLET A small *corm* arising
at the base of a mature one.

COROLLA The part of a *flower*
formed by the *petals.*

COTYLEDON A seed leaf;
the first leaf or pair of leaves
to emerge from the *seed*
after germination.

CROWN The part of the
plant at or just below the soil
surface from which new *shoots*
are produced and to which
they die back in autumn.

CUTTING A section of a plant
that is removed and used for
propagation. For the various
methods, see pp. 173–183.

CULTIVAR (CV.)
A contraction of "cultivated
variety". A group (or one
among such a group) of
cultivated plants that are clearly
distinguished by one or more
characteristics that are retained
when propagation is performed.

DEADHEAD To remove
spent *flower heads* so as to
promote further growth or
flowering, prevent seeding,
or improve appearance.

DECIDUOUS Losing its
leaves annually at the end of
the growing season.

DIEBACK Death of the tips
of *shoots* due to frost or disease.

DISC FLORET, DISC FLOWER
A small and often individually
inconspicuous, usually tubular
flower, often making the central
portion of a composite *flower
head*, such as a dahlia.

DIVISION A method of
propagation by which a
clump is divided into several
parts during *dormancy.*

DORMANCY The state of
temporary cessation of growth
and slowing down of other
activities in whole plants,
usually during winter.

ELLIPTIC (of leaves)
Broadening in the center and
narrowing toward each end.

ENTIRE (of leaves) With untoothed margins.

EVERGREEN Retaining its leaves at the end of the growing season, although losing some older leaves regularly during the year. **Semi-evergreen** plants retain only some leaves or lose older ones only when the new growth is produced.

EYE The center of a *flower*, of particular note if different in color from the *petals*.

FALL The drooping or horizontal *petals* of irises.

FILAMENT The stalk of an *anther*.

FLORET A single *flower* in a head of many flowers.

FLOWER The part of the plant containing the reproductive organs, usually surrounded by *sepals* and *petals*.

FLOWER HEAD A mass of small *flowers* or *florets* that, together, appear to form a single flower, for example, as seen in a daisy.

FORCE To induce artificially.

GENUS (pl. genera) A category in plant classification, consisting of a group of related *species*.

GLAUCOUS Bluish-white, bluish-green, or bluish-gray.

HABIT The characteristic growth or general appearance of a plant.

HARDY Able to withstand year-round climatic conditions without protection.

HERBACEOUS Dying down at the end of the growing season.

HYBRID The offspring of genetically different parents,

usually produced accidentally or artificially in cultivation, but occasionally arising in the wild.

LAYERING A propagation method whereby a *stem* is induced to root by being pegged down in the soil, still attached to the parent plant.

LEAF MOLD Fibrous, flaky material derived from decomposed leaves, used as an ingredient in potting media and as a soil improver or mulch.

LIME Compounds of calcium The amount of lime in soil determines whether it is *acid*, *neutral*, or *alkaline*.

LINEAR (of leaves) Very narrow with parallel sides.

LIP A lobe, with 2 or more flat or pouched perianth segments.

LOAM Well-structured, fertile soil that is moisture retentive but free draining.

MONOCOTYLEDON A flowering plant that has only one *cotyledon* in the seed; also characterized by narrow, parallel-veined leaves, and parts of the flower in threes or multiples of three.

MULCH A layer of organic matter applied to the soil over or around a plant to conserve moisture, protect the *roots* from frost, reduce the growth of weeds, and enrich the soil.

NATURALIZE To establish and grow as if in the wild.

NEUTRAL (of soil) With a *pH* value of 7, the point at which soil is neither *acid* nor *alkaline*.

NODE The point on a *stem* from which leaves arise.

OFFSET A small plant that arises by natural vegetative

reproduction, usually at the base of the mother plant; in *bulbs*, offsets are formed initially within the bulb *tunic* but later separate out.

OFFSHOOTS See *offsets*.

OPPOSITE (of leaves) Borne 2 to each *node*, one opposite the other.

ORGANIC 1. Compounds containing carbon derived from decomposed plant or animal organisms. 2. Used loosely of *mulches* and soil mixes that are derived from plant materials.

OVARY The part of the female portion of the *flower* containing *ovules* that will form the fruit.

OVULE The part of the *ovary* that develops into the *seed* after *pollination* and fertilization.

PALMATE Lobed like a hand, arising from the same point.

PAN A shallow, free-draining pot in which *bulbs* are grown.

PERENNIAL Living for at least 3 seasons.

PERIANTH The outer part of the *flower*, consisting of the *calyx* and the *corolla*. Often used when the calyx and the corolla are very similar in form, as in *Tulipa* and *Lilium*.

PERIANTH SEGMENT One portion of the *perianth*, resembling a *petal* and sometimes known as a *tepal*.

PETAL One portion of the usually showy and colored part of the *corolla*.

PETIOLE The stalk of a leaf.

pH The scale by which the acidity or alkalinity of soil is measured. See also *acid*, *alkaline*, and *neutral*.

PINNATE (of leaves) Compound, with *leaflets* arranged on opposite sides of a central stalk.

POLLINATION The transfer of pollen from the *anthers* to the *stigma* of the same or different flowers, resulting in the fertilization of the ovules in the *ovary*.

PROSTRATE With spreading or trailing *stems* lying flat on the ground.

RAY FLORET, RAY FLOWER One of the *flowers*, usually with strap-shaped *petals*, that together form the outer ring of flowers in a composite *flower head* such as a dahlia.

RAY PETAL The *petal* or fused petals, often showy, of a *ray flower*.

RECURVED Applied to *petals* of *flowers* and florets that curve backward.

REFLEXED Applied to *petals* that are bent sharply backward at an angle of more than 90°. They are sometimes called fully reflexed.

RHIZOME An underground, creeping *stem* that acts as a storage organ and bears leafy *shoots*.

ROOT The part of a plant, normally underground, that functions as anchorage and through which water and nutrients are absorbed.

ROSETTE A group of leaves that radiate from approximately the same point, often borne at ground level at the base of a very short *stem*.

RUNNER A horizontally spreading, usually slender *stem* that forms *roots* at each *node*, often confused with *stolon*.

SCALE A dry leaf or bract, usually pressed flat to the axis to which it is attached.

SEED The ripened, fertilized *ovule*, containing a dormant embryo capable of developing into an adult plant.

SEEDHEAD Any, usually dry, fruit that contains ripe *seeds*.

SEEDLING A young plant that has developed from a *seed*.

SELF-SEED To release viable seed which germinates around the parent to produce *seedlings*.

SEPAL Part of a *calyx*, usually insignificant, small, and green, but sometimes colored, showy, and *petal*-like.

SHOOT The aerial part of a plant, which bears leaves.

SIMPLE (of leaves) Not divided into leaflets.

SPATHE One, or sometimes two, large *bracts* that surround a flower cluster or individual *bud*.

SPECIES A category in plant classification, the rank below *genus*, containing closely related, very similar individual plants.

SPRAY A group of *flowers* or *flower heads* on a single, branching stem.

SPUR A hollow projection from a *petal* that often produces nectar.

STAMEN The male reproductive organ in a plant, consisting of the *anther* and usually its *filament* or *stem*.

STEM The main axis of a plant, usually above ground and supporting leaves, *flowers*, and fruits. Sometimes referred to as a stalk.

STERILE Infertile, not bearing spores, pollen, or *seeds*.

STIGMA The part of the female portion of the *flower*, borne at the tip of the *style*, that receives pollen.

STOLON A horizontally spreading or arching *stem*, usually above ground that roots at its tip to produce a new plant.

STYLE The part of the *flower* on which the *stigma* is borne.

TEPAL A single segment of a *perianth* that cannot be distinguished as either a *sepal* or a *petal*, as in *Crocus* or *Lilium*.

TOOTH A small, marginal, often pointed lobe on a *leaf*, *calyx*, or *corolla*.

TENDER Of a plant that is vulnerable to frost damage.

TEPAL See *perianth segment*.

TRUE (of seedlings) Retaining the distinctive characteristics of the parent when raised from *seed*.

TUBER A thickened, usually undergound, storage organ derived from a *stem* or *root*.

TUNIC The fibrous membranes or papery outer skin, which is sometimes thick and leathery, of *bulbs* or *corms*.

UPRIGHT (of habit) With vertical or semi-vertical main branches.

WHORL The arrangement of 3 or more organs, for example, leaves or flowers, arising from one point.

WINTER MOISTURE Excessive amounts of water that accumulate in the soil during the winter months.

INDEX

Each genus name is shown in **bold** type, followed by a brief description. Species, varieties, and subspecies are given in *italics*; cultivars are in roman type with single quotes. Common names appear in parentheses.

A

Acidanthera bicolor var.
  murielae see
  Gladiolus callianthus
Acidanthera murielae see
  Gladiolus callianthus

Albuca
Half-hardy to frost-tender, spring- or summer-flowering bulbs that produce loose spikes of tubular flowers.
  humilis 144

Allium (Onion)
Fully to frost-hardy perennials, some of which are edible, with bulbs, rhizomes, or fibrous rootstocks. Most of them produce small flowers that are packed together in a dense, shuttlecock-shaped or rounded cluster.
  albopilosum see *A. cristophii*
  acuminatum 130
  aflatunense (of gardens) see
    A. hollandicum
  akaka 120
  azureum see *A. caeruleum*
  caeruleum 107
  cernuum (Nodding onion,
    Wild onion) 103
  christophii see *A. cristophii*
  cristophii 106
  cowanii see *A. neapolitanum*
  cyathophorum
    var. *farreri* 146

Allium continued
  farreri see *A. cyathophorum*
    var. *farreri*
  giganteum (Giant onion) 35
  hollandicum 35
  karataviense 120
  moly (Golden garlic) 149
  murrayanum see
    A. acuminatum
  narcissiflorum 146
  neapolitanum 59
  oreophilum 130
  ostrowskianum see
    A. oreophilum
  pedemontanum see
    A. narcissiflorum
  schoenoprasum
    (Chives) 146
  stipitatum 34
  unifolium 76

× **Amarcrinum**
Hybrid genus *(Amaryllis*
× *Crinum)* of one robust, frost-hardy, evergreen bulb, grown for its large funnel-shaped flowers.
  × *A. howardii* see
    × *A. memoria-corsii*
  memoria-corsii 57

× **Amarygia**
Hybrid genus *(Amaryllis*
× *Brunsvigia)* of stout, frost-hardy bulbs, grown for their showy, autumn flowers.
  × *Brunsdonna parkeri* see
    × *A. parkeri*
  parkeri 57

Amaryllis
Frost-hardy bulbs, grown for their funnel-shaped flowers. which appear in autumn.
  belladonna
    (Belladonna lily) 57
  'Hathor' 56

Amazon lily see
  Eucharis × *grandiflora*
American turkscap lily see
  Lilium superbum

Angel's fishing rod see
  Dierama
Angel's tears see
  Narcissus triandrus

Anemone (Windflower)
Fully to frost-hardy perennials, sometimes tuberous or rhizomatous. Grown mainly for their shallowly cup-shaped flowers, which bloom in spring, summer, or autumn.
  blanda 'Atrocaerulea'
    see 'Ingramii'
    'Ingramii' 140
    'Radar' 130
  × *fulgens* 130
  pavonina 76

Apennine anemone see
  Anemone apennina

Arisaema
Fully to half-hardy perennials, grown for their large, hooded spathes, each enclosing a pencil-shaped spike. Fleshy red fruits are produced in autumn before the plant dies down.
  atrorubens see *A. triphyllum*
  candidissimum 144
  consanguineum 36
  griffithii 107
  jacquemontii 107
  sikokianum 107
  triphyllum (Jack-in-
    the-pulpit) 108

Arisarum
Frost-hardy, tuberous perennials, grown mainly for their hooded spathes, each enclosing spikes with minute flowers.
  proboscideum
    (Mousetail plant) 131

Aristea
Half-hardy, evergreen, clump-forming, rhizomatous

D

Nectaroscordum
Frost-hardy, flowering
bulbs with long, linear,
erect leaves. A relation
of *Allium*, plants exude
a very strong smell of
onion when bruised.

Neomarica
Frost-tender, evergreen,
rhizomatous perennials
producing iris-like, short-
lived flowers in summer.

Nerine
Frost to half-hardy bulbs,
some of which are semi-
evergreen, grown for their
rounded heads of wavy-
petaled flowers.

Nomocharis
Fully hardy bulbs with
a lily-like habit and, in
summer, loose spikes of
flattish flowers.

Notholirion
Frost-hardy, summer-
flowering bulbs, grown for
their funnel-shaped flowers.

**Ornithogalum
(Star-of-Bethlehem)**
Fully hardy to frost-
tender bulbs, grown for
their mostly star-shaped,
white flowers.

P

Pamianthe
Frost-tender, evergreen
bulbs, grown for their large,
scented flowers in spring.

Pancratium
Frost- to half-hardy bulbs,
with large, fragrant, daffodil-
like flowers in summer.

Patersonia
Half-hardy, evergreen,
clumping, rhizomatous
perennials that flower in
spring and early summer.

**Phaedranassa
(Queen lily)**
Half-hardy bulbs, grown for
their colorful, tubular flowers
in spring and summer.

Veltheimia continued
their drooping, tubular
flowers, which are similar
to those of red hot pokers
(*Kniphofia*), and their rosettes
of thick, wavy leaves.
  bracteata 115
  undulata see *V. bracteata*
  viridifolia see *V. bracteata*

W

Watsonia
Half-hardy, clumping corms,
grown for their showy spikes
of horizontal, tubular flowers
borne on erect stems.
  beatricis see
    W. pillansii
  borborica 30
  pillansii 31
  pyramidata see
    W. borborica
  rosea see *W. borborica*

Y

Z

Zantedeschia
Frost-hardy to frost-tender,
tuberous perennials that
produce unusual spathes
in spring and summer.
  aethiopica
    'Crowborough' 18
    'Green Goddess' 21
  elliottiana (Golden
    arum lily) 39

Zephyranthes
Frost- to half-hardy,
clump-forming bulbs
with crocus-like flowers.
  candida (Rainflower,
    Windflower) 150
  carinata see *Z. grandiflora*
  grandiflora (Rainflower,
    Windflower) 112
  robusta see
    Habranthus robustus
  rosea see *Z. grandiflora*

Zigadenus
Frost-hardy bulbs that
produce sprays of small, star-
shaped flowers in summer.
  fremontii 101
  venenosus
    (Death camas) 103

Acknowledgments

Key: t=top; b=bottom; r=right; l=left; c=center; cra=center right above; cla=center left above; crb=center right below; clb=center left below

The publishers would like to thank the following for their kind permission to reproduce the photographs:

Alpine Garden Society 98cl, 122br, 126l, 128cla, /
H Baumann 26cr, /**Mike Ireland** 127tl;
John Amand 134tl; **Ayletts Nurseries** 49clb;
Gillian Beckett 36br, 65tl, 76tr 7 bl, 79br, 84b, 105bl, 109br,
133tr & bl, 135cra & bl, 139bl, 141tl, 144tr, 156 tr & br, 157br;
Pat Brindley 24tr, 66tl, 71bl & br, 73tl & 73tr, 126b, 127br, 135tl;
Ray Cobb 128br; **Eric Crichton** 10, 13b, 21bl,
26tr, 52cla, 62cr, 101tl & tr, 129cla;
Philip Damp 50tr, 51br, 55cr; Alan Edwards 123cla;
Garden Picture Library/Howard Rice 3;
John Glover 42crb, 160br;
Derek Gould 19br, 71cla, 80, 90tl, 120tr; **Hortico** 90br;
International Flower Bulb Society 135cla;
Andrew Lawson 11, 14, 15, 40br, 41tr, 44tl, 46br;
Brian Matthew 35tr, 79bl, 95 tr & br, 98tl, 105br, 109tl,
110l, 113bl, 119bl; **Photos Horticultural** 72b, 83bl, 89b, 111bl;
Howard Rice 89tr; **Arthur Smith** 28tl, 29cl & br ;
Harry Smith Collection Front jacket (cla), 19tr, 22c, 25cr & br, 27tr,
28cl, cr & br, 29bl, 30cr & br, 34br, 35br, 39bl & br, 41tl , cra, crb & br,
45cla, crb & br, 47bl, 59bl, 64tl, 68tr, 70cl, 74tl, 77bl, 79tl, 103tl,
107tr, 108tr, 109bl, 113br, 114, 117tr & br, 118br & tr, 123b & tr,
124tl, 125bl, 127tr, 128bl, 129tl, 131cl, 133tl & br, 137br, 143br,
144br, 146tr, 148tl, 149bl, 152tl & tr, 155bl, 160tl, 161bl & br.

In addition to the above, the publishers would also like to thank
the staff of the Royal Horticultural Society Publications.

Abbreviations

C	centigrade	in	inch, inches
cm	centimeter	m	meter
cv.	cultivar	mm	millimeter
F	Fahrenheit	oz	ounce
f.	forma	sp.	species
ft	foot, feet	subsp.	subspecies
g	gram	var.	variant